African Perspectives on
Governance

D0950805

African Perspectives on Governance

Edited by Goran Hyden,
Hastings W. O. Okoth-Ogendo,
and Bamidele Olowu

Africa World Press, Inc.

P.O. Box 1892
Trenton, NJ 08607

P.O. Box 48
Asmara, ERITREA

Copyright © 2000 Goran Hyden, Dele Olowu, Hastings W. O. Okoth-Ogendo

First Printing 2000

All rights reserved. No part of this publication may be reproduced, stored in a retrieval system or transmitted in any form or by any means electronic, mechanical, photocopying, recording or otherwise without the prior written permission of the publisher.

Cover design: Jonathan Gullery

Library of Congress Cataloging-in-Publication Data

African perspectives on governance / edited by Goran Hyden, Dele
    Olowu, and Hastings W. O. Okoth Ogendo.
        p.   cm.
    Includes bibliographical references and index.
    ISBN 0-86543-718-1. – ISBN 0-86543-719-X (pbk.)
    1. Sociology, Urban--Africa. 2. Cities and towns--Africa.
3. Spatial behavior--Africa. 4. Human geography--Africa.
5. Africa--Politics and government.   I. Hyden, Goran, 1938-
II. Olowu, Dele. III. Okoth-Ogendo, H.W. O.
HT148.A2A344 1998
307.76'096--dc21   98-41115
                                                             CIP

This book is dedicated to our friends and colleagues,

the late Dan Mudoola, and Ronald Cohen, who made

such valuable contributions to the projects that helped

produce this volume.

Contents

Introduction

This volume grows out of two separate projects, one in East Africa, the other in Nigeria, devoted to research on governance issues. The former was conceived at a meeting of researchers from universities in East Africa and the University of Florida as early as 1988, before much attention had been paid in academic or political circles to the current political reform agenda. The purpose of the project in East Africa was to facilitate for younger scholars in the region to engage in research on issues that they thought were politically pertinent and feasible to carry out. We chose "governance" as the overall umbrella concept for this effort, mainly on the premise that it was sufficiently indicative of our interests in political reform issues, yet broad enough to invite scholars from a wide range of disciplines.

After several rounds of correspondence between those involved in East Africa and at the University of Florida, a project proposal was submitted to the Ford Foundation, more specifically its regional office for Eastern and Southern Africa. A two-year grant of $180,000 was approved in late 1990—supplemented two years later by another $165,000—with the Center for African Studies at the University of Florida serving as the administrative agency. Running the project was a committee made up of three scholars from East Africa—one from each country—and two from the University of Florida. During the first two years this committee consisted of H. W. O. Okoth-Ogendo, University of Nairobi, chairman; Goran Hyden, University of Florida, secretary; Samuel Mushi, University of Dar es Salaam; Dan Mudoola,

1

Makerere University; and Ronald Cohen, University of Florida. Dr. Mudoola was unfortunately killed in 1992 by a grenade thrown into a restaurant which he visited in Kampala, Uganda. Following his untimely death, he was succeeded by Joan Kakwenzire, a historian also from Makerere University. This was the only change in the leadership of the project during its five-year existence. This committee had the dual purpose of managing the project and evaluating incoming research proposals for funding.

We received a total of one hundred applications, submitted in four separate rounds. Out of these, 21 were awarded research grants. One of the objectives of this project was to see what governance issues scholars in the region identified as particularly important. We wanted, as the title of this volume confirms, to help mobilize African perspectives on governance. We were generally struck by the fact that the issues that these scholars grapple with are not very different from those that people in other regions of the world take an interest in. Nonetheless, their interpretation and analysis may differ in that they build on the contextual factors that are especially significant in contemporary Africa. Research projects ranged from the role of language in national integration in Tanzania, the political attitudes of Rwandese refugees in Uganda, and the growth of an imperial presidency in Kenya to such (more political-economy-oriented) topics as structural adjustment and governance. We were particularly pleased to see not only a considerable number of applications from female researchers but also a pronounced interest among men in the role that women play in the governance field in East Africa.

The relative success of the project in East Africa in generating research interest in governance issues encouraged us to respond to a request for a similar project in Nigeria in 1992. With Professor Dele Olowu as chairperson, Professor Adebayo Williams and Dr. Kayode Soremekun at the Obafemi Awolowo University in Ile-Ife serving as catalysts, and Professor Ronald Cohen—with assistance from Professor Goran Hyden—taking the lead at the University of Florida, a proposal was submitted to the United States Information Agency (USIA) for funding under its "Democracy and Governance" program. A grant of $60,000, later supplemented by another $30,000, was received in 1993. The leadership of this project was provided by the five persons listed above, and its mode of operation resembled that of the East Africa project, the difference being that instead of having a single seminar at which all grantees reported on their findings in a preliminary fashion, this one included a workshop for the successful applicants before they ventured into the field to do their research. Like its East African counterpart, the Nigerian project operated with a broad definition of the concept of governance, again with a view to soliciting as many interesting and pertinent proposals as possible. It funded a total of twelve researchers out of a pool of some fifty applicants.

The final research papers produced by the grantees in the East African project have been bound into one volume entitled *Governance Issues in East Africa: Highlights from the Field.* This volume has been distributed to university libraries and other relevant institutions in East Africa. A limited number of remaining copies are available through the Center for African Studies at the University of Florida. The Nigerian papers have been assembled and published in two separate volumes. One is titled *Governance and Democratization in Nigeria,* and published by Spectrum Press in Ibadan, Nigeria, in 1995, the second *Governance and Democratization in West Africa* and published by CODESRIA Press in Dakar, Senegal, in 1999.

This volume is different from those publications in that it draws not on the research reports produced by the projects, but on fresh pieces written by a cross-section of the best grantees and the senior scholars who served as project leaders and resource persons. It combines scholars from East Africa and Nigeria in an effort to provide a comparative perspective on issues deemed most important by the two groups. As the subsequent chapters indicate, the comparison among countries in Africa has been easier and more effectively done in some cases than in others. All the same, this volume is devoted to an inter-African comparison focused first and foremost on the similarities and differences between the three East African countries, Kenya, Tanzania, and Uganda on the one hand and Nigeria on the other. Some authors go beyond the boundaries of these four countries to include references also to other relevant African cases. We are particularly anxious to underline that this volume is meant to provide a platform for African scholars to engage the issues of governance and provide their interpretation of what is relevant and how some of the problems facing the countries on the continent might be tackled more effectively. Although the contributions in this volume are not tightly held together by a common definition of governance, we believe that collectively they offer valuable contributions in their own right to our understanding of the principal issues with the ongoing political reform process in African countries. What is more, many chapters also include ideas and suggestions for further research.

This book is more specifically a product of a conference that was held in Arusha in May 1996, where the authors and a number of other academics and policy analysts were assembled to discuss first drafts of their papers. This meeting was financed by the Carnegie Corporation of New York and the Ford Foundation. We wish to thank both these organizations for enabling us to produce this volume.

Finally, we wish to thank Dr. Peter Wanyande, University of Nairobi, who was hired by the African Academy of Sciences, the recipient of the Carnegie grant for this project, to prepare and administer it. Our gratitude also goes to Dr. Stephen Snook and Richard Marcus at the University of Florida, who assisted with the editorial work of this book, and to Ms. Susan Mickelberry for final copy-editing and producing a camera-ready verision of the manuscript.

The Editors

1

The Governance Challenge in Africa

Goran Hyden

Introduction

The purpose of this chapter is twofold. It serves to place the subsequent contributions in context, but its aim is also to draw on the insights from the various chapters in this volume with a view to providing a sense of where governance research may be particularly useful and rewarding in the future. It is important to underline here that this project is exploratory. In this respect, the authors have been primarily asked to come up with perspectives on governance that may serve as inputs into the development of theory in this field. A principal task here, therefore, is to pick up the more important insights provided and see how they relate to existing conceptual and theoretical discussions on governance, democratization, and the broader literature on regime transition. Before embarking on this aggregative task, however, it is important to provide the reader with a sense of how the concept of governance has been used in this volume. The insights discussed in this introductory chapter will indicate some of the more interesting issues that are ripe for further research.

The Various Dimensions of Governance

This volume reflects the basic premise on which the projects that laid the foundation for this exercise rested, namely, the eclectic and open-ended use of the term governance. Because the whole effort aimed at encouraging African perspectives on this set of issues, we did not want to bring to bear on these researchers a concept that was not only developed by analysts elsewhere but which also lacked precision in the way the latter used it. No attempt was made *a priori* to adopt the definition of governance that the present author has provided elsewhere (Hyden 1992 and 1997). "Governance" was never allowed to become a conceptual straight-jacket but was expected to function as a rather loose framework within which each researcher could creatively explore political issues of significance. The problem that we have encountered in this venture, therefore, is not the limitations stemming from the imposition of a confining concept, but rather the opposite: the challenge of making sense of the wide range of interpretations of governance that the authors bring to the agenda.

At first glance, this multitude of views may be confusing. The usage of the concept varies from being focused on issues of the state as well as the regime. Several authors think of it primarily in relation to the state and how it carries out its economic and social development mandate. This span, however, is no broader than what one finds in other literature where the concept of governance features. Scholarly analysts as well as those involved in making policy are yet to find agreement on what governance really stands for (see, e.g., Carter Center 1989 and 1990; World Bank 1992). Beyond the general observation that governance refers to how power is being exercised and with what results, there are other interesting common threads that emerge in the critical analysis provided by the contributors to this volume.

In trying to do justice to these, we find one common denominator in the frequent reference, both explicit and implicit, to the weakness—if not absence—of a genuine civic public realm, in which such basic principles as the rule of law, justice, and respect for others (including things public) are being embraced and enforced. Okoth Ogendo alludes to this shortcoming in his reference to the absence (in the past, at least) of a sense of constitutionalism in African countries. Suberu, in his analysis of ethnicity, comes at it from a different angle when he uses Peter Ekeh's (1975) thesis about the two publics in Africa, one "primordial" that is moral and strong, and another "civic" that is weak and legitimate only to the extent that it serves the former. The same concern is repeated in the contributions by Kakwenzire on human rights, Olokotun on the media, and Williams on the intellectuals. Although it is less explicit in the contributions by Enemuo, Soetan, and Wanyande, the poor performance of central and local government institutions is attributed to the lack of public accountability—i.e., a sense that being a public servant carries with it certain obligations not found in the private realm. Enemuo, for instance, quotes Mabogunje (1995:2), one of the resource persons for the U. S. Information Agency-funded Nigerian Governance Project, arguing with reference to that country that people "strain themselves to pay levies and contribute or donate generously to the coffers of their community development associations," but feel they owe local government no obligation, hence are unwilling to pay taxes or rates and may even encourage or condone local councillors to misappropriate funds meant for local services. There is little in other contributions that really serves to qualify this point. The public realm lacks the civic qualities that typically help generate a sense of responsibility and accountability among government officials.

There has been much discussion among comparativist political scientists about the weakness of the state. In a major contribution, Migdal (1988) suggested that there is a positive correlation between a weak state and strong society—i.e., the weaker the former, the stronger the latter. Our investigations here indicate that this thesis is not sufficient for understanding African politics today. One reason is that it is not only the state that lacks capability to get things done. The same applies to society, or civil society, as it is now more often designated. Although there are frequent references in the literature to non-governmental organizations as promising substitutes for governments (e.g., Clark

1991), our more cautious position, as illustrated here by Soetan and Wanyande, is that civil society itself is undeveloped and weak and thus lacks the capability to implement policy. This is manifest in the deteriorating conditions in which large groups of citizens—not the least, women—find themselves as a result of both inadequate state performance in the past and the current frailty of non-governmental organizations.

The second reason why Migdal's thesis is insufficient is that the state is not only weak in terms of capability but also in terms of legitimacy. The rules of rational and legal authority that invariably have served to strengthen—and, typically, legitimize—the state are far from institutionalized in Africa and have, if anything, weakened in recent years. This concern is reflected in Olowu's emphasis on the need to reaffirm ethical norms in African public services. The question that arises as a result of the contributions made here, however, is whether this is a problem confined to the state alone. There is evidence to suggest that such norms as Olowu mentions—professionalism, political impartiality, and representativeness—are being threatened not only in the public services but also elsewhere. Several of the authors, notably Suberu, suggests this is a pervasive problem affecting also civil society. Because it transcends the boundary of the state, it is a regime issue (i.e., it relates to the framework of rules that guide both state and society). Weakness at this level is not so much a matter of capability as it is orientation. In this respect, it may be better conceived in terms of "softness" than weakness. Whatever term is chosen to analyze this phenomenon, however, the main point that we wish to make here is that governance, as typically used in this volume, like regime, transcends the boundaries of government and state to incorporate a regime focus. In this respect, we follow O'Donnell and Schmitter (1986), when they argue that democratization of the state is only one aspect of a wide-ranging process that involves civil society; hence their interest in regime.

This, again, is not a unique perspective. Regime has experienced a renaissance in the study of politics in recent years both in international relations and comparative politics. This is to a large extent the result of the growing significance of norms in both practical politics and the study thereof. This trend to bring "regime back in" is sufficiently marked that it has the potential of providing a new line of research in political science where those studying politics cross-nationally and internationally are likely to find common ground.

The important contribution that this volume makes is to emphasize that the interesting issues in this area go beyond those of regime transition. Virtually all studies (at least in comparative politics) in recent years that have centered on the concept of regime (e.g., O'Donnell and Schmitter 1986; Bratton and van de Walle 1997) deal with it in the context of democratization. While such a focus is understandable, given the widespread interest that democratization efforts around the world have acquired among students of politics, it is limiting in that it concentrates only on studying the way societies are grappling with the task of "capturing the democratic moment." Our contributors, notably Olowu, Soetan, Soremekun, and Wanyande, also draw attention to another side of regime studies, namely how norms and rules that are changed influence policy and its implementation. This is a more permanent theme that gives the concept of regime—and, by implication, "governance"—a significance in the study of both policy and politics that it currently does not enjoy.

What emerges quite clearly from the range of studies included here is the usefulness of not only distinguishing between "state" and "regime" as analytical concepts but also between "policy" and "governance." The study of policy, whether formulation, decision, implementation, or evaluation, is inevitably associated with the activities of public organs, i.e., the state. Most such studies tend to focus on specific aspects of policy, using methodologies that highlight such aspects of policy-making as its efficiency (costs and benefits) and effectiveness (impact). They rarely include references to the institutional framework within which policy is made. In recent years, however, there are increasing calls for the need to transcend these narrow parameters so as to include references to how this framework facilitates or impedes the successful implementation of policy. One such advocate is Majone (1989), who argues not only for the need to combine policy analysis with advocacy but also for the incorporation of institutional analysis—and change—to achieve policy outcomes.

Our studies point in the same direction as Majone's analysis in that understanding policy (particularly) at a time of regime transition, but even at other occasions), is insufficient without attention to how change of rules affects policy. More concretely, how changes in the rules of the political game in African countries influence implementation of policy is a critical issue, particularly for those who are interested in how these countries can reach greater success in their efforts at national development. It is now frequently assumed that the more participatory the policy-making process is, the greater the probability that policies will be legitimate in the eyes of the potential beneficiaries and more effectively implemented. On the basis of the studies presented here, we do not necessarily take that for granted, but pose it as a hypothesis worth more empirical illustrations.

For the purpose of understanding the relationship between the many concepts that are typically used in the discussion of development, it may be useful to make the following analytical distinctions:

Table 1. Conceptual distinctions in the study of development.

Level	Institutional focus	Concept
Meta	Regime	Governance
Macro	State	Policy-making
Meso	Sector	Administration
Micro	Project	Management

This volume does not really penetrate all these levels, although theoretically the relations between all of them are interesting. What we are concerned with here is, primarily, how regime and state interact, and, in the case of Olowu's, Soetan's, and Wanyande's chapters, how regime changes also affect the implementation of specific policies. As these chapters demonstrate, governance is closely wedded to policy in that the two empirically interact with each other all the time. For example, it is quite possible that a particularly important policy may stand in the way of changing the rules of the game. Such has been the case as Soremekun also argues in his chapter with economic policies that have been given a stronger weight than the need for political reform.

To capture these distinctions in a slightly different manner, it may be helpful to go back to Seymour Martin Lipset's discussion of legitimacy and effectiveness (1959). In arguing what explains the stability of democracy, he maintained that it is not only economic development but also effectiveness and legitimacy of the political system. In his system's perspective, effectiveness refers to actual performance—i.e., the extent to which the system satisfies the basic functions of government as both leaders and followers see it. Legitimacy, on the other hand, involves the capacity of the system to engender and maintain the belief that the existing political institutions are the most appropriate for society. While effectiveness is primarily instrumental and can be assessed in objective terms, legitimacy is evaluative and assessed, therefore, in subjective terms. Our distinction here between "state" and "regime" as well as between "policy" and "governance" runs along the same lines. Issues of policy at the state level can be evaluated in objective terms, whether the concern is efficiency or effectiveness, while issues of governance are likely to require attitude surveys or other instruments aimed at tapping subjective perceptions.

Knowledge regarding the relative degree of legitimacy of a country's rules and institutions is, as Lipset also emphasizes, important in any attempt to analyze the stability of the system in face of a crisis in effectiveness. As this volume highlights and many other studies before have illustrated (e.g., Sandbrook 1985; Rothchild and Chazan 1988), governments or states in Africa have proved very ineffective. A major reason, however, why so many political systems in Africa have experienced turbulence (in some cases, like Liberia and Somalia, total breakdown) is that this crisis of the state has been accompanied by an equivalent crisis in legitimacy of the regime. Although effectiveness and legitimacy are not independent of each other, it is useful for analytical purposes to keep them apart. One can anticipate situations where, for example, the state is ineffective while the regime remains quite legitimate, a factor which gives the government a higher degree of maneuverability than in a situation where the regime lacks legitimacy. Drawing again on Lipset's treatment of the relationship between effectiveness and legitimacy, it is possible to indicate the association between the key variables here as follows:

Table 2. Relationship between state/regime, policy/ governance, and effectiveness/legitimacy.

		State/Policy/Effectiveness	
		+	-
Regime/	+	A	B
Governance/			
Legitimacy	-	C	D

When Lipset originally provided his matrix along these lines, the principal challenge was to modernize society in the Third World. Economic development was viewed as the prime mover of progress and as a catalyst both for greater state effectiveness and greater regime legitimacy. Forty years later, the challenges are different. Long gone are the dreams of a linear process of development towards democracy boosted by economic development. In the African context, in particular, underlying much of the present state of affairs are two parallel developments: a decline in the economic sector (much of it attributable to ineffective state institutions) and a lack of confidence in the political institutions that African countries took over from departing colonial powers (and never bothered to reform beyond the relatively superficial act of deracialization). Today's governance challenges in Africa, therefore, can only be fully appreciated and understood if we take into consideration the political legacy that these countries are coping with today.

The next section of this chapter will analyze a number of aspects relating to this legacy and discuss, with the help of the contributors to this volume and other sources, how they are being handled today. Those aspects that have been selected for special attention here are: (1) the breakdown of the public realm, (2) the emergence of neo-patrimonial forms of rule, and (3) the resurgence of external forces.

The Breakdown of the Public Realm

As we have suggested above, the public realm is not merely the state but also civil society. It is the arena in which both state and civil society associations interact and compete for influence. It is the place where the regime is put directly to test. If norms and rules are not adhered to, it is immediately noticeable; and if such behavior cannot be punished, the victim is not only a particular actor but the regime, and (by extension) the system as a whole. The public realm, therefore, is like a football field where the game cannot be effectively played unless players and teams adhere to the rules and there are referees present to enforce them. To serve its function as the principal policy arena, actors must be assured of access, fair treatment, and the prospect of influence. Without adherence to rules that guarantee these principles, actors will withdraw or rebel with the objective of changing the rules in such a direction.

The story of the public realm in Africa begins with colonization in that the nature of this realm became a major issue primarily as a result of the emergence of the colonial state. This is not to imply that there was no public realm in precolonial societies or that there was no controversy surrounding its nature. With regard to the present, however, it is primarily colonial rule and its legacy that seem to matter.

Colonialism and its relevance to contemporary politics in Africa has recently been the subject of two well-written books (Young 1994 and Mamdani 1996). Both emphasize the importance of formal structures and argue that these have changed very little since independence. As such, both these contributions to the literature may be viewed as rebuttals of the predominant line of analysis since the early 1980s, which has focused on the informal nature of African politics. Mamdani's book is particularly interesting because it is a first attempt to incorporate a study of South Africa into the analysis of African politics. His main thesis is that while African nationalists managed to deracialize civil society, democratization after independence never succeeded because they failed to break the tribal logic of "native authorities" that had been established in the name of "indirect rule" by the British. This dual arrangement— whereby the urban-based nationalists, on the one hand, were able to indigenize civil society and use it to overturn the colonial system of rule while the rural population, on the other, was confined to perpetuating local traditions within narrow ethnic parameters set for them by the departing colonial state—served as a structural barrier to the development not only of democracy but also a public realm of a civic kind. Mamdani pursues this argument with reference to the cases that he knows best: South Africa and Uganda. He maintains that Uganda is the home of the most serious attempt yet to democratize "native authority" through the efforts by President Museveni's National Resistance Movement to institute local councils that transcend the sectarian boundaries of the previous system of traditional rule. That country, however, has also fallen short of fully addressing the democratic demands of civil society, he argues. In South Africa, by contrast, though the home of the strongest and the most imaginative civil-society-based resistance on the continent, democratic reform has floundered on the walls of customary power (Mamdani 1996:296-97).

His analysis may be criticized for painting the African situation in too broad strokes. This tendency to overgeneralize is apparent in the weight he attributes to indirect rule—which, after all, was applied only by the British and by no means everywhere. He can also be accused of assuming too much linearity in societies where the history is much more complex. Such (and other) types of criticism notwithstanding, Mamdani's thesis cannot be ignored. It certainly can serve as the starting point for further analysis of the problems African countries face in trying to democratize.

Of special relevance here is the question of how far the breakdown of the public realm is the result of the nationalists' failure to break the hold of customary power, pursued as it has been in the name of defending tradition against alien encroachment. A similar argument has, of course, been made earlier by

Ekeh (1975) with reference particularly to West Africa, and it is being applied in this volume by Enemuo. Both Ekeh and Enemuo, however, seem to say something that Mamdani is not, at least explicitly, and that is that nationalists, after having indigenized control of government, were not interested in defending the civic nature of the public realm. Instead they preferred to strengthen the primordial, i.e., community-based public, thereby severely weakening the civil society project and the prospect of African countries being able to modernize and democratize.

It is the articulation of this experience that has internally driven African societies in the direction of regime change today. Because of the prominent role that the state officially was allowed to play in national development after independence, much of the deterioration of the moral fabric that had existed at the time of independence has centered on the state. State effectiveness has continuously waned as a result of ongoing parochialization of the public realm. Resource allocation by government and other state institutions has typically come to follow ethnic or religious lines. Although this does not mean that these countries have always been characterized by what Suberu in his chapter calls "hegemonic repression," the alternative mode of rule— "hegemonic exchange" (Rothchild 1986)—also has parochializing effects as it tends to overrule norms that underpin the civicness of public action.

This use of state power has been detrimental to the nationalist regimes, typically based on rule by a single party, not only because it created a skewed distribution of resources in favor of those groups that have power and wealth, but also because the state has lost its capability to implement policies that have been promised. The segmentation of society that has followed in the wake of politically responding to the ethnic factor in so many African countries has impeded the many reforms of the public services that possibly could help these institutions to be revived. Olowu's concern with these issues in this volume are timely, since the political circumstances have changed in the 1990s, but both in his analysis and that of, for example, Enemuo point to the probability that any reform, at central or local level, will be difficult because of the institutionalization of highly parochialized patterns of rule since independence.

Although it has taken a long time for international finance institutions to recognize that the causes of Africa's crisis is as much political as anything else, it is clear that a major reason why African economies had to undergo structural adjustment in the 1980s was a result of the rapidly declining levels of efficiency and effectiveness in state-driven and state-controlled operations. These large-scale interventions to modify the structures of African economies would not have been necessary had the state functioned in a satisfactory manner. It is no coincidence that governments that continued to operate quite well (e.g., Botswana) never had to subject themselves to the painful cure that structural adjustment programs (SAPs) are. There is little disagreement today that these adjustment programs have been necessary for Africa, but, as Soetan illustrates in her chapter, the costs have often been high, not the least for already underprivileged groups like women and children, whose living conditions have deteriorated considerably. This is one significant part of the cost that Africa has had to pay for the shortcomings of its political leaders after independence—and the gullible orientation of external donor agencies in uncritically supporting them. The bitterness of the medicine is only one aspect of Africa's current suffering. More fundamental and equally difficult to accept is the self-inflicted wounds that Africa's political leaders caused their countries by undermining the rational and legal foundation of state policy after getting to power.

It is also these leaders who have demonstrated the greatest reluctance to accept SAP prescriptions. Few African governments have accepted them willingly, as Wanyande stresses in his chapter, the primary reason being that these leaders have feared that liberalizing the economy would weaken their control of resources that are crucial to their staying in power. There was understandably, at least in the initial phase, little domestic support for these programs, and leaders tended to use this as justification for not embarking on economic reforms. By remaining recalcitrant, the political leadership in these countries had to swallow the pill the hard way—i.e., by being forced to do so by the international finance institutions in collaboration with the dominant countries in the Organization for Economic Cooperation and Development (OECD).

Much of the crisis that Africa has gone through for almost two decades now (with no end in sight) can be attributed, as several contributions to this volume confirm, to an inadequate performance at the policy level. With almost all resources dedicated to the state, it is no surprise that it has been forced to take a major hit. People have lost confidence in public institutions and have increasingly experienced the public realm as a very insecure place. The rules have become more and more arbitrary and participation in public affairs often associated with personal risks and losses. The state is no longer fulfilling the role of protector of life; even such basic functions as law and order have in the 1980s been communalized in the sense that local vigilante groups are emerging in many places to carry out the tasks that in a functioning state belong to the police and other relevant security organs. The *sungu sungu* movement in Tanzania is one of several such phenomena that became significant in the face of state collapse in the 1980s. In this context, it is worth bringing in the Ugandan case. There, what remained local expressions of security concern were translated into a full-scale liberation movement which decided that the shortcomings associated with state performance in the past were on such a scale that the only way forward was to reform the state in a radical fashion. Museveni's National Resistance Movement achieved such a transformation in 1986 after it seized power in the country; one of its significant moves, as Mamdani and others have demonstrated, was the introduction of local resistance councils with a mandate to reverse past shortcomings, including threats to security of individuals and communities in the rural areas. Although this task is still not completed in the northern part of the country (as Kakwenzire indicates in her chapter), it has nevertheless given the Ugandan state a new measure of legitimacy that exceeds that of either Nigeria, Kenya, or Tanzania. It might, of course, be argued that the deterioration of state performance in Uganda had gone so far that it did not take much to provide the impression of things becoming better. This point has sometimes been used by critics of the "economic miracle" that Uganda has produced under Museveni's leadership. The case of Uganda, however, rests on more solid ground than what can be deduced from economic figures only, notably the change in the quality of the political leadership away from sectarianism and parochialism. In the context of the four countries discussed as primary cases in this volume, Uganda stands out as being further ahead, not only in terms of economic reform but also with reference to changes in the public realm. While it may still be some distance away from being really "civic," the public realm in Uganda has been cleared of many questionable dimensions that continue to plague politics in other countries. Especially significant is that political leaders have been forced to resign after pressure from a critical parliament. Nonetheless, neo-patrimonial patterns of rule prevail also there, and it is time now to turn to the question why this phenomenon has been so prevalent in post-colonial Africa.

The Emergence of Neo-Patrimonialism

In the previous section we were primarily concerned with the deterioration in state performance and the effects it has had on the political systems in Africa. We are now turning to the regime level to assess how the subversion of norms and rules associated with the maintenance of a civic public realm has ruined the legitimacy of the regime and exacerbated the trend towards instability in these countries.

The contributors to this volume may not all use the concept of neo-patrimonialism, but they do implicitly confirm the thesis that has been advanced by others (most recently by Bratton and van de Walle 1997) that the institutional hallmark of African politics since independence has been neo-patrimonialism. This concept is derived from Max Weber's notion of patrimonial authority which he associated with the exercise of power in small-scale, face-to-face types of traditional communities. In such patrimonial systems, a person rules due to his personal power and prestige. Others are followers or subjects with no rights and privileges other than those bestowed upon them by the ruler. Authority is wholly personalized, shaped by the ruler's own preferences rather than a codified system of laws. The ruler ensures political stability and personal political survival by providing security in an uncertain environment and by selectively allocating favors and material benefits to loyal followers who are not citizens but merely the ruler's clients.

It has been necessary to qualify the original Weberian concept by referring to "neo-patrimonialism" because what we have witnessed in Africa—and some other places—in recent years has taken place not in a typical traditional setting but in the context of a modern state. In fact, because rulers have had access to the enormous resources that a modern state can mobilize, neo-patrimonial rule has rested on a more extensive base than was ever possible to acquire in traditional settings. Medard (1982) is among several scholars who have suggested that neo-patrimonialism has been institutionalized as a curse that is very difficult to do away with. Christopher Clapham (1985) echoes the same point when he argues that neo-patrimonialism is the most salient type of authority in the Third World because it corresponds to the normal forms of social organization in precolonial society, and these still prevail in many of these countries. These authors all insist that it is critical to the countries' hold on power.

What we are saying here is not as, for example Jackson and Rosberg (1982) did, that Africa lacks institutions. Neo-patrimonialism sustains itself through institutions, albeit typically informal ones. The point about neo-patrimonialism, as compared to classic patrimonialism, is that it twists formal institutions to serve its own purposes. The "imperial presidency" that was the subject of one of the studies funded by the East African Governance Project focused on how—in this case in Kenya—the presidential system was used to enhance the power of the head of the state. In this situation, as in so many others around Africa, the formal rules of the system are being flouted and highly personalized, dyadic relations between the "strong man" and his acolytes allowed to take their place. The full dimensions of this system of rule have been analyzed by several other students of African politics (e.g., Callaghy 1984, Joseph 1987, and Bayart 1992).

What has been typically missing in most of the literature are meaningful references to the costs of these systems to the societies in which they operate. Academics have typically satisfied themselves with describing and analyzing these costs but have refrained from talking about their implications for human welfare or national development. Policy analysts in various international think tanks have largely identified the means to make systems *formally* more efficient and effective. Their rationale for calling for reform has been to compare per capita growth across regions and conclude that Africa is falling behind others. For a long time, however, these analysts refused to accept that the system of rule was part of the problem. They focused on such more easily manipulable variables as shortage of trained manpower, lack of infrastructure, or wrong economic policies. It is only recently that these analysts have come around to acknowledging that the nature of the political system is a main reason for Africa's current dire predicament. It must be added here that the first agency in the international system to highlight this problem was the Addis Ababa-based United Nations' Economic Commission for Africa (ECA). Under the leadership of its former Executive Director, Dr. Adebayo Adedeji, it spoke out on the shortcomings of the political leadership and governance systems in Africa much earlier than the World Bank or the bilateral donors, which in the 1990s have joined the choir calling for reform. Especially influential in this direction was the conference that the ECA organized in Arusha, Tanzania, in 1989—which, in calling for greater participation by non-governmental organizations and civil society, also identified the costs associated with a system of rule that is unpredictable.

The authors contributing to this volume do not come up with hard facts to demonstrate what the costs are, but they do provide additional information to indicate the need for further research on the question of actual costs both for individuals and for the societies from the perpetuation of neo-patrimonial systems of rule. There are three dimensions of this rule that are particularly important for further work: (1) unaccountability, (2) patriarchy, and (3) ascription.

Neo-patrimonialism is the opposite of democracy in that it is characterized by the absence of public accountability. It lies in the very nature of this system that it is kept private and secret (Jackson 1977). Personalized exchanges, involving favors that are not regularized in budgets or other public documents, are being hidden at any cost. That is why the neo-patrimonial ruler will do everything to cover up any traces of such "deals" and punish those (e.g., in the media, as Olokotun demonstrates in this volume) who attempt to search for the truth or who point to the fact that matters are illegal or unconstitutional. The most damaging aspect of this tendency to "privatize" politics and treat it as a "closed shop" is that it becomes virtually impossible to punish some one who has been an insider but for some reason proves to be a political liability. Instead, such persons are typically "rewarded" with another prestigious appointment (e.g., as ambassador) so that he will not divulge any information that may be harmful to the ruling clique. Because there is no public accountability—and to the extent one can talk of accountability at all, it is to the "strong man" at the top—irregularities, including in some cases rampant corruption, continue. The full costs of this inability to deal with the lack of public accountability in neo-patrimonial systems have yet to be fully appreciated, but our hypothesis is that it is one of the most pertinent factors explaining Africa's economic decline. In this African perspective on governance, the authors do not have confidence that the introduction of multi-party politics has changed the situation much, if at all. The neo-patrimonial tendencies are as evident in the governments that have been chosen in competitive elections as they were in the days of one-party rule.

Neo-patrimonialism is also patriarchal. Although it might be argued that such a system of rule does not preclude participation by women, the way most of Africa's modern rulers have interpreted their traditions is to treat women as second-class subjects, not even second-class citizens. Funmi Soetan in her chapter shows how marginal female participation—in economy and politics alike—

has remained after independence. In neo-patrimonialist systems, women suffer even more than men from the frailty—if not absence—of a "rights" culture in society. Although some women come to serve in responsible positions, they are typically doing so at the discretion of men, not the least that of the "strong man" himself. Because they have no guaranteed avenues for advancement and because the male leadership tends to give them only marginal attention by insisting on their role in the private rather than the public realm, African societies fail to make full use of their human resources. We believe that this pertinent feature of African society today is another reason why neo-patrimonialism, as long as it prevails, must be seen as responsible for the continent's failure to move forward.

Neo-patrimonialism is ascriptive in that it encourages recruitment based not on merit, but on such factors as ethnicity. This tendency of favoring certain groups is by no means unique to Africa and in some countries, like the United States and New Zealand, is institutionalized in the name of affirmative action to give priority in hiring to certain ethnic groups. Neo-patrimonialism, however, is different in that consideration of factors other than merit is not formalized in law but treated in a discretionary fashion by those in power. This practice has two detrimental implications. One is that the probability that the most qualified person for a particular job really gets it is smaller than in other systems. For this reason, neo-patrimonial systems can be said to be wasteful of scarce human resources. Ascription, however, also has another sinister effect. It tends to generate conflicts between primary social organizations, where the principal reason for membership is clan, ethnicity, or race. Such conflicts, which build on vertical as opposed to lateral cleavages in society (the latter typically being socio-economic in nature) are more difficult to manage and therefore pose greater risks for society. Students of ethnicity in Africa, e.g., Young (1977) and Kasfir (1979), have pointed to the relatively pragmatic use of ethnic identity in Africa. They are right so far as individuals have a chance to determine themselves, how to handle their identity. Such an interpretation, however, is less applicable to situations in which identity is deliberately politicized by a neo-patrimonial leadership to serve their own purposes in power. Africa is full of such examples, some more glaring than others, but they span all the way from Siyad Barre's nefarious manipulation of clan relations in Somalia, to Daniel arap Moi's use of low-intensity ethnic violence to strengthen his party's election fortunes, and to the Nigerian military's refusal to accept the outcome of the 1993 presidential election, in which a man from the "wrong" ethnic group was poised to win. Especially important to emphasize here is that ascription has not disappeared with democratization. In fact, the accounts provided here indicate that it may have been further enhanced. Our hypothesis is that the more competitive elections are, the greater the risk of falling back on ascriptive criteria for conducting politics. In short, there is a complex relationship between the introduction of democratic forms, on the one hand, and the elimination of neo-patrimonialism, on the other, that needs to be more extensively explored. In this volume, Suberu draws attention to the role of the electoral system. The prevailing "first-past-the-post" or plurality system tends to have the effect of reinforcing zero-sum attitudes in politics. How far the electoral system really is part of the problem is an issue that is still worth more attention, although there are some analysts (e.g., Barkan 1996) who see so many other virtues with the plurality system that they consider it worth retaining.

Particularly relevant here is the style of governance or rule. Neo-patrimonial rule rests on a zero-sum approach to politics, according to which there is no scope for compromise. This is a very crude way of conducting politics and one which is especially detrimental to reasoned deliberations and policy-making. Nonetheless, African rulers to this day continue to look upon compromise in politics as a sign of weakness: a compromise is never a victory, as it often is in democratic systems based on reasoned debate; on the contrary, it is seen as a loss, something that one can agree to only in the very last resort. In most cases, rulers will do whatever they can to preempt such a situation from arising, hence the frequency of political detentions and other breaches of human rights that Joan Kakwenzire discusses in her chapter.

What we have been trying to argue in the foregoing is that the problems of African development cannot be attributed only to state performance, but are due to the replacement of the civic nature of the public realm, which African countries inherited at the time of independence (however imperfect it was then) with a parochial, neo-patrimonialist set of rules that has proved totally inadequate for the task of governing a modern state. It is the widespread dissatisfaction with these norms in African countries that is as responsible as any other factor for the calls for political reform, including the pressures from the international community.

The Resurgence of External Factors

External forces have come to play a disproportionately large role in African development in recent years. Although political independence was meant to enhance African self-reliance and such ambitions have continued at the rhetorical level to this day, the fact is, of course, that most African countries have become increasingly dependent on external forces, notably the international finance institutions. The financial or economic dependence on these organs has been accompanied in the 1990s by a degree of political dependence that was not there formerly. To be sure, at a very general level there was always a certain degree of dependence, even when African countries lined up behind one of the superpowers in the Cold War, as Kayode Soremekun discusses in his chapter. This dependence, however, manifested itself primarily in behavior in the international arena; it was hardly intrusive at the national level. State sovereignty was never really questioned in the days of the Cold War. This is what has changed in the 1990s. The dependence that African countries now experience includes measures aimed at influencing not only domestic policies but the very constitution of the political order. It is a level of intrusiveness that African countries have not witnessed since the days of colonialism, and it is no coincidence that some critical observers see in the extension of this situation the prospect of re-colonization of the continent.

We do not hold the opinion that such a scenario will necessarily develop, but our study points to the fact that the new dependency is largely the result of self-inflicted measures, notably the virtual collapse of norms and rules that sustain both a functioning state and a vibrant civil society. The loss of legitimacy that is associated with this decline has led to governance emerging as a critical field of research. Although our use of the concept here has remained rather loose, each author in his or her way alludes, explicitly or implicitly, to the breakdown of the civic nature of the public realm.

The restoration of political order in Africa, therefore, is first and foremost a matter of instituting new norms that are embraced broadly enough that they might withstand attacks from forces interested in perpetuating neo-patrimonialism. There is no convincing evidence, at least yet, that the introduction of competitive elections—often considered the real "gateway" to democracy—produces the conditions under which such new regime norms and rules can be effectively implemented. Students of African politics in the 1990s will not necessarily find the answers to the problems of regime transition if their interest is confined largely to the study of elections. While these obviously are important events in every country's domestic politics, they seem, however, less promising as objects of research if the overall concern is what counts in constituting a more democratic political order.

We have a situation in Africa, as the first decade of democratization efforts is coming to an end, where the regime issues remain least satisfactorily tackled in those countries which have made a gradual transition to multi-party democracy; where, according to some critical observers, the changes have been largely cosmetic. Thus, the legacy of neo-patrimonialism has been most difficult to erase where there has been the least radical turnover of the existing order. The regime issues have been addressed most thoroughly in those countries which have gone through what an increasing number of African observers call a "second liberation." These countries include Eritrea, Ethiopia, and Uganda. We do not argue here that these countries are necessarily more democratic today than other countries are, but they have at least taken a more consistent approach to how to contain the adverse effects of neo-patrimonialism. For this reason, they may also stand a better chance in the long run to consolidate the gains they have made towards instituting a new political order in which governance practices are likely to be more effective and legitimate.

One thing that Eritrea, Ethiopia, and Uganda share with South Africa is that they have all undertaken a comprehensive constitutional review. These broad-based exercises have not only allowed members of the public to become more familiar with constitutional issues and also come forward with proposals of their own, but they have contributed to the evolution of the kind of constitutional consciousness that Okoth-Ogendo argues has been lacking in much of Africa to date. A recent study of these experiences does indicate that constitution-making with a view to creating a consensus about which rules should prevail is a constructive precursor to the holding of elections and a "safer" approach to regime transition than the mere holding of elections (Hyden and Venter, forthcoming).

These cases are also interesting because they have allowed the African actors to remain in the "driver's seat." By seizing the initiative, the governments of the countries mentioned above have placed the external actors in a situation where they have fewer opportunities and less leverage to shape the process. In the majority of Africa's countries, however, where the old order is being perpetuated by the same style of neo-patrimonialist rule, the role of the external actors is both more exposed and more controversial. Because there is nowadays a broad consensus in international circles that the neo-patrimonialist system of rule does not help African countries solve their social and economic problems—and because an increasing number of Africans themselves realize this —the moral claim by African leaders that state sovereignty must not be violated (a call that was widely respected until recently) no longer carries much weight. This is particularly so because the African continent is full of examples where the adverse effects of corrupt and inefficient governance are manifest to all. This presents the external actors with a moral dilemma. Many would like to withdraw from Africa altogether because they have seen very few results, if any, of their previous actions. It is no secret that, strategically, Africa means very little today to those who were once its colonizers. At the same time, there is still a measure of humanitarian concern that transcends national and cultural boundaries which makes many governments in other parts of the world ready to intervene in African affairs to save human life and help promote a return to normalcy where political conflicts have led to widespread suffering. These external actors, however, whether governmental or non-governmental, also realize that interventions after conflicts have broken out rarely ever become anything but a "band-aid" exercise. For these reasons, one of the catchwords in the international community today is conflict prevention or preventive diplomacy. This posture inevitably implies taking an active stand against the very causes of deadly conflict, among which neo-patrimonialist rule is one of the more prominent. That is why in countries where this type of rule continues virtually unchallenged (e.g., Kenya and Nigeria) external actors believe they act in the interest of the country's citizens by openly criticizing the government for its failure to introduce and/or respect the rules of democratic governance. The relative weight of these interventions is enhanced by the fact that the political opposition has proved incompetent. The external actors have become an agency of last resort, which citizens in these countries increasingly accept have a vital role to play in correcting some, if not all, of the arbitrary measures taken by the "strong men" in power. This is most likely not the way they would like things to be, but the perpetuation of neo-patrimonialism has caused a sense of disillusionment and frustration among large groups of people in these countries; hence, a new readiness in many circles to accept the role that foreign diplomats and external aid agencies play in many African countries today.

The degree of resurgence of external forces in African affairs therefore is, we argue, correlated to the extent that a neo-patrimonialist system of rule continues. If the old regime and system of governance has not been subject to radical overhaul, the outside pressures on government leaders are much stronger than in places where such a radical rupture with the past has taken place. The latter finds it easier to deal with external actors and can hold them at bay more easily. To the extent that they accept a degree of transparency and respect for human rights, they can get away with other demands for democratic governance—e.g., multi-party politics, as the case of Uganda illustrates. The notion that the external actors apply double standards, arguing for multi-party politics in one country but not in another, has been used by the Kenyan Government (comparing itself with that of Uganda). The significant thing is that such an argument has carried little or no weight in the domestic Kenyan debate. Those pressing for constitutional and legal reform there believe that they have a strong case regardless of what the external actors have to say about their country and others.

Conclusions

Adebayo Williams concludes this volume with a review of the changing intellectual context in which governance and development issues have been discussed in Africa since the days of nationalism. Using strong words, he stresses the "programmed self-destruction" that has characterized the political leadership since independence. But he is also worried about the complicity that African intellectuals have had in this degeneration by allowing themselves to serve the interests of opportunistic rulers. While others may not necessarily express it in the same strong words, it is difficult to deny that Williams is right in noting that African intellectuals have not always stood up strongly enough to oppose the destruction of the civicness of the public realm. Too many have been co-opted by the system through acceptance of short-term benefits produced by the discretionary measures of neo-patrimonialist rule.

The full consequences of this trend for the intellectuals may be evident only now that universities suffer from a shortage of creative and upright leadership. The very institutions that could play a key role in helping to bring about a shift away from neo-patrimonialism are currently so weak that their own perpetuation, as Williams argues, is in question. It is hard to escape the conclusion of his analysis, therefore, that the battle for a new form of governance begins close to home, as far as all intellectuals go. Some may argue that this is placing too heavy a burden or too high an expectation on what intellectuals can achieve, but, given the paucity of other forces in society, there is little doubt that (with the exception of external actors discussed above) intellectuals constitute the most promising group to lead a reformation of the political order. This may mean that African intellectuals have to get directly involved in political organizations created to achieve such an end, as happened in Uganda, where the National Resistance Movement was above all a movement of frustrated intellectuals. Apart from the contribution they can make towards such an overhaul of neo-patrimonial systems of rule, their concern with governance reforms is also warranted for reasons that are more directly related to their own profession. Neo-patrimonial systems have proved to be inherently hostile to free and objective inquiry. If we are interested, therefore, in academic freedom and the emergence of a culture that sustains it, there is no way these issues can just be left to others to settle.

As the two governance research projects that preceded the production of this volume and the contributors here all indicate, the agenda for future investigations can easily be made very long. We particularly stress the connection between governance and regime on the one hand and state and policy on the other as an interesting and potentially productive area of further research. For example, getting policy to work for the benefit of ordinary citizens is an issue closely tied to the nature of the rules that guide political action. The authors of this volume also indicate the need for the research agenda to transcend the currently predominant interest in how formal institutions like elections help democratization. For example, how democratic governance may be fostered from below through initiatives taken by groups of citizens or communities is not only a practical but also a scholarly concern. In short, the African perspective on governance that we provide here calls for an expansion of the research agenda beyond what mainstream scholarship on democratization in Western countries treats as most important. In this respect, the individual contributions that follow this introductory chapter are all of interest to students of comparative politics interested in knowing how their counterparts in another region of the world look at some of the most pertinent issues of the day.

Works Cited

Barkan, Joel D. "Debate PR—Southern Africa: Elections in Agrarian Societies," *Journal of Democracy* 6, 4 (1995):106–116.

Bayart, Jean-Francois. *The State in Africa: The Politics of the Belly.* New York: Longman, 1992.

Bratton, Michael and Nicolas van de Walle. *Democratic Experiments in Africa.* New York: Cambridge University Press, 1997.

Callaghy, Thomas. *The State-Society Struggle: Zaire in Comparative Perspective.* New York: Columbia University Press, 1984.

Carter Center. *Beyond Autocracy in Africa.* Atlanta, Ga.: The Carter Center of Emory University, 1989.

Carter Center. *African Governance in the 1990s.* Atlanta, Ga.: The Carter Center of Emory University, 1990.

Clapham, Christopher. *Third World Politics: An Introduction.* Madison, Wis.: University of Wisconsin Press, 1985.

Clark, John. *Democratizing Development.* London: Earthscan, 1991.

Ekeh, Peter. "Colonialism and the Two Publics: A Theoretical Statement", *Comparative Studies in Society and History* 17, 1(1975):91–117.

Hyden, Goran. "The Study of Governance" in G. Hyden and M. Bratton, eds., *Governance and Politics in Africa.* Boulder, Colo.: Lynne Rienner Publishers, 1992.

Hyden, Goran. "Governance and the Reconstitution of Political Order" in Richard Joseph, ed., *State, Conflict, and Democracy in Africa.* Boulder, Colo.: Lynne Rienner Publishers, 1998.

Hyden, Goran, and Denis Venter, eds. *Constitution-Making in Africa: Lessons from the Second Liberation.* Oxford University Press, forthcoming.

Jackson, Robert H. *Plural Societies and New States.* Institute of International Studies. University of California, Berkeley, 1977.

Jackson, Robert H., and Carl G. Rosberg. *Personal Rule in Black Africa: A Conceptual Analysis.* Berkeley and Los Angeles: University of California Press, 1982.

Joseph, Richard. *Democracy and Prebendal Politics in Nigeria.* New York: Cambridge University Press 1987.

Kasfir, Nelson. "Explaining Ethnic Political Participation," *World Politics* 31, 3(1979):369–385.

Lipset, Seymour Martin. "Some Social Requisites of *Democracy: Economic Development and Political Legitimacy,"* American Political Science Review* 53, 1(1959):69–105.

Mabogunje, Akin. "Institutional Radicalisation, Local Governance and the Democratisation Process in Nigeria" in Dele Olowu, Kayode Soremekun, and Adebayo Williams, eds. *Governance and Democratisation in Nigeria.* Ibadan, Nigeria: Spectrum Books, 1995.

Majone, Giandomenico. *Evidence, Argument, and Persuasion in the Policy Process.* New Haven and London: Yale University Press, 1989.

Mamdani, Mahmood. *Citizen and Subject: Contemporary Africa and the Legacy of Late Colonialism.* Princeton, N.J.: Princeton University Press, 1996.

Medard, Jean-Francois. "The Underdeveloped State in Tropical Africa: Political Clientelism or Neo-Patrimonialism" in Christopher Clapham, ed., *Private Patronage and Public Power: Political Clientelism in the Modern State.* London: Frances Pinter, 1982.

Migdal, Joel. *Strong Societies and Weak States: State-Society Relations and State Capabilities in the Third World.* Princeton, N.J.: Princeton University Press, 1988.

O'Donnell, Guillermo, and Philippe C. Schmitter. *Transition from Authoritarian Rule: Tentative Conclusions about Uncertain Democracies.* Baltimore, Md.: Johns Hopkins University Press, 1986.

Olowu, Dele, Kayode Soremekun, and Adebayo Williams, eds. *Governance and Democratisation in Nigeria.* Ibadan, Nigeria: Spectrum Books, 1995.

Olowu, Dele, Kayode Soremekun, and Adebayo Williams, eds. *Governance and Democratisation in West Africa.* Dakar, Senegal: CODESRIA Press, 1999.

Rothchild, Donald. "Inter-Ethnic Conflict and Policy Analysis in Africa," *Ethnic and Racial Studies* 9, 1 (1986):66–86.

Rothchild, Donald, and Naomi Chazan, eds. *The Precarious Balance: State and Society in Africa.* Boulder, Colo.: Westview Press, 1988.

Sandbrook, Richard. *The Politics of Africa's Economic Stagnation.* Cambridge: Cambridge University Press, 1985.

World Bank. *Governance and Development.* Washington, D.C.: The World Bank, 1992.

Young, Crawford. *The Politics of Cultural Pluralism.* Madison, Wis.:

University of Wisconsin Press, 1976.

Young, Crawford. *The African Colonial State in Comparative Perspective.* New Haven and London: Yale University Press, 1994.

2

The Quest for Constitutional Government

H. W. O. Okoth-Ogendo

The Problem

Written constitutions have come to assume a pivotal role in the organization of the modern state and the conduct of government worldwide. The primary reason for this is that contemporary societies have become so complex that relations between various organs of the state, *inter se,* and with spheres of civic freedom and responsibility can no longer be left to age-old conventions and practices, but must, instead, be reduced to rules and objective principles to which all relevant parties can appeal and aspire. Indeed, the doctrine of the "unwritten constitution," even in the context of the Westminster model, is now no more than an elegant fiction.

The constitutional history of Africa in the course of this century, especially South of the Sahara, while attesting to the centrality of written constitutions and the complexity of issues surrounding constitutions and governance, has generated an intriguing and remarkable paradox. For while there is clear evidence of commitment to

33

the idea of written constitutions, we are yet to see an equally firm commitment to constitutional government across the region. Because such commitment is an important indicum of popular sovereignty, it follows also that governments throughout this region have not yet attained a full measure of political legitimacy.

What factors explain these phenomena? What will it take for Sub-Saharan Africa to move from mere declarations of constitutional intent to a vibrant and broadly internalized system of constitutional government? Will the current waves of plural politics and demands for constitutional reform provide a framework for that transition? This paper will explore these issues by examining emerging trends in governance over the last four decades, and by assessing prospects for constitutionalism and governance in the twenty-first century.

Constitutions and Constitutionalism

The Idea of a Constitution

There is no single or authoritative definition of what a constitution is; nor is there a minimum set of principles that defines the content of a "model" constitution. Throughout history, different societies at particular stages of development have pronounced varying factual, philosophical, or theological conditions as equivalent to a constitution. Thus any of the following phenomena can be as much a constitution as a document which bears that nomenclature:
- a single constitutive act,
- a fundamental norm, value, or moral principle,
- a set of common aspirations or expectations,
- a social and economic programme, or
- an important juridical fact.

A "constitution" need not, therefore, be embodied in a single written document, even though most of them now are (Van Maarseveen and Van der Tang 1978). The point to emphasize is that what is recognized as "the Constitution" should have some organic or generic character, or that it should be generally recognized as the primary point of reference for governance in society.

No society is, therefore, without a constitution even though not every constitution is adequate for the society to which it applies. In Africa, where the nation-state is an amalgam of semi-autonomous communities and nationalities, the so-called "state constitution" is only one among many other instruments that answer to the description of "a constitution." The meekness of the written state constitution, therefore, is that it is treated as the primary referential instrument for governance only at the supranational level. In other words, virtually all African states are polyconstitutional rather than military. The implications of this for governance will be examined later.

The Concept of Constitutionalism

To have a constitution (written or unwritten) is not the same thing as enjoying or living under a system of constitutional government. That depends on whether society in general and those responsible for the management of public affairs in particular, adhere to basic principles of constitutionalism. The classic, basically Western Liberal conception of constitutionalism connotes both stability in the organization of the state and adherence to a political ideal about how best to organize the state (Zoethout 1995). In the one case constitutionalism entails the codification of the various organs of the state, and in the other it has come to imply the existence of restraints on the powers of government. The notion that constitutionalism implies limitation of state power derives from the fact that, without it, the operation of government can easily relapse into arbitrary rule.

In my view, codification and the existence of constraints on governmental power, though important, are not the hallmarks of constitutionalism. The idea of constitutionalism must, in the very first instance, imply that a society acknowledges its constitution as a living standard with which the conduct of public behavior should conform and against which it must be evaluated. The minimum evidence of adherence to the principles of constitutionalism is therefore public respect for the constitution, in whatever form, of the society of which one is a member. At a more fundamental level, constitutionalism involves habitual acceptance of the rules enshrined in the constitution or consistent with constitutional principles as the ultimate bases of political choice. Fidelity to life under law is thus a fundamental principle of constitutionalism. Constitutionalism in this sense is not merely a legal concept; it is a political principle of great importance.

Do Constitutions Matter?

The road to the orderly process of government thus commences with a publicly acknowledged constitution, even though it does not terminate there. In this sense, therefore, constitutions matter. But there is more. According to Finer, even when constitutions are being violated, subverted, or otherwise ignored, one must not lose faith in them and this for several reasons.

The first is that while no one constitution is an entirely realistic description of what actually happens in society are one hundred percent unrealistic fictions bearing no relationship whatsoever to what goes on (Finer 1979)

There will always be some fundamental social, economic, or political concern buried in the text of every constitutional instrument in operation at any point of a nation's history. Those who abrogated and replaced the many constitutional instruments that have littered the political landscapes of Central African Republic, Togo, Gabon, Nigeria, Benin, Sudan, Ethiopia, and Ghana, for example, must have believed that they were creating new structures and norms for their respective societies. Whether these new instruments were appropriate or not at those particular points of history is another matter.

The second reason is that the mere fact that constitutional texts may not change over a considerable period of time does not mean that the fundamental concerns of society remain static. Finer cautions that different historical contexts have generated different pre-occupations; different preoccupations have generated different emphases (op. cit.). Hence, although certain basic and cross-cultural functions are and should be expected of any constitution, no single constitutional model is good for all societies at all times. A constitution is therefore appropriate or inappropriate only to the extent that it does or does not embody the basic concerns of a given society either in general terms or in respect of particular interests.

The third reason, which is of particular relevance to post-colonial societies, is that the constitution is quite often also the instrument which constitutes the state. In its constitutive function, the constitution is the instrument that pronounces the existence of the state and defines the extent of its territorial borders. Articles 1 and 2 of the Constitution of the United Republic of Tanzania, 1977, is typical of nearly all first post-colonial constitutions. It declares as follows:

- Tanzania is one State and is a United Sovereign Republic
- (i) The territory of the United Republic consists of the whole of the area of Mainland Tanzania and the whole of the area of Tanzania Zanzibar, and includes territorial waters.

Although this assertion is quite unnecessary, it serves the important function of demonstrating the sovereignty of the state. It is an announcement to all and sundry that a new state is born.

The issue for Africa, therefore, is not whether constitutions matter, but what it will take to develop a vibrant tradition of constitutionalism and a process of constitutional government.

The Meaning of Constitutional Government

The Concept of Governance

History is replete with evidence demonstrating that the transition from declarations of constitutional intent to a full state of constitutional government is essentially a function not of law *per se,* but of the political-economic environment in general. Central to that environment is how social systems are organized and managed, how resources are allocated, managed, and consumed, how power is acquired, distributed, and exercised, and how lifestyles of present and future generations are determined. In other words, governance has always been and remains a central factor in the quest for constitutional government.

Although the concept of and concern with governance is not new, its entry into the discourse on the nature of government in Africa is relatively new. A number of definitions have emerged in recent times as to what this concept entails and its relevance to decision-making in public affairs. In a rather unhelpful passage, the World Bank, in attributing Africa's development problems to a crisis of governance, defined that concept simply as "the exercise of political power to manage a nation's affairs" (World Bank, 1989). Hyden and Bratton have, on the other hand, explained governance in terms of the conscious management of regime structures with a view to enhancing the legitimacy of the public realm (Hyden and Bratton 1992).

That latter definition sees governance as a systematic and processional framework within which legitimate public enterprise activities are conducted. More specifically, it implies creative interaction designed to promote full and effective participation by the citizenry in public affairs, accountability by the state to civic activism, continuous state-society and intra-society nexus, and ultimately, the existence of institutional arrangements founded on and designed to sustain those values.

As an analytical concept, therefore, governance is both a standard of measurement and an outcome of what constitutes acceptable conduct of public affairs, at several levels. In the context of political decision-making, governance is a crucial variable in the distribution of power and the allocation of resources in virtue of that power distribution. Further, to the extent that economic and social planning depends on an appreciation of the interplay between human needs and the stock of resources available to society, to that extent will governance as a standard and an outcome determine the values that must enter into the calculus of development. Finally, governance is also about how society builds and sustains structures and institutions necessary for the management of its affairs.

As a practical matter, the quality of governance in any given society will, of necessity, vary with the empirical manifestations of particular regimes of management or mismanagement of public affairs. Governance as a standard of measurement need not therefore be confused with government which may be "good" or "bad" depending on who is in charge of public affairs at a specific point in time.

Constitutions. Governance. and Constitutional Government

For the purpose of this paper, governance will be viewed as the link between statements of constitutional intent and a full state of constitutional government. For it is the quality of governance which *per force* must determine the extent of commitment to or the level of habitual acceptance of constitutional rules or principles. Constitutional government means, therefore, that regime behavior as a whole (as measured by particular structural, organizational, or normative expressions of government) is a reflection of its avowed constitution, and the processes derived from that conduct answer to the essence of constitutionalism as earlier defined. In other words, governance is the contextual variable which society requires before public respect for "the Constitution" and the other elements signifying commitment to constitutionalism (see Supra) can be translated into a vibrant system and process of constitutional government. There will, of course, be practical difficulties in determining whether or not a given society has internalized the minimum threshold of values necessary for that linkage. We think, however, that the absolute indispensable minimum must be a high degree of commitment in public discourse to the essence of constitutionalism. That commitment should pervade the ideology of statecraft even if not immediately acted out in the arena of public decision-making as a matter of obligation. Only upon the attainment of that threshold can it be said that a process of constitutional government is on the horizon. Constitutional government is therefore not simply about the production, distribution, and exercise of power, or the aggregation and allocation of resources in accordance with the terms stipulated in the constitution; the governance context in which these activities take place is an integral part of that enterprise.

How well have African countries fared in this whole calculus? Judged by the criteria set out in the preceding sections, it is clear that—although virtually all African states, at one point or another, have had constitutions (most of them more than one)—the full state of constitutional government is yet to be attained in any of them. The reasons are both historical and contemporary.

Constitutional Atrophy and Collapse[1] in Africa

Historical Antecedents

For over a century now, Africa has been undergoing a number of traumatic experiences. The first is the trauma of colonialism and extractive imperialism that commenced in the middle of the nineteenth century and continued well into the decade of the 1980s. The second is the trauma of irresponsible politics that started soon after political liberation in the late 1950s and deepened in the 1970s. The third is the trauma of economic stagnation and reversal that started to register in the 1980s and is expected to continue well into the twenty-first century.

The consequences of colonialization and imperial extraction are everywhere. The very foundation of the development gridlock in which Africa now finds herself is rooted in that particular experience. It is this experience which all but destroyed Africa's capacity for endogenously creating a viable political order.

The constitutional structures that departing colonial authorities imposed as media of power transfer in both English- and French-speaking Africa had precedent neither in the system of colonial government itself nor in whatever remained of the social and cultural ideology of the colonized peoples. The entity created by the constitution was, in essence, no more than a "constituted state" (Okoth-Ogendo 1993, 1996) perched precariously on top of fragile and fractionalized nationalities or cultural domains. The so-called national constitution was thus virtually incapable of domestication let alone internalization, whatever quality of governance regime structures might adopt. That, however, was only one problem.

Contemporary Factors

Irresponsible politics and economic stagnation after independence made the development of constitutional government not merely impossible, but, for many governing elites, cumbersome and undesirable. The persistent dissipation of national treasuries by rent-seeking elites; the propensity to resolving political conflicts through coups, counter-coups, irredentism, and ethnic chauvinism; the reckless experimentation with foreign ideologies; and the total disregard of organs of civil society in matters of governance are some of the factors that readily come to mind (Wunsch and Olowu 1990; Zartman 1995).

The "constitutional order" as designed at independence thus functioned, when it did at all, mainly as a costly irrelevance which the new states were best rid of! But just as colonial authorities made little or no attempt at creating minimum conditions for the establishment and operationalization of a constitutional order, post-colonial elites equally made no attempts at the design of appropriate structures and institutions of government. What should have been an opportunity for reflective constitution-making or constitutional reform became instead an excuse for the dismantling of independence constitutions.

The Dismantling of the Constituted State

The dismantling of the constituted state, when it came, was rapid and virulent in most parts of Africa. Within a span of less than thirty years, various African states underwent:
  • in excess of seventy-five military takeovers and more than two hundred attempts at abrogation of the written

constitution in at least one country (Swaziland);
- numerous amendments to the power structure of the constitution in more than five countries (Kenya, Tanzania, Zambia, Malawi, Sierra Leone);
- disregard of constitutional and especially human rights principles by both the executive and judicial arms of government on numerous occasions; and
- massive centralization of power through increased use of discretion, public-order, and public-security legislation, and reduction of the political space available to governmental critics.

In nearly all of these cases, the independence constitutions were often cited by the military and civilian rulers alike as the primary impediment to the operation of governmental functions. What is intriguing, but not entirely surprising, is that attempts to re-enact fresh constitutions showed no clear understanding of what the necessary and sufficient principles of a constitutional order should be. Repeatedly, what the African military and civilian rulers came up with were remarkably similar to what they were rejecting. The exception always was that the power structures in the new constitutions were carefully rearranged so as to remove the fetters upon central authority which characterized the old. A number of states (for example, Ghana, Tanzania, Zambia, Malawi, and Kenya) went so far as to legislate political competition out of the constitution altogether through the establishment of the one-party state. Others, like Zaire, Togo, and Benin simply issued decrees to that effect.

The result is that constitutional structures, where they remained or were re-established, became little more than instruments of political warfare. Appeal to constitutional authority by ruling elites, thereafter, was being made only if it reinforced their own narrow view of state power. In other words, the constitutional structure was quickly turned by the ruling elites into a shield for the protection of their interests and a sword to be used against their enemies rather than a framework for the enhancement of social, political, and economic rights of the polity as a whole. In addition, the power structures in all countries, whether under civilian or military rule, were reorganized in such a way as to confer on ruling elites authority far in excess of what colonial administrators ever exercised. The effect of this was not only to weaken the autonomy of the civil service bureaucracy but also to isolate organs of civil society from any meaningful participation in government. The centralized state, as Wunsh and Olowu (1990) point out, soon found itself, under the weight of the inefficiency arising from constitutional, administrative, and political concentration of power, unable to discharge any useful functions in society. Indeed the state as an instrument of power and a framework for the management of public affairs (including resources) simply atrophied and all but collapsed in many parts of Africa (Zartman 1995).

The Reconstruction of the State in Africa

The Challenge

The above scenario suggests that the reconstruction of the state in Africa is an essential first step in the transition to constitutional government. There are, in our view, two important parameters to consider: the first is the nature of the political discourse, which forms the platform for that step; and the second, its normative and institutional (i.e., constitutional) agenda. The first addresses the issues of what is currently on the table, who is engaged in that discourse, and what their specific targets are. Because politics is generally an affair of strategic brinkmanship, it is important that attention be paid to the "language" in which that discourse is conducted. The rhetoric may, however, conceal poorly articulated but nonetheless important expectations. The second parameter, therefore, focuses on the specific outcomes, expressed or implied, which that discourse contemplates.

The Discourse

We have argued above that governance must be viewed as the link between constitutional intent and constitutional process. Consequently, the discourse of reconstruction itself needs to be presented and resolved in that language. What that means is that it is not enough merely to understand and condemn or vilify what has gone wrong with the business of statecraft in Africa. Perhaps more fundamental is the need to articulate a clear, corrective path for the future. Is there evidence that this is happening?

Current debates on reconstruction in Africa are organized, by and large, around one primary message: the need for democratization (or liberalization or, less normatively, good governance). Within that general rubric, a great deal is also being said about the need for "the strengthening of civil society," "minimum constitutional reforms," and "human rights" issues. Organizing political discourse around the general call for democracy has brought a number of important but old issues into sharp focus. These include the dangers of excessive concentration of power, the nature and character of democratic space in relation to politics, economy, and culture; the "proper" role of the state in development; and the nature of popular sovereignty (Buijtenhuijse, and Rijnierse 1993; Hyden and Bratton 1992).

The resolution of that debate in terms of a concrete framework for governance in a reconstructed state is, however, far from clear. As Crawford Young has observed, although many important changes have occurred by virtue of these discourses, the results thus far fall far short of consolidated[2] democracy by any reasonably rigorous criteria (Young 1996; see also Linz and Stepan 1996). There are, perhaps, several reasons for this. First, members of the political class participating in that discourse still associate democracy largely with plural politics. The fact that in this decade alone nearly all one-party or military regimes in Africa have succumbed to multiparty elections is therefore considered more or less the terminus of the struggle. Indeed, supplementary discourses continuing in Kenya, Zambia, Zimbabwe, and Uganda, for example, are concerned primarily with how to improve the integrity of the electoral process—freedom, fairness, "level playing fields," etc. Second, the discourse of democracy itself appears limited in terms of its expected impact on social organization in general and the organization of statecraft in particular. Power transfer as opposed to power transformation is still the dominant theme of discourse. This, as we shall see below, has narrowed considerably the constitutional agenda emerging from it. Finally, the public domain remains relatively excluded from that discourse. Although there is a lot of language about the importance of civil society in the process of democratization; civil society itself is not properly engaged in that discourse. The social forces, both internal and external, which are active in that discourse can in no way be described as "organs" or "agents" of civil society (Shivji 1991).

This third reason requires some elaboration. Linz and Stepan (1996) have defined civil society as "that area of the polity where self-organizing and relatively autonomous groups, movements, and individuals attempt to articulate values, to create associations and solidarities, and to advance interests."

They go on to indicate that that arena may contain "manifold social movements," such as women's groups, neighborhood associations, religious groupings, intellectual organizations, trade unions, entrepreneurial groups, and professional associations. The problem with this approach, and one which appears to becloud the discourse on democracy in Africa, is the assumption that the existence of those movements, *ipse dixit,* constitutes an active civil society realm. And yet many of these movements have always been and some still are either part and parcel of Linz and Stepan's other conceptual category—political society, or essentially creations of political society. Trade unions, professional cartels, church hierarchies, and non-governmental organizations, have a particularly established association with governments throughout Africa. Indeed, many of them often demonstrated their loyalty to political society by eschewing active politics on grounds that this was the domain of professional politicians and political parties, even when they operated as instruments of the state in respect of service (material and moral) delivery to communities at the grassroots level.

The fact that these movements are internal and have in the last several years reversed course and are now active participants in the arena of politics (usually against the ruling classes), though of great importance to the discourse on democracy, in no way makes them organs of or manifestations of an active civil society realm. The problem is not simply conceptual; it is fundamentally about membership and legitimate attribution.

This brings us to the fourth reason why the current discourse on democracy has not, thus far, produced a clear governance framework for the future; namely, that the discourse itself has been hijacked by and converted into a sectarian agenda by these movements in association with powerful external forces. For this reason the language of discourse is often framed in global generalities, hence is anything but contextual. As a result, the agenda appears elegant, but deceptively universal. Not only have internal movements managed to relocate themselves into the arena of active politics, especially in the formulation of national social economic policies, they have also claimed and largely won the right to call the state and its organs to account in respect of the implementation of those policies. Specifically, they argue that the state should create an enabling environment for development through, *inter alia,* responsible political behavior, respect for human rights and the rule of law, transparent governments, and public responsiveness. What is missing here is a clear account of how those values can be internalized in particular social, political, cultural, and economic contexts.

External pressures emanating from international political developments in general and donor country policies in particular have given further credence to this universal language. The most significant development on the international scene is the collapse of the communist/socialist regimes of Eastern Europe, in general, and the dismemberment of the Union of Soviet Socialist Republics (USSR), in particular. What that development has meant for Africa is perhaps twofold. For one, it made those African countries that depended on the USSR for political, military, and economic support extremely vulnerable to internal social and political pressures for change. It is not surprising that many of the "satellite" states of Eastern Europe in both English- and French-speaking Africa were quickly overridden by insurgencies fueled by internal movements (Riley 1991). For another, the collapse of Eastern Europe was also read as a demonstration that the model of economic growth and development, political organization, and constitutional order developed there (which many African countries had copied) was fundamentally flawed. African scholars and elites that had idealized that model were thus forced to re-examine its basic tenets and, in particular, the central role it assigned to the state and its bureaucratic apparatii (Riley 1991) The effect of this is that the political and economic ideology of western democratic liberalism became the universal language—indeed, the only organizing idiom—of state recon- struction or design everywhere in Africa (Hyden and Bratton 1992).

Changes in donor community policies and politics has provid- ed another important leverage. Donor communities, their agencies, and the Bretton Woods institutions, particularly the IMF, have in the last few years insisted that African countries should liberalize their economies, adopt transparent and responsible political behavior, and undergo political change. Democratization has thus become the entry point in the politics of international aid in Africa. The World Bank argued as long ago as 1989 that political legitimacy and pub- lic consensus were a pre-requisite to sustainable development. Africa's development agenda in the 1990's, the Bank added, must include the restructuring of state institutions. This is a theme which is now being pursued by all countries which provide major aid funds to Africa (World Bank 1989).

It is generally assumed that donor countries, which only a decade earlier had provided the main backstopping support for repressive regimes in Africa, suddenly realized that democratic values were universal phenomena and that it was their moral duty to propagate them on the international plane. But it is also likely that change in donor policies may well have been motivated by the desire to globalize the market economy. For Western countries in particular, the competitive advantage that their own industries had accumulated during this century would certainly have been better served by a global free market system. The discourse on international trade issues, environmental governance, technology transfer and adoption, and global investment promotion suggests that economic liberalization rather than democratization *per se* has been a stronger motive for exerting pressure on Africa. For this reason, donor communities and agencies have been more than ready to apply:

- threats of or actual aid freezes;
- proactive, if at times unconventional, diplomacy;
- candid appraisal of internal political practice; and
- observation, monitoring, and reportage of significant political events in an effort to cajole or even force African countries to "democratize."

The current discourse on the reconstruction of the state in Africa, though important both in itself and in its immediate effects, is incomplete and its long-term impact far from discernible. We are particularly worried about its deceptive universality, its lack of operational specificity, and its inability to progress beyond power-transfer politics. Particularly worrisome is its continued marginalization of the public realm and, in particular, its failure to fully engage grassroots opinion. It is in every respect a typical liberal democratic discourse—a discourse confined almost exclusively to the political elites on either side of the power calculus (Hutchful 1993).

The Agenda

The discourse we have outlined above is therefore basically one among the political elite. There is, of course, a much wider and more comprehensive conversation going on among academics and other observers of the African political landscape.[3] But that wider discourse has not and may not immediately shape the actual agenda which actors are currently negotiating in specific countries. What that agenda is, the strategies being employed by protagonists on both sides of that landscape, and its normative and institutional outcomes are essentially contextual and country-specific.

What is generally agreed upon among practitioners and observers alike, however, is that, whatever the content of that discourse, its outcomes must be captured in some juridical form.

The form most often discussed is constitutional, even though ordinary legal mechanisms are sometimes considered acceptable. Because of the rather limited focus of the political discourse, however, there is no clear indication, except most recently in South Africa, Uganda, Ethiopia, and possibly Eritrea, as to the precise constitutional form which that discourse should take.

Nonetheless, there are obvious advantages for insisting that the reconstruction of the state should assume a juridical as opposed to a merely ideological focus. The most important is that it would legitimize both the discourse and its outcomes. It is intriguing that even in countries formerly under military or pseudo-civilian rule,[4] the first step in the reconstruction process has always been the search for a "founding norm," (i.e. Grundnorm) for the new edifice. The Benin Doctrine of the "Sovereign National Convention," which brought Mathieu Kerekou's pseudo-civilian rule to an abrupt end in 1990, was an early attempt to posit a basis of legality in the absence of a pre-existing norm on which to anchor the reconstruction process. It is not surprising that the Benin Doctrine has been repeated in similar circumstances and has succeeded in all of French-speaking Africa except Togo and Zaire. In Kenya, Zambia, Malawi, and Tanzania, where original constitutions or derivations thereof still exist, attempts to apply that doctrine has (not surprisingly) failed.

The second is that in a continent that has seen so much disregard of the role of law and human rights abuses, legality is regarded as a mark of political maturity. That has more than just a propaganda value; it brings international respectability (Spiro 1959). Even in Zaire and Liberia, where the state is in total collapse, the predominant discourse around the sporadic gunfire, is not so much about the restoration of "law and order" or "democracy" *per se,* but about return to "constitutional" government. The third advantage is the expectation that the outcomes of political discourse are most likely to survive, this time around, if embodied in a set of principles that are autochthonous and autonomous, thus beyond the reach (as it were) of partisan politics. In a sense, the constitutionalization of the current discourse has a remarkably familiar ring to it, namely that only an acceptable and publicly acknowledged pre-eminent statement of political values can guarantee orderly political conduct among constituent groups in the future.

The normative and institutional agenda derived from the current discourse is thus as specific as it is admittedly narrow. It consists essentially of three items, all of which are concerned with the issue of power. The first is the reorganization of government, the second the reform of associational life, and the third the restoration of liberties.

Demand for the reorganization of government is, not surprisingly, the most hotly contested item on that agenda. Specific targets include the presidency and the administrative bureaucracy through which executive authority is exercised. Because the overconcentration of power in these organs in the last three decades is seen as a fundamental cause of political and economic decay, the primary concern here is how to dismantle and reconstitute them in a forum that is likely to engender efficiency, accountability, and public responsiveness. What the discourse is looking for are organs that can be relied upon to discharge public trust. The specific jural form in which this concern is stated is in terms of limitation of executive power through *inter alia,* increase in parliamentary controls, decentralization of authority, and the institutionalization of independent "watchdogs" outside the legislature. The model that appears to inform that discourse is the constitutional practice of the United States of America, even though that arrangement originated from very different political considerations (Thach 1969). Beyond that, there is very little clarity about the nature of the presidency; its functions and powers, its relationship to other organs of government, the procedure for its constitution, and its role in the legislative process. There is reason to be cautious about this particular aspect of the discourse. Trends emanating from Zambia, Malawi, and even Zaire, though inconclusive, indicate that demands for the reconstitution of the presidency may only be "skin deep!" The culture of the "imperial presidency" (Okoth-Ogendo 1993) could re-assert itself after the dismantling of current structures.

In regard to the bureaucracy, however, there is substantial agreement that what Africa needs is an efficient and "legal-rational" mechanism in the Weberian sense (Weber 1954). The concern here is to delink the administrative bureaucracy, especially the civil service and the uniformed forces, from the politically constituted executive. Specifically, the discourse is calling for a system of public administration which redesignates the service as facilitative frameworks for local autonomy as opposed to their current function as coercive instruments of centralized executive authority. In many African countries, that redesignation need not involve radical or any constitutional change. What is required, and what political elites not in government are asking for, therefore, is comprehensive revision of administrative law.

Tied up with, but necessarily more complex than the issue of bureaucratic reforms, *per se,* is the second item in the reconstruction agenda—namely, the reform of associational life. Central to this item is the liberalization of political space and the basic rights associated with it. Given the ideological, legal, and administrative baggage associated with decades of one-party rule, this issue has raised the greatest passion in recent years. A lot of ground has been conceded by ruling elites, however. This includes return to multiparty politics, leadership turnovers, state financing of political parties (e.g., in Tanzania, Uganda, and South Africa), and the rise of a relatively free press. Two areas, however, remain contentious.

The first is over whether or not regulatory machinery should continue to exist in respect, *inter alia,* of the formation (including registration) of political parties, the convening and conduct of public meetings, the security of party cadres and property, the requisition of resources for use by political parties, and the recruitment of party membership. Sufficient clarity is still lacking, however, as to whether the preference is for complete self-regulation or a special, if protective, legal response in this area. The proliferation of "political party laws" in East and Central Africa would indicate, however, that resolution may well be in terms of the latter.

The second contention is over the conduct of electoral politics. The issue here is how to ensure that a framework exists for the administration of free and fair elections. Although almost every country in Africa has an "Electoral Commission" or institution discharging similar functions, many of them are either substantially dominated by the ruling elites or do not have the resources (at once human, material, and financial) and the capability to conduct such elections. Consequently, much of the discourse here is also about delinkage from the state not merely in terms of procedural safeguards against executive interference, but also in terms of participation by all shades of the political spectrum in the appointment to membership in and supervision of the operations of electoral commissions. This clearly is a crucial item in the agenda of reconstruction, if only for the simple reason that elections lie at the heart of democratic government as well as affording opportunity for recruitment to all levels of political leadership (Okoth-Ogendo 1978).

The third item in the agenda of reconstruction is the restoration of civil liberties. This, many would argue, should have emerged as the essential core of the current political discourse in Africa. With a human rights record that has produced "endless tear drops" (Cohen et al. 1993), it is not surprising that the active phase of the human rights discourse preceded the "democratization" wave by almost a decade. What is ironic, however, is that power-transfer politics has virtually eclipsed constructive dialogue in this important area. The reason why may well be that, this being the one area in which elaborate constitutional provisions have always existed in both French- and English-speaking Africa, very little institution-building is called for here. The primary concern therefore, is not with the constitutionalization of civil liberties and other forms of human rights; rather, it is with the creation of organs for the enforcement or guardianship of those rights. The design of those organs and their relationship to other structures of government, especially the courts, must however, be clarified. In addition, a clearer notion of the governance framework within which state agencies and other institutions must operate in order to give effect to those rights is also needed here.

It is our assessment that because the normative, and institutional agenda drawn from the current discourse on democratization is directed mainly at power—its production, distribution, exercise, regulation, and effects—opportunity could be lost for a more wholistic reconstruction of viable structures for constitutional government. Important as power is to the organization and operation of the state, a constitutional edifice that revolves exclusively around that dynamic is not likely to survive, unless it is buttressed by conventional norms which address issues surrounding when and in what contexts particular outcomes of that power are legitimate. Such conventions can and should, over a long period of time, evolve in society. They can also be crafted or imposed, in which case, they must form part of the agenda of reconstruction itself. African countries cannot afford to wait for history to resolve that issue. Consequently, we offer the following suggestions.

Prospects for Constitutional Government in Africa

A Sense of *Deja Vu?*

Let us, at the risk of repetition, start by restating what the problem is. For more than forty years Africa's political leadership has failed to attain an acceptable level of internal and external legitimacy in the management of public affairs. As a result, decision-making in the public domain remains largely an affair of power rather than of law, of expediency rather than of essential justice, and of discreetly determined impulses rather than of social necessity. For that to change, conscious attempts must be made by all segments of society (political, economic, civil, and bureaucratic) to internalize and articulate a minimum level of "constitutionalist" discipline necessary for the creation of a just and fair social order. That will require more than active participation in the "correct" discourse. Care must be taken to ensure that that discourse is institutionalized in a manner that is both legitimate and sustainable.

Much of what is going on, however, is little more than a re-enactment of the past—some sort of *deja vu* in which the mistakes of the last forty years are again being reproduced under new guises and idioms. Most of these mistakes are the result of a number of fallacies in constitution-making dating back to colonial training and socialization. Four of these, which have been examined at length elsewhere (Okoth-Ogendo 1996) need only be summarized here. These include the mistaken notion that colonialism was itself a phase in the evolution of colonial government which is worth drawing on; that African elites are committed to the task of building a viable constitutional order; that the imposition of a unitary constitutional (i.e., nation-state) model is the best strategy for national integration; and that the reception of Western constitutional and legal models is the only way to consolidate democracy.

There are two more recent fallacies. One is the assumption that reform of the instrument called "the Constitution" is all that is required to rectify the mistakes of the past. In South Africa, for example, while the constituent Assembly was fully aware that the apartheid ideology was embedded essentially in the domains of property and administrative law, they left the task of ridding the post-1996 legal system of past attitudes and prejudices to the creative but slow initiative of the courts. Despite efforts before 1994 to rid that country of the more obvious aspects of apartheid legislation, comprehensive reform of the legal order as a whole remains as important as the momentous constitutional developments that have taken place there in the last two years.[5]

The sixth fallacy is the assumption that constitutional reform, especially if properly conducted, will cure all the ills of society. There is a strand in the on-going discourse which would want the constitution to solve a whole array of specific, essentially temporary and short-range problems. They are not prepared to leave anything to the test of time and circumstance, to creative adaptation by both judicial interpretation and executive administrative application, or indeed to future generations to write their own ideologies into the fabric of the instrument without discarding it altogether. As a result, some of the newer constitutions, such as those of South Africa, Uganda, Ethiopia, and Malawi, are not only lengthy but also fairly rigid in their prescription of certain jural principles. The 1995 Ethiopian Constitution, for example, goes so far as to prohibit its own violation or overthrow (Article 9-3)!

Some Rules of "Constitutional Prudence"

There is serious danger in raising the stakes of constitution-making to such a lofty level. A number of "constitutional prudence" rules are therefore in order as African countries define the conditions necessary for the transition to constitutional government.

The first and most important rule is to understand that constitution-making is very serious business. As a major exercise in the design and redesign of a nation, constitution-making must not be undertaken merely to achieve some short-term or sectarian goals, even though such goals may and often are the factors that trigger such an exercise. The fundamental problem of African countries which never went through military rule, such as Kenya, Malawi, Tanzania, and Senegal, is that because ruling states often "ran to amend the constitution" whenever political conflicts arose, that otherwise fundamental instrument soon lost its legitimacy. Ripe as the conditions for the redesign of the African state are, and whatever the sense of urgency, many of the current protagonists for constitutional reform feel a broad and long range view of change is clearly indispensable; and that, for two other reasons.

Constitution-making must look both to the past and to the future. Consequently, an assessment should first be made of a nation's past history, its contemporary political and legal structure, the shared values and future aspirations of its people, and its level of tolerance to ideas and ideologies before that exercise is undertaken. Further, current constitution-makers must understand that the rules they settle on are essentially about the regulation of the political conduct of future generations. Constitution-making necessarily involves substantial pre-commitment intended to last several generations. Although that has led to lively debates about the so-called "counter-majoritarian dilemma" (Tribe 1978), there is general agreement that pre-commitment— even by a minority—is a crucial starting point in the design of a constitution. The more reason there is that constitution-making should proceed on a holistic agenda.

The second rule is that constitution-making must secure an informed and active participation of the public, both in the determination of the agenda, and the promulgation of its outcomes. Public participation is particularly important at the beginning of the exercise before particular options are presented for evaluation and discussion. Further, it is important that the discourse on constitutional change be conducted in languages accessible to the public on whose behalf change is often sought. That means that the format for discourse as well as participation in the identification of basic issues should reflect not merely the influence of so-called "organs of civil society," but the general public at large— the real constituent power. Since that public cannot participate in the process as a collectivity, it must, at the very minimum, determine the rules by which active participants are to be identified. What appears to be happening instead is that political elites are basically looking for popular reaction to items of agenda drawn up in the privacy of political party, civilian cabinet, or military board rooms!

The third rule is that constitution-making outcomes must be framed in such a way as to operate in harmony with the rest of the legal order. Consequently, where, as is the case in Africa, the legal order has a more established tradition than the constitution itself, conscious attempts must be made initially by the legislative branch, and on a case-by-case basis by the courts and administrative agencies, to eradicate obvious inconsistencies and conflicts, and to imbue the former with the ideology of the latter. The fact that constitutions often pronounce themselves the supreme law has not, in Africa, prevented the judicial and executive branches from enforcing rules that are patently repugnant to constitutionalist principles.

The fourth rule is that constitution-makers must understand that, in the final analysis, it is not the intrinsic quality of a given constitution that will determine its durability or sustainability. No constitution, says Duchacek, "can cure a sick society nor protect it against usurpers" (Duchacek 1973). Hence, apart from the expectation that a constitution will work well if it works at all— if it is an accurate or, at any rate, ideologically relevant approximation or interpretation of a people's history, is accepted as the pre-eminent norm in society, is a broad summary of social consent, has mechanisms for restraint of power, and enables society to demarcate its political relationships in an orderly manner—it is the extra-constitutional realities of a given society that will determine its durability. This is what in the older constitutional regimes are referred to as "conventions" or as the "unwritten constitution" (Ryn 1992). A constitution can never be a substitute for the judicious exercise of the ordinary skills of political compromise, social responsiveness, and fidelity to the "constitutional rules of the game" (Elster 1995).

In Search of Paradigms

For the reconstruction of the state in Africa to be meaningful and for the transition from statements of constitutional promise to a full measure of constitutional government to occur, the fallacies outlined above will need to be deconstructed and the rules of "constitutional-prudence" given herein taken seriously. New paradigms of constitution-making are therefore badly needed. We have argued elsewhere that a number of such paradigms are in fact implicit in the current reconstruction debate (Okoth-Ogendo 1996). These revolve around four sets of relationships, namely, those between form and content, structures and processes, political behavior and the management of public affairs, and the need to balance autochthonous with universal principles of constitutionalism. It is important to emphasize that, while implicit in the discourse, these relationships do not as yet form part of the agenda of reconstruction. The design of what the prospective constitutional orders might look like is therefore still fuzzy. Nonetheless, by tilting discussion away from leadership paradigms to social processes, a solution may yet be found to the intractable problem of how to broaden and legitimize the outcomes of the current constitutional agenda.

Concluding Remarks

The concern of this chapter has been to examine the linkages between constitutions, constitutionalism, and governance in the current discourse on the reconstruction of the state in Africa and to assess the prospects of a viable system of constitutional government in the future. It should be evident that constitutions, but not particular species of constitutional arrangements, are important. Like Finer, while we believe that constitutions do matter, they should not be regarded as a textbook on the governance of a particular country.

Rather, a constitution resembles a sharp pencil of light which brightly illuminates a limited area of a country's political life before fading into a penumbra where the features are obscured—even if that surrounding darkness may conceal what are the most potent and significant elements of the political process. (Finer et al. 1995)

Consequently the discourse and agenda for change must emphasize values rather than structures, political "hygiene" rather than sterile institutional craftsmanship, and commitment to acceptable principles of governance rather than design of complex power-limitation mechanisms. To move from constitutional *formalia* to constitutional *realia* will take much more than a technically sound instrument.

Notes

1. Some of the materials in this and the next sections have been published in C. M. Zoethoet et al. 1996, under the title "Constitutionalism Without Constitutions: The Challenge of Reconstruction of the State in Africa." Propelled development, stunted her capacity for technological growth and adaptation, and squandered her natural and human resources. Social relations, family organizations, systems of production and reproduction, and indeed Africa's very moral universe were fundamentally shattered by the

colonial experience. A syndrome of dependency on the North for virtually every aspect of survival and a deep sense of insecurity thus became an important characteristic of the African social landscape.

2. The expression "consolidated democracy" implies, *inter alia,* a governance outcome that goes beyond mere pluralism.

3. The pages of the *Journal of Democracy* and other, specifically Africanist media are full of exciting material on this.

4. That is, military regimes that had "civilianized" themselves.

5. In Kenya, opposition elites are not even clear as to whether what is needed are "constitutional" or "legal" reforms, or both.

Works Cited

Buijtenhuijse, R., and E. Rijnierse. *Democratization in Sub-Saharan Africa (1989-1992): An Overview of the Literature.* Leiden: African Studies Centre, 1993.

Cohen, R., Hyden, G., and Nagan W. P. eds,. *Human Rights and Governance in Africa.* Gainesville, Fla: University Press of Florida, 1993.

Decalo, S. "The Process, Prospect and Constraints of Democratization in Africa." *African Affairs* 91, 362 (1992):7–36.

Duchacek, L. D. *Power Maps: Comparative Politics of Constitutions.* London: Clio Press, 1973.

Elster, J., and R. Slagstad. *Constitutionalism and Democracy.* Cambridge: Cambridge University Press, 1988.

Elster J. "Forces and Mechanisms in the Constitution-making Process," *Duke Law Journal* 45 (1987):364–396.

Finer, S. E. *Five Constitutions.* Harmondsworth: Penguin, 1979.

Finer, S. E; V. Bogdanor, and B. Rudden, eds. *Comparing Constitutions.* Oxford: Clarendon, 1995.

Huntington, S. P. "Democracy for the Long Haul," *Journal of Democracy* 7, 2 (1996):3–14.

Hyden, G., and M. Bratton, eds. *Governance and Politics in Africa.* Boulder, Colo.: Lynne Rienner Publishers. 1992.

Lane, Jan-Erik. *Constitutions and Political Theory.* Manchester: Manchester University Press, 1996.

Linz, J. J., and Stepan, A. "Toward Consolidated Democracies," *Journal of Democracy* 7, (1996):14–34.

Marseveen, Henc Van, and Ger van der Tang. *Written Constitutions: A Computerized Comparative Study.* Dobbs Ferry, N.Y.: Oceania

Publications, 1978.

Okoth-Ogendo, H. W. O. "The Politics of Constitutional Change in Kenya Since Independence: 1963–1969," *African Affairs* 71, 282 (1972): 9–34.

Okoth-Ogendo, H. W. O. "Succession to Leadership in Africa: Some Thoughts on Political Recruitment," 1978. Mimeographed.

Okoth-Ogendo, H. W. O. "Constitutions Without Constitutionalism," in D. Greenberg ed., *Constitutionalism and Democracy: Transitions in the Contemporary World.* New York: Oxford University Press, 1993.

Okoth-Ogendo, H. W. O. "Constitutionalism Without Constitutions?" in C. M. Zoethout, Carla M. Zoethout, Marlies E. Pettermaat-Kros, and P. S. Akkermans, eds. *Constitutionalism in Africa: A Quest for Autochthonous Principles.* Gouda: Quint, 1996.

Riley, S. P. "The Democratic Transition in Africa: An End to the One-Party State," *Conflict Studies* 245 (1991):1–37.

Ryn, C. G. "Political Philosophy and the Unwritten Constitution." *Modern Age* 34, 4, (1992):303–310.

Shivji, I. G., ed. *State and Constitutionalism: An African Debate on Democracy.* Harare, Zimbabwe:SAPES Books, 1991.

Spiro, H. J. *Government by Constitution: The Political System of Democracy.* New York: Random House, 1959.

Thach, C. C. *The Creation of the President 1775–1789.* Baltimore, Md.: Johns Hopkins University Press, 1969.

Tribe, Laurence H. *American Constitutional Law.* Mineola, N.Y.: Foundation Press, 1978.

Weber, Max. *Law and Economy in Society* (translation by Edward Shils and Max Rheinstein). Cambridge, Mass,: Harvard University Press, 1954.

World Bank. *Sub Saharan Africa: From Crisis to Sustainable Growth.* Washington, D.C., The World Bank, 1989.

Wunsch, J. S. and D. Olowu, eds. *The Failure of the Centralized State: Institutions and Self-Governance in Africa.* San Francisco: ICS Press, 1990.

Young, C. "Africa: An Interim Balance Sheet," *Journal of Democracy* 7, 3 (1996):53–69.

Zartman, I. W. ed. *Collapsed States: The Disintegration and Restoration of Legitimate Authority.* Boulder, Colo.: Lynne Rienner Publishers, 1995.

Zoethout, Carla M., Marlies E. Pietermaat-Kros, and P. W. C. Akkermans, eds. *Constitutionalism in Africa: A Request for Autochthonous Principles.* Gouda: Quint, 1996.

3

Human Rights and Governance

Joan Kakwenzire

Tsze-kung asked about government. The Master said, "The requisites of government are that there be sufficiency of food, sufficiency of military equipment, and the confidence of the people in their ruler." Tsze-kung said, "If it cannot be helped, and one of these must be dispensed with, which of the three should be foregone first?" "The military equipment," said the Master. Tsze-kung again asked, "If it cannot be helped, and one of the remaining two must be dispensed with, which of them should be foregone?" The Master answered, "Part with the food. From of old, death has been the lot of all men; but if the people have no faith in their rulers, there is no standing for the state."

Confucius, *Confucian Analects* (500 B.C.)

Introduction

The above quotation from Confucius clearly indicates that the relationship between basic human rights and governance of the people is a very old one. Although people must sometimes bend to the will of the sovereign, much like grass to the wind, such "bending" will only be productive when people are assured of their basic rights (such as to their lives, property, or food) and

61

have faith and trust in their leaders (Alston 1979). This means that people must not only be given material rights, but must also enjoy the immaterial freedoms of the individual such as right to privacy, freedom of conscience, and the right to choose their leaders and ways of being governed. The idea of separation between social and economic rights on the one hand, and civil and political ones on the other, therefore, is fallacious.

In Africa, and the countries we consider here in particular, most people do not have even basic rights and suffer daily abuses from their governors. How can they be expected to have faith in their governments? This chapter undertakes the difficult task of assessing and comparing the dynamics of the human rights and governance issues in the East and West African regions in the past ten years. The West African experience is analyzed by looking at the Nigerian situation, in particular, since it is the most populous and influential country in that part of Africa; the East African situation is evaluated by looking at the human rights experience of Kenya, Tanzania, and Uganda. The picture that emerges in this chapter is that while there may have been temporary improvements in the human rights situation in these countries (and people's awareness of human rights may have grown), it is still characterized by uncertainty and turbulence. Thus, the human rights needs of people are often in conflict with the interests and ambitions of political leaders. Efforts by international organizations to influence these leaders to acknowledge the importance of respect for human rights notwithstanding, little has happened so far in terms of institutionalizing systems aimed at protecting human rights in these countries. The main argument of this chapter is that the reason for the weakness, if not absence, of a viable human rights regime is the lack of strong democratic institutions at the grassroots level. Their absence enables political leaders to personalize and corrupt offices and roles and perpetually engage in "top-down" policy-making. The international community has been ineffective in altering this situation for reasons such as too narrow program goals (Archer 1994), improper implementation of projects (Paul 1989, Robinson 1994), and lack of follow-up of implemented projects (Human Rights Council of Australia 1995; CIDA 1995).

From an African perspective, it is important to recognize that the shortcomings of the international community are also the result of a double standards that it has adopted when it comes to support for democratization. "The West is so keen on the universalization of liberal democracy that it accepts easy and remarkably flexible standards of pluralism and free elections. To all appearances, the West has been generally satisfied with the form rather than the content of elections and is undisturbed that, in Africa, people are voting without choosing" (Ake 1994).

This double standard extends to almost all areas of human rights and has undermined the rapid progress made in the late 1980s and early 1990s by the urban and rural poor towards "a second liberation," that is, a march towards emancipation not from colonial masters, but from incompetent and exploitative indigenous rulers. African leaders, after an initial confusion under the sudden onslaught of mass demands for democracy, have been rescued by the amorphous political conditionalities of Western donors applied by "reducing democracy to governance and governance to the political correlates of structural adjustment, particularly the rule of law, transparency, and accountability" (Ake 1994). Donor conditionalities "remain a market-driven, competitive model which favors the strong in every area and fails in practice because it fails the poorest people and the poorest countries" (Archer 1994). The result is that African governments have found it easy to pay lip service to democratization and ignore a long-term commitment to proper governance and protection of human rights. For example, it has become possible for these governments to suppress freedom of speech and peaceful assembly and to use the criminal justice system to detain and harass advocates of "the second liberation" without stepping heavily on the toes of donors. Democratization has failed to deliver the benefits, material as well as immaterial, that people in Africa have expected. Many have become worse off than before. Without greater attention to what needs to be done in addition to institutionalizing the forms of democracy, the latter effort will continue to be in vain.

Methodology

This paper provides examples of violations of human rights in recent years by ostensibly pluralist as well as military governments in Kenya, Nigeria, Tanzania, and Uganda against their opponents and critics. The performance of these governments may be compared because their legal systems have much in common, having originally been shaped by British colonial rule. To avoid confusion of facts and issues, each country's experience is discussed separately. A conclusion is drawn at the end of each sub-section.

This chapter relies on basic documents, such as those from human rights commissions and international human rights organizations, reports in newspapers as well as scholarly books and articles. In taking an African approach to human rights, I recognize that in Africa the custom has always been that individual rights are exercised and enjoyed through family and clan. While this strong linkage between individual and social rights has been weakened by the advent of Western thinking, it is clear that it has by no means been totally wiped out. In my analysis of human rights and governance issues, therefore, I start from the assumption that Africa finds itself in a transitional stage, in which a human rights culture that corresponds to the aspirations of the people is still absent or very weak. The challenge, therefore, continues to be in African countries how much effort should be given to enforcing universal human rights standards as compared with adapting these standards to conditions that are more in accordance with the socio-economic and cultural realities of contemporary Africa. Preaching human rights, as if the issue needs not be problematized, is a simplistic and mistaken approach.

Following an overview of what has been written on human rights in Africa to date, this chapter proceeds to examine a cross-section of human rights abuses and violations that have taken place in the four countries under study here. It concludes by making an overall assessment of the contemporary situation and offering a set of recommendations about what might be done.

Human Rights in Africa: A Review of
Past Contributions

Although the literature on the human rights situation in East Africa or Nigeria is relatively scant, a fair amount of more general, and theoretical, material has been produced over the past two decades. This literature can be dissected in many different ways. I have chosen here to break it down into four separate segments, that will be subject to discussion:

A. Human rights protection and promotion by governments, including the balance and demarcation between economic and social rights on the one hand, and civil and political rights on the other, the effectiveness of the separation of powers (i.e., between executive, legislative and judicial branches of government), and the extent of the desire by leaders to meet people's human rights needs.

B. The opportunity for people to participate in the promotion and protection of human rights, a focus that raises such issues as accountability and transparency, freedom of speech and association, freedom of conscience, and freedom of the person.

C. The role and ability of foreign parties to promote human rights in aid-recipient countries.

D. The role that the conflict between human rights and human obligations may play in lowering the minimum human rights threshold.

Promotion and Protection of Human Rights
by Governments

A general observation of the human rights situation in Africa is that the factors, which historically in other regions of the world, notably Europe and the Americas, have been mutually reinforcing in promoting the growth of a human rights culture, are absent, or very weak. For example, the linkage between social and economic development on the one hand, and democratization, including the evolution of a human rights culture, cannot be demonstrated in Africa to date. The absence of these structural conditions is cited as a reason for human rights abuses in Africa. The point that a respect for human rights is part of a more broadly conceived development process has been made by several authors, for example Forsythe (1989).

The independence of parliament and the judiciary in promoting and protecting human rights receives much attention in academic literature and at specialized seminars, but little else. Judges are routinely muzzled, and parliaments commonly act as rubberstamps. The notion of an independent judiciary is commonly recognized through specific constitutional provisions or through appropriate legislation, but these clauses are not necessarily respected if the interests of government, or individual political leaders, are threatened. The latter often act as if they are above the law, including the supreme laws of the land. This does not mean that the cause is totally lost. In some countries, recent democratization efforts have included measures to strengthen both judiciary and parliament. African countries, both in the west and the east, have, for example, provided clauses in the constitution stipulating that a certain percentage of public funds must be allocated to the judiciary on the assumption that such a guarantee means reducing the influence of the executive over the judicial court system. The point here, however, is that such initiatives notwithstanding, much of what the literature and experts have to say about the separation of powers is still more rhetoric than reality in Africa.

People's Participation

What possibilities do citizens, and especially the poor, have to affect the social, economic, and political processes of their governments, and the subsequent human rights consequences of those processes? The answer to this question is an obvious "none." In all four countries, with the possible exception of Tanzania, people have historically had a limited impact on their government's policies.

It has been argued that in poverty-stricken countries, basic rights like food, clothing, and shelter are what is crucial, not political rights. There is substantial evidence, however, that the issue is more complex than that. Alston (1979), for example, argues that only when non-material needs, which would include civil and political rights, are seen as indivisible from material needs can human rights be promoted and enforced. Dias (1994) shows the crucial relationships between human rights, development, and democracy, and notes that at the grassroots level there is a lack of awareness of these relationships. Development itself has become a major source of human rights violations. He notes that both international, national and local non-governmental organizations (NGOs) have been struggling with imposing human rights accountability upon development decision-makers, but only to little avail. Referring to the 1990 Houston meeting of "The Other Economic Summit", he introduces the concept of "people's conditionalities," which invokes existing obligations under international human rights law to protect people from being treated as an expendable resource in the development process. He argues that people's conditionalities need to be developed out of a process of learning from the lives of affected peoples. Arat (1991) provides a thorough analysis of the forces affecting democratization in developing countries, including how civil-political rights and socio-economic rights factor into the development process. She argues that only when a correct balance between these categories of rights has been established can democracy be maintained and development be fostered.

The Role of Foreign Parties

The conditioning of aid on human rights has received much attention by the international community in recent years. Both multilateral and bilateral agencies have devoted considerable intellectual energy to devising strategies and indicators that bring the human rights issue into democratization and, more indirectly, development. Like so many other agencies, Canada's official Canadian International Development Agency (CIDA) states that respect for human rights, democratization, and good governance are integral to the organization's purpose as a development agency (CIDA 1995). The Human Rights Council of Australia (1995), as an NGO, recognizes the value of linking human rights protection to the disbursement of foreign aid and argues that this applies not only to the official development agencies but also to NGOs working in the development field. Danchurchaid, a Danish human rights NGO, is a case in point. It takes human rights into account in all its activities and relationships with partners. Its primary policy objective is the promotion of human rights considerations in identification, planning, implementing, and evaluating development activities (Madsen 1994).

Paul (1989) provides perhaps the most powerful statement when he insists that human rights considerations must be made at all stages of the development project cycle. Failure to do so can result in a number of social and economic ills. The fundamental solution, therefore, is to make sure that people can participate at all stages in a development project cycle. To be sure, not all NGOs agree with the conditionalities that are being imposed on African governments, because they are not always very well-conceived and these organizations do not want to be "typecast as stooges of Western donors bent on imposing inappropriate and possibly unpopular reforms" (Robinson 1994). Other critical voices of these conditionalities point to the danger of making them permanent and the need to consider how such demands can be turned into constructive instead of punitive measures (e.g., Hill 1991).

The growing interest in governance has provided an opportunity to pursue a human rights agenda within a new context, as the World Bank (1993) notes. No global review of these issues, however, is being issued, one reason being that many governments regard such a "grade card" an inappropriate interference in the sovereign affairs of a state. With more attention paid to the full range of human rights, however, the compilation of such a record would make it easier to identify reform-minded governments and reward them with increased aid (Waller 1992). Such a gain notwithstanding, aid organizations working on these issues realize the problems of establishing meaningful links between indicators of human rights performance and policy decisions for development.

Conflict Between Human Rights and Human Obligations

This issue is of special interest in the African context for two reasons. The first is the legacy of nation-building that is still being invoked by government leaders to emphasize that human rights take a second place to human obligations. African countries cannot "afford" the individualist conception of human rights because they are in a hurry to catch up with the rest of the world and to that effect a definite measure of self-sacrifice is needed (An-Naim and Deng 1990). While this argument carries less weight today than it did in the first two decades after independence, it is still being referred to to justify strong-hand measures that imply violations of human rights.

The other reason for the interest in the conflict between human rights and human obligations is the communalist orientation of African society. No individual exists in isolation from the community and it is natural, therefore, that a person first and foremost feels an obligation toward his community. This distinction between individual and group rights is usually described as being irreconcilable and at the bottom of much human rights abuse by governments in Africa (Howard 1986). As part of this cultural argument, authors also propose that Africans are more concerned about human dignity than human rights. These dichotomies seem less strong today, as the international community has recognized that social and economic rights are important, and Africans acknowledge the value of individual rights. It would be wrong to assume, therefore, that these different sets of perspectives cannot be reconciled.

Country Backgrounds

It is now time to turn to a brief introduction of each of the four countries covered in this chapter. Some of this information has appeared in previous chapters and the account here will be brief. Yet, in order to set the stage for a discussion of the human rights performance in these countries, it is important to provide a select cross-section of information of relevance to the subject matter.

Nigeria

Nigeria is among the many countries in Africa that have been subject to alternating periods of military and civilian rule for most of the post-independence period, the most recent change taking place as late as 1998. It is significant that Nigeria has been governed by civilians only one quarter of the period the country has been independent. In spite of being one of the main oil producers in the world, Nigeria has experienced continued inflation, unemployment and other related social and economic problems. A major reason for this has been the inept manner in which the government has managed the economy. It has failed to take account of the implications of its 90 percent reliance on oil for its foreign exchange earnings and its 75 percent dependence on the same commodity for budget revenues.

Nigeria's civil rights record since independence has been far from exemplary and was outright dismal during much of the 1990s. It turned from bad to worse in 1993, when the presidential election, held as a transition to civilian rule, was declared invalid by the military rulers and a coup later that year brought a new military junta under the leadership of General Sani Abacha to power. The latter disbanded all elected legislative bodies, replaced civilian state governors with military administrators, and banned all political activity. In subsequent years the Government announced a series of harsh decrees restricting press freedom and civil liberties which, like other military decrees, contained clauses prohibiting judicial review of any government action with the intention of consolidating the military's hold on power. Security forces stepped up routine harassment of human rights and pro-democracy groups, including labor leaders, journalists, and student activists, as is further discussed by Olokotun in Chapter Four. According to Amnesty International (1994), security forces also killed civilians, as many as fifty in a single incident in the Lagos area. False arrests and torture of civilians have also been reported as common during the Abacha regime.

It is hard to know how long his regime would have lasted, had he not died by stroke in 1998. Plans had been announced to reintroduce civilian rule but the conditions under which this was being considered were such that few people in Nigeria trusted the intentions of the military leaders. Recognizing the alienation of the military government from both its own population and the international community (Nigeria had been ostracized by the British Commonwealth because of its human rights record), the new military rulers decided in 1998 to embark upon an accelerated return to civilian rule, including competitive elections of legislators, governors, and the president. These elections had been completed in early 1999. Nigeria had only its third civilian president since independence—not surprisingly, a former military head of state, Obasanjo, who had retired from office in 1978 after paving the way for the second civilian republic.

Kenya

Kenya is in many ways a microcosm of modern Africa. Its economy, though based on agriculture, is, relative to that of its neighbors, diversified. Though pressed by a growing population, Kenya is relatively prosperous, comparatively stable, and host to international organizations serving other countries experiencing turmoil.

Kenya won its political independence from the United Kingdom in 1963. Since then it has remained under civilian rule under two presidents: Jomo Kenyatta, a Kikuyu (the country's largest ethnic group) and leader of the Kenya African National Union (KANU), who ruled until he died in his sleep on 22 August 1978, and Daniel arap Moi, who has been the country's president since then. Kenyatta left a legacy of potentially explosive ethnic discrimination which Moi, a Kalenjin, who initially enjoyed considerable success, later compounded until it exploded into civilian violence in the 1990s.

In 1982, following attempts by government critics to form an opposition party, the government altered the constitution and made Kenya a one-party state. This led to an attempted coup led by disgruntled groups within the country's air force, but it never succeeded and instead Moi reinforced his personal control of the state machinery. Government security forces arbitrarily arrested and detained hundreds of citizens who criticized the one-party rule. University students and professors, journalists, teachers, and even farmers, were detained and tortured to sign confessions.

In the early 1990s democratization initiatives around Africa caught up with Moi and Kenya. While initially trying to resist, Moi had no choice but to yield to international and domestic pressure to reintroduce multi-party politics. Moi won the first such elections in 1992 and was re-elected again for his second (and last) term in 1997, a major reason for his victory being the divided nature of the political opposition. Suppression has continued under Moi's rule in the 1990s, and he has done little to instill confidence and faith in his government's readiness to protect and promote human rights. With his government's tacit sponsorship of ethnic violence, Kenya has endured a period of duress that has caused a deterioration in both social and economic indicators in the country. At the same time, however, concerned groups of citizens have organized in order to protect the rights of citizens, and Kenya may have one of the strongest civil societies in Africa.

Uganda

Uganda has probably suffered more human rights abuses since independence than any of the other countries covered here.

The present author had the honor of serving on the Commission of Inquiry into Violations of Human Rights, which was set in 1986 after the National Resistance Movement (NRM) under the leadership of Yoweri Museveni toppled the corrupt and inept military regime which in turn had overthrown civilian president, Milton Obote, in 1985. The mandate of the commission was to investigate human rights abuses from 1962, when Uganda gained independence, to 1986. From the thousands of verbal and written reports received from all parts of the country, it can only be said that Uganda's human rights record before 1986 was disastrous.

The human rights provisions in the post-independence constitutions of 1966 and 1967 were compromised by wide-ranging rights of derogation in a state of emergency, which the government could call on relatively flimsy grounds and get away with. In such states of emergency, the state suspended observance of all human rights, which meant, in practice, a license to override the rule of law. The situation deteriorated after Idi Amin, Obote's military commander-in-chief, overthrew him in 1971 and seized power himself. His human rights excesses between 1971 and 1978, which led to the death of as many as half a million Ugandans, are now well-recorded. The Commission of Inquiry was able to hear about not only these abuses but also those committed by Obote, when he was fraudulently returned as President of Uganda in 1980 and ruled until his overthrow five years later. The violations during these years were in many respects as bad as during the Amin period, so it is fair to state that gross violations of human rights had become the way of life in Uganda since 1970.

The human rights record of the NRM, has been comparatively good, except with regard to northern Uganda, and some parts of eastern Uganda, where armed opposition to the new rulers has continued. Instead of declining, these abuses have been on the increase, as these "dissidents" have stepped up their fights against the government. The Lord's Resistance Army (LRA) under Joseph Kony in the north has itself been involved in serious human rights violations by harassing and torturing (including cutting off ears and noses) civilians who oppose the LRA. Its leaders have also been accused of abducting children to employ as soldiers in the field.

A new constitution was adopted in Uganda in 1995 after a special Constitutional Commission had toured the country and a special Constituent Assembly had been popularly elected to approve it. This constitutions establishes for the first time in Uganda's history a permanent human rights commission, which is now operational. Its mandate includes investigating at its own initiative complaints of violations of human rights and recommending to parliament effective measures for the promotion of these rights. The Commission is operating independently of any executive authority and is self-accounting to parliament. Still, many human rights observers are disappointed that this new commission does not have wider powers. It may not be as effective in protecting human rights as the legacy of abuses in the country warrants.

Tanzania

Tanzania is the most stable of the four countries included in this study. It has been ruled by the same political party (originally Tanganyika African National Union, later renamed *Chama cha Mapinduzi*). CCM, as it is popularly referred to, was created in 1977 as a vanguard party functioning in a constitutional one-party state, established already in 1965. This was also a period of socialist construction. The ruling party did not wish to see any opposition or challenge to its hegemony. Consequently, it detained a number of leading politicians who criticized its socialist strategy. The media were all state-owned, and freedom of both association and expression was seriously constricted. The worst human rights violation during this period took place in the years 1974-76, when a few million, rural inhabitants were forcefully removed from their homesteads and told to establish residence in planned communal villages. In addition to a great loss of property during this campaign, people's rights were trampled on by the authorities. Local livelihoods were seriously threatened. On balance, living conditions in the countryside deteriorated as a result of this bold, but ill-conceived project.

In spite of these incidents, it is fair to maintain that, comparatively speaking, Tanzania's human rights record looks better than its East African neighbors, not to mention that of Nigeria. There has been very little brutality of the kind that people have experienced in the other three countries. The political leadership has violated rights not because of feeling threatened as much as being too ambitious in their development efforts.

Tanzania remained a one-party state until 1992 when the constitution was changed to incorporate, among other things, multi-party politics. The first competitive elections were held in 1995 with CCM winning over two thirds of the seats in the legislature, and its candidate, Benjamin Mkapa, winning the presidency. While some of the old authoritarian features of rule still continues in Tanzania, there have been considerable changes as privately owned media have been allowed to compete with the government-owned ones. The judiciary, although it remains corrupt at least at the lower levels of the system, has enhanced its independence and role in governance.

The country's most difficult issue remains the relationship between Zanzibar and the rest of the republic. Tanganyika and Zanzibar were united into a single republic in 1964 and the country named Tanzania (after the three initial letters in each name). Ever since the union was first established, Zanzibar has insisted on a great measure of sovereignty. How much the Union Government should concede has been a thorny issue on and off. In the 1990s, Zanzibar has made consistent moves to demonstrate its autonomy. It has done so, for example, by harassing members of the political opposition and ignoring demands from the rest of the republic and the international community to engage in a dialogue with its representatives. The Zanzibar government has arrested and retained in prison several leading members of the political opposition and houses belonging to people presumed opposition loyalists have been burned. Civil servants suspected of such preferences have been summarily dismissed from their jobs. In sum, therefore, while the human rights situation has improved in Tanzania at large, it remains unsatisfactory on the islands of Zanzibar.

The brief review above gives an overall sense of what has happened in the human rights and governance field since independence. I shall now turn to a somewhat more detailed account of what has happened with regard to the following specific areas: (1) abuse of the criminal justice system to suppress opposition; (2) detention without trial and alleged treason; and, (3) civil freedoms. Illustrations will be sought from countries where these violations have been especially serious in the last ten years.

Abuse of the Criminal System to Suppress Opposition

One of the more common methods in Africa and elsewhere to discredit political opponents is to trump up charges and politically stage-manage trials in the official courts. In the last decade, the governments in Nigeria and Kenya have engaged in such activities in an effort to tarnish the name of their critics. This does not mean that similar efforts have been totally absent in Tanzania or Uganda, but they have not been allowed to abuse the judicial system to the extent that they have in the former two countries. I shall now turn to a review of the most prominent incidents or cases in Nigeria and Kenya.

Nigeria

The case that attracted widespread attention in Nigeria as well as outside that country is the conflict between the Federal Government and the Ogoni people in the southeastern part of the country over the revenue rights and related issues stemming from the production of oil in the area. The local people had joined in a quasi-political organization named the Movement for the Survival of the Ogoni People (MOSOP), led by a well-known Nigerian writer and intellectual, Ken Saro-Wiwa. This movement has been in existence for some time, but its confrontation with the federal government escalated after increased violence, including the death of some local government officials, in April 1994. The government responded by deploying large numbers of police and military in Ogoniland. Credible reports of increased killings by the security forces and beatings at police check-points accompanied this development. During raids on villages in Ogoniland during the months of May and June, 1994, some fifty people were extra-judicially executed by the security forces and as many as 600 persons detained without trial. In order to quell the upsurge of violence in the area, the military administration of Rivers State (where Ogoniland is located) promulgated a draconian decree imposing the death sentence for "civil disturbances occasioning death." For crimes such as "attempted murder" the administration set up a special court, the Civil Disturbances Tribunal. This tribunal had the power to impose death penalty, not only for capital offenses committed in connection with the unrest, but also apparently for previously non-capital crimes such as "attempted murder." Although chaired by a retired judge, the tribunal's other members were not required to have legal training and could include armed forces officers of as low a rank as captain. It was this tribunal that was used to try Ken Saro-Wiwa and nine other MOSOP leaders for murder. Their trial focused attention on the human rights situation in Nigeria like no other violation has done in recent times. Although Nigeria's military leaders had promised world leaders, including South Africa's Nelson Mandela that Saro-Wiwa and the others would not be executed, they were all secretly hanged in December 1995, leading to an international outcry and Nigeria's suspension from the Commonwealth.

Kenya

There are more than 40 ethnic groups in Kenya, and ethnic divisions have been exploited for political gains ever since independence. The situation, however, has deteriorated after the introduction of multi-party politics in the 1990s. The Government has, if not outright supporting it, quietly endorsed ethnic violence in the Rift Valley, pitting local Kalenjin and Maasai people against Kikuyus and other who have moved into the province in search of livelihood. A major reason behind this ethnic cleansing has been to ensure a victory for the ruling party in constituencies where the ethnic composition, because of the immigrants, looked as if it may lose. During October 1993, twenty people were killed in Narok District, reigniting a campaign that already started the year before in preparation for the 1992 general elections. By the end of 1994, when the campaign was again temporarily halted, 1,500 people had been killed and as many as 300,000, mainly women and children, had been displaced. President Moi has blamed the violence on the political opposition, trying to demonstrate the harmful effects of multi-party politics, but there is strong circumstantial evidence that the violence has been instigated by individual politicians in the government. Attempts by the National Democratic Human Rights Organization, formed by a Kikuyu politician from the Province, Koigi wa Wamwere, was harassed, and he himself arrested together with a number of other prominent Kikuyu politicians from the area. When students at Kenyatta University in Nairobi demonstrated to demand an end to the violence and the resignation of the Minister for Local Government, they were violently attacked by the police. Several students were injured, and some female ones raped.

Torture of prisoners is widespread and systematic in Kenya and political killings have claimed several hundred lives in the 1990s. In 1993 the Government began using capital criminal charges instead of political ones as a way of covertly silencing non-violent government critics. The capital charges of actual or attempted robbery, one set of charges that have been applied to political cases, are non-bailable and carry a mandatory death sentence in Kenya. By summer 1995, at least ten prisoners, three of them women, were held under false charges carrying the death penalty.

Detention Without Trial and Treason

Detention without trial is one of the most common ways of silencing dissent in Africa. It is typically used to remove rival politicians who pose a threat to the head of state. It may also be used by the authorities against less prominent politicians if they constitute a threat to local, vested interests. Thus, in addition to the head of state, provincial governors may also have the right to detain people. Detention is legally time-bound, typically to twenty-four hours, before it is necessary to present the detained person before a court judge. In many instances across Africa, however, persons have been detained indefinitely simply for political convenience or as a matter of personal punishment. Most detainees are normally tortured at the time of their arrest and held in harsh, life-threatening conditions with inadequate food, over-crowded and unsanitary cells, and no washing facilities, exercise, or fresh air. They are normally denied visits from families, lawyers, or doctors. When detention has not been appropriate, governments have not hesitated to trump up charges of treason, as I will demonstrate with illustrations from Nigeria, Kenya, and Uganda.

Nigeria

A well-known case of detention without trial in Nigeria is that of Sylvester Oidion-Akhaine, General Secretary of the Campaign for Democracy, an alliance of pro-democracy groups, and a staff member of the Committee for the Defence of Human Rights (CDHR), an affiliated non-governmental organization, at the time of his arrest in January 1995. He was arrested at the CDHR Secretariat in Lagos along with three other staff of the same organization who were released the same day. Considered a threat to state security, Oidion-Akhaine was held under the State Security (Detention of Persons) Decree No. 2 of 1984, which allows for indefinite detention without charge or trial. Five months later, the government ignored the orders from the High Court in Lagos that he be brought before the court and his detention justified, and that he be given access to his lawyers, family, and doctor. The reason for his detention was believed to be his non-violent expression of pro-democracy views, his opposition to military rule, and his advocacy of the annulment of the 1993 presidential election, in which Chief Mashood Abiola was denied victory by a unilateral decision by the military junta to cancel the election.

Abiola was eventually detained after having made claims that he was the rightful head of state of the country. This angered the military leaders, who decided to charge him with treason and treasonable felony for declaring himself head of state. His trial was orchestrated and constantly interfered with by the military regime. The latter showed no mercy and denied Abiola bail despite his appeal on grounds of health. Despite his ordeal, Abiola has maintained his integrity and has shown tremendous courage. For instance, on August 5, 1994, he rejected a court offer of conditional release on terms that would have prevented him from political campaigning. In an ironic twist of history, Abiola died in prison in 1998, only a month after his principal tormentor, General Sani Abacha, the Nigerian head of state, himself had unexpectedly passed away, paving the way for a return to civilian rule.

Kenya

The right to a fair trial is one of the most important human rights of detainees and is provided for in the International Covenant on Civil and Political Rights, to which Kenya acceded, as well as in the African Charter on Human and Peoples' Rights, to which Kenya acceded in February 1992. These commitments notwithstanding, the Kenyan authorities have denied many political detainees anything near a fair trial.

Well-publicized cases in point are those of Wamwere (mentioned above) and Josephine Nyawira Ngengi. Wamwere's sixteen-months trial ended in October 1995 with the accused being sentenced to four years' imprisonment and "6 strokes of the cane." Their defense counsel were reportedly denied the right to present their final summations orally, and Wamwere and his three co-defendants were not allowed to be present in the court-room to hear the judgement. Expecting foul play, international and local human rights observers attended the trial, and they raised a number of concerns which related specifically to its conduct, the nature of the evidence presented, and the impartiality of the court. They concluded that by national or international standards, Wamwere's trial could not be described as fair.

Josephine Nyawira Ngengi, who was arrested in May 1994 in Nakuru in the Rift Valley Province, is the sister of Njuguna Ngengi and a member of the Release Political Prisoners group in Kenya. She actively campaigned on behalf of political prisoners in Kenya, participated in the Mothers' Hunger Strike for the release of political prisoners in Nairobi, and publicized her brother's case. At the time of her arrest, she was held illegally and incommunicado for twenty-two days before being charged with robbery with violence, a totally absurd charge. She stated that she was tortured while in police custody. Her case came to court three times, and on each occasion she was released and then re-arrested on the same charges.

Uganda

Political detention in Uganda in the 1990s has been much less common than it was in previous decades, as indicated above. The government, however, has been forced to resort to this method in conjunction with the ongoing insurgency in the northern part of the country. There has also been abuse of the judicial process, for example, by charging people with treason without any evidence other than having been captured by the authorities in the northern war zone.

According to an Amnesty International report published in 1996, at least 168 suspected government opponents had been detained since 1994 by the Fourth Division of the National Resistance Army. These detentions occurred in the content of intensified counter-insurgency operations. The detainees had been taken into military custody for "screening" by military intelligence officers. These detentions were a clear violation of Ugandan law, which stipulates that a prisoner should be charged within twenty-four hours with a recognizably criminal offense, or otherwise released. There is a constitutional provision for administrative detention in a state of emergency, but no such state of emergency had been declared in the North at the time.

The detentions also violated Uganda's international treaty obligations under the African Charter of Human and Peoples' Rights.

These and other unlawful detentions in northern Uganda have raised a question-mark over the otherwise significant progress that has undoubtedly been made in Uganda since the days of Amin and Obote, but more recently there has been a reported reduction in the number of suspected extra-judicial executions or detentions of civilians by soldiers. It should also be mentioned here that attempts by the authorities to prosecute "rebels" have been rejected by the courts and the government has abandoned any further such prosecutions.

Civil Freedoms

Civil freedoms here include references to freedom of speech and association, two rights that people in African countries have found governments ready to violate to protect their interests. In this section references will be made to how these rights have been trampled upon in all four countries covered by this project.

Nigeria

Constitutional provisions providing for freedom of speech and association were not enforceable for the whole of the 1990s until the Abacha regime was overturned in 1998. Despite its public declarations of support for these freedoms, and its attempts to continue public political dialogue on constitutional issues, the Abacha regime consistently increased its systematic intimidation of the press through legal and extra-legal means. The government directly took over newspapers and shut down others. Those few that could survive as independent media were regularly subject to harassment. Journalists were forced underground, and much of the alternative press in the 1990s survived by operating from makeshift offices that could not easily be traced by the security forces. Newspaper editions that have been critical of government have been intercepted and re-published after the critical items had been deleted and new pro-government pieces inserted in their stead.

As regards the freedom of association, the situation during the 1990s was less serious for religious, professional and social organizations. There was no need for these non-governmental bodies to register with government, but open-air religious services were prohibited in most states of the Federation due to a legacy of religious tensions in those places. During the Abacha regime, political parties were banned on the grounds that they tended to be formed along ethnic, religious, or other parochial lines. It is only after the 1998 transition to civilian rule that political parties were allowed again.

Kenya

Many actions by the Kenyan authorities have seriously undermined the right to freedom of expression. Editions of newspapers and publications critical of government have been impounded. In 1994 alone, more than eighty journalists, human rights activists, and other government critics were detained, many alleging torture. However, most non-violent critics of the government who have been arrested have been either held for short periods of time and then released without charge or charged with "sedition" or related offenses such as "subversion" and released on bail after a few days or a week. Both charges permit the imprisonment of non-violent critics of government. As indicated above, different laws and charges are increasingly being used so that critics appear to be detained not for their non-violent political activity but on grounds that they are criminals. The government can then pretend that there are no political prisoners in the country, since all are held under criminal laws.

Non-governmental organizations in Kenya are constantly under attack in Kenya. Women's self-help groups have been prevented from holding meetings on several occasions through violence by security forces. In June 1993 armed police beat women attending a seminar organized by the League of Kenyan Women Voters. In the first three months of 1995, *Kituo cha Sheria,* a legal education and aid organization, had its offices subjected to fire-bomb attacks at six separate occasions. In the political arena, as many as fifty-six opposition members of parliament were arrested during 1994, mostly when they attempted to hold public meetings. The political paranoia was also illustrated in the case of *Safina,* a proposed political party, which was refused registration for a period of three years because it was alleged to have foreign links.

Tanzania

B ecause the violations of human rights in Tanzania have been less frequent and serious than in the other countries I have had no reason to refer to it in the earlier sections, but when it comes to protection of civil freedoms, Tanzania does not escape without some blemish. Many of its problems in this field stem from the legacy of an autocratic form of socialism that the ruling party established in the 1970s. Individual liberties were for a long time frowned upon because they contradicted the collective principles associated with socialism.

Although there was an amendment in the Constitution to allow for multi-partyism in 1992, no comprehensive review of the country's national laws and legal procedures was undertaken. In its 1992 report, a presidential commission that had been appointed to look into what constitutional and legal amendments were necessary to accommodate multi-party politics identified a broad range of laws on the books that needed to be repealed or amended. In spite of inaction by the government, a series of independent decisions by the high courts of the country have ruled several laws unconstitutional. These include laws relating to the issuance of the death penalty, corporal punishment, and sedition, the right to stand as an independent candidate in elections, and a law which requires that official permits must be obtained before a political rally or demonstration can be held.

Although the government has retained the right to discipline and possibly ban journalists and media outlets that are considered threats to the "public interest," the media situation in Tanzania has improved considerably. For example, in 1993 a law was passed to permit privately owned radio and television stations as well as newspapers. Since then a very vibrant press (in both English and Swahili) as well as several radio and television stations have started operating in the capital and some of the major regional towns. The press corps, in consultation with the authorities, has also established one of Africa's first independent media councils, a self-regulating body. This does not mean that there have been no incidents of trying to muzzle the media. For example, Paschal Shija, editor of the *Express* newspaper, and Riaz Gulamani, its publisher, were arrested in 1994 after an editorial was published accusing the Tanzanian Government of incompetence. They were released on bail after ten hours, but were again briefly detained soon after and charged with sedition before being granted bail once more. It is the situation on the islands of Zanzibar, as indicated above, however, that has given rise to the most serious worries.

During 1994, repression by the Zanzibar Government focused less on high-profile opposition leaders than on rank-and-file opposition supporters and on obstructing political activities of the opposition. That year, the government issued a circular permitting the authorities to bar journalists with "questionable qualifications," a term that could be applied with the widest of discretion. In 1996, the same government banned the Dar es Salaam-based Swahili newspaper, *Majira,* and in 1998 another Swahili paper, *Mtanzania,* after both had published critical articles about the human rights conditions on the islands.

The Zanzibar Government has also been accused of charging its critics, including members of the official political opposition, on very flimsy and unclear grounds. For example, in August 1994, 52-year old Zubari Haji Tandeu appeared in court on a charge of obstructing the presidential motorcade at Kitopi, eleven miles (eighteen kilometers) north of Zanzibar town. According to independent reports, this charge was brought against Haji Tandeu by the police at Mahonda Station when they learned that he was a supporter of the opposition party (Civic United Front). He was allegedly beaten up while in detention. He was released on bail after two days.

Uganda

Journalists have been prominent targets of politically motivated criminal charges in Uganda. Although the consequences for those detained have typically not been serious, at least four separate cases have attracted attention in the 1990s because they have contradicted the ambitions of President Museveni's Government of being different from the preceding regimes. The first case involves the late Hussein Auks, former editor in chief of the *Shariat* newspaper and Haruna Kunabi, a sub-editor of the same paper, who were held for eleven days and nearly three weeks respectively, in 1993 before being charged with sedition. The reason was that the *Shariat* had carried an article critical of a number of government ministers. Although no further official action is known to have been taken, the charges have never been dropped.

The editor in chief of *The Monitor,* Wafula Ogutu, was arrested on three charges of defamation and one charge of "publishing false statements likely to cause alarm" in October 1994, after printing a story claiming that President Museveni had strongly criticized government ministers at a meeting three months earlier. Ogutu was detained overnight and taken to court next morning, at which point the charges were withdrawn by the authorities.

In the same year, two leading representatives of the opposition party, Uganda People's Congress (UPC), Haji Badru Kendo Wegulu and Patrick Rubaihayo, were briefly detained and charged with sedition on the grounds that they were responsible for claims in a party manifesto that Uganda was being ruled by Tutsi of Rwandese origin. This was viewed by the authorities as being intended to discredit and incite opposition to President Museveni and the ruling National Resistance Movement (NRM).

After the case had been adjourned several times, because the prosecution claimed that it had not finished its investigations, the chief magistrate of Kampala dismissed the case on the grounds that evidence had not been presented to him to sustain the charges in a court of law.

The most serious incident took place in 1995 when Sam Njuki, a reporter, died while being arrested. This caused an international outcry which had the effect of making the government much more hesitant to continue harassing journalists. The president himself declared what he called a "cease fire" with the media representatives.

Uganda is officially a non-party state, where only the NRM is allowed to conduct political campaigns. Although political parties are not officially banned, those in existence, like the UPC, are not allowed to conduct campaigns, only run their internal affairs. The freedom of association, therefore, is circumscribed in a manner that is not the case at present in any of the other three countries (although in Nigeria only since 1998). A number of incidents of violations of rights have occurred when people with an alleged political agenda have tried to hold rallies or meetings. For example, in August 1994, the Sheraton Hotel informed a group called *Abaana ba Buganda* (Children of Buganda) that it had withdrawn its agreement for a meeting of the group after having been advised to that effect by the police. In December the same year, a rally by the Democratic Party Mobiliser Group in Kampala was dispersed by about 100 armed policemen on the grounds that official permission had not been sought by the organizers. A rally organized by the same group the year before had met with the same fate. Dispersal of opposition meetings and violent treatment of the opposition by Local Defence Forces personnel intensified during the presidential campaigns in 1996. At one occasion, the main opposition candidate, Dr. Paul Ssemogerere, had to be given heavy police protection to escape harassment by the local security forces that operated under the control of local government units.

Conclusions

This chapter has painted a somewhat ambiguous picture of the human rights situation in Nigeria and East Africa. While there have been improvements, especially in Tanzania and Uganda, violations of basic human rights, whether civil-political or socio-economic, have continued in all countries. Notably, governments have remained sensitive to criticism by the media of members of the political opposition and have not hesitated to abuse the rights of these people. Incidents of the kind that have been reported in this chapter raise doubts about the depth of these governments' commitment to proper governance and human rights observance.

At a minimum, the breaches of citizens' rights in Africa indicate the absence of a human rights culture. People are not yet ready to stand up to defend these rights if such actions are associated with risks for one's own life. In this respect, African countries still have some distance to go before the protection of human rights can be taken for granted.

This raises the question of how the outside world can help to accelerate this process. There is reason to be critical of the way that especially Western donor governments have treated human rights as part of a packet of political conditionalities imposed to induce African governments to adopt more democratic forms of governance. This approach has had the effect of limiting their effectiveness in promoting human rights through local organizations. Instead of taking a comprehensive look at the human rights situation and treating it on its terms, whether cultural or material, and try to build on such a foundation, they have tried to enforce an adherence to only the set of rights that suits their current political agenda. It is impossible to build a human rights culture from above. It is equally foolish to try to accelerate the process without recognizing where the windows of opportunities lie in the local culture or economy. As Zehra Arat (1991) has noted in her thorough study of the relationship between human rights and democracy in three developing countries (Costa Rica, India, and Turkey), the stability of democratic systems is threatened if the elected government cannot reinforce socioeconomic rights at levels comparable to those of civil-political rights. This chapter suggests that her observation is also applicable to the situation in Nigeria and East Africa. An African perspective on human rights and governance, therefore, implies a greater sensitivity to the need for a comprehensive approach to the subject matter and a greater interest among intellectuals on the continent on how an ideology of human rights can be developed that can achieve a viable balance between individual and group rights. The agenda for future research along these lines alone could become very rich and rewarding.

Works Cited

Ake, Claude. *Democratization of Disempowerment in Africa.* Port Harcourt: Malthouse Press, 1994.

Alston, P. "Human Rights and the Basic Needs Strategy for Development." *Working Paper No 2.* London: Anti-Slavery Society, 1979.

Amnesty International. "Nigeria: Resumption of Public Executions." London: Amnesty International, 1994.

An-Naim, Abdullahi Ahmed, and Francis M. Deng, eds. *Human Rights in Africa: Cross-Cultural Perspectives.* Washington, D.C.: The Brookings Institution Press, 1990.

Arat, Zehra F. *Democracy and Human Rights in Developing Countries.* Boulder, Colo.: Lynne Rienner Publishers, 1991.

Archer, Robert. "Markets and Good Governance." Paper prepared at the 9th INFID Conference, Paris, 1994.

Canadian International Development Agency (CIDA)."Human Rights, Democratization and Good Governance." Ottawa: CIDA, Good Governance and Human Rights Division, 1995.

Cohen, Ronald, Goran Hyden, and Winston Nagan. *Human Rights and Governance in Africa.* Gainesville, Fla.: University Press of Florida, 1993.

Dias, Clarence. "Relationship between Human Rights Development, and Democracy: South/North NGO Solidarity in Fostering Popular Participation" in Manfred Nowak, ed. *World Conference on Human Rights: The Contribution of NGOs.* Vienna: Ludwig Boltzmann Institute of Human Rights, 1994.

Forsythe, David P. ed. *Human Rights and Development: International Views.* New York: St. Martin's Press, 1989.

Hill, Dilys. *Development Assistance and Human Rights: Principles, Criteria and Procedures.* London: Commonwealth Secretariat, Human Rights and Development Series, 1991.

Howard, Rhoda. *Human Rights in Commonwealth Africa.* Totowa, N.J.: Rowman and Littlefield, 1986.

Human Rights Council of Australia. *The Rights Way to Development: A Human Rights Approach to Development Assistance.* Marrickville, Australia, Human Rights Council of Australia. 1995.

Madsen, Hanne L. *Lessons from Human Rights Assessments in Evaluations of Development Projects.* Copenhagen: Danchurchaid,1994.

Paul, James. "International Development Agencies, Human Rights and Humane Development Projects," *Alternatives 14,* 1 (1989):78–107.

Republic of Uganda. *Verbatim Record of the Proceedings of Report of Commission of Inquiry into Violations of Human Rights in Uganda, 1962–1986.* Kampala, Uganda: Fountain Publishers, 1996.

Robinson, Mark. "Governance, Democracy, and Conditionality: NGOs and the New Policy Agenda: in Andrew Clayton, ed. *Governance, Democracy and Conditionality: What Role for NGOs?"* Oxford: INTRAC, 1994.

Waller, P. P. "After East-West Detente: Towards a Human Rights Orientation in North-South Development Cooperation," *Development* 1 (1995):24–32.

World Bank and Lawyers Committee for Human Rights. *Governance and Human Rights.* Washington, D.C.: The World Bank, 1993.

4

Governance and the Media

Ayo Olokotun

The Problem

One area where there is a dearth of scholarship on global socio-political change in the scholarly enterprise of producing an intellectual map is the role, profile, and morphology of the media and their relationship to the ebbs and flows of democratization in various countries. This is an especially acute problem in Africa (Zelizer 1993; Herbert 1993). This is so because, at least in part, most of the books and publications in this area are produced by scholars in mass communication who are preoccupied with such matters as news gathering, the status and role conceptions of media workers, and changing communication policies in various countries.

In a review of three recent books on the African media, Les Switzer (1995:132) remarks on the qualitative and quantitative deficiencies as well as the lack of theoretic originality in most studies of the African media. Following this, the prospects for carrying forward scholarly work on the African media are related, in my view, to success in steering away our analytical lenses from "media-centric" explanations and categories in order to refocus

91

them, as one scholar suggests, on "a series of processes and institutions such as economic forces, international relations, the state and political movements" (Jakobowicz 1995:129). Drawing on Nigerian and East African case studies, this paper examines the relationship between the media and governance, as well as its conceptual sibling, democratization, for the period between 1990 and 1996. The choice of this time-span is dictated by the intensity and efflorescence of prodemocracy movements and demands, as well as the efforts of states to accommodate, bargain with, or divert their pressures.

In Nigeria, pro-democracy agitation, backed by international pressures, combined to push out General Ibrahim Babangida after he cancelled the presidential elections of June 1993; in Kenya the same duo of forces broke down president Moi's resistance to multiparty elections, which were held in December 1992. Tanzania and Uganda have had to mount constitutional changes and elections as status quo responses to mounting demands for democratization and improved governance.

The media were and remain in the vanguard of these changes. By constructing audiences for democratic change, setting the agenda for public debate and responding in general to an internationalist ethic of open governance, the media, in the face of official persecution and intimidation, has provided impetus and direction to the governance and democratization ferment in their respective countries.

This paper seeks to demonstrate the linkages between media combativeness bred of a Jeffersonian framework which prioritizes unimpeded flow of information and the rising crescendo of calls for democratization in these countries. If, as theorists of hegemony remind us, society is "a battlefield" of contending "representations" of reality (Clark 1984: 6), then the Nigerian and East African media helped a great deal in fostering those "speech communities" knit together by democratic aspirations and anti-authoritarian images (Sorlin 1994:36).

In the struggle to "improve politics" and create regimes that can "strengthen the contribution of politics to development," thereby enhancing the "legitimacy of the public realm," (Hyden

1992:25) the role of the media is critical in two major senses. First, by acting as "watchdogs" of governments in keeping with their historical and sociological responsibilities, they, at the limits, reduce the propensities of leaders towards neo-patrimonial politics. Second, the media calls for new rules, thereby accelerating movement towards regimes that manifest the indices of good governance: accountability, respect for human rights and the law, openness, and decentralization.

In Nigeria and the three East African countries under consideration a good deal of the media are state-owned (although Nigeria and Kenya have gone further in developing traditions of private ownership and outspokenness). But even in these countries, as in the others, the price for dissent is quite high and many journalists had to pay that price in the shape of imprisonment, job loss, intimidation, and the torching of newspaper houses.

One scholar captured a crucial dimension of this harsh reality when he wrote that "Access to public media in Africa always was, and still is denied to any group challenging the existing authorities. In most countries the press laws either implicitly or explicitly allow censorship" (Monga 1995:367).

When, in February 1993, the Tanzanian Minister for Information and Broadcasting, Dr. William Shija, announced the banning of two Kiswahili newspapers, *Michapo* (palaver) and *Cheka* (laughter), or when the Nigerian government proscribed three prominent opposition newspapers in 1994, the authorities were sending clear messages that they will not infinitely bear with media of a critical bent *(New African,* April 1993, p. 41). As we shall see, the troubles of the media in their struggle for governance and democratization also included the escalating cost of printing, underdeveloped or rickety infrastructure in an age of telematics, ethnically driven pressures reflecting the imbalance of national polities, as well as an insecure employment situation which again is related to economic doldrums in the countries studied.

Finally, this paper addresses the international media and the underground press which, given the vicissitudes of domestic politics and anti-press laws, emerged to play, at certain junctures, definitive roles in the struggle for democratization and open politics.

In the next two sections, I draw a profile of the media in Nigeria and East Africa as well as indicate the theoretical backdrop from which derive the perspectives and central assumptions of the chapter.

The Media: Profile and Overview

As a result of high illiteracy levels, meager and dwindling incomes, and the capital intensity of newspaper production, radio remains the preeminent medium of information dispersal in Nigeria and East Africa, as indeed all over the continent. In view of its accessibility and suitability in agrarian settings, it has tended to suffer the most from regulation by government. In radio, and the popular but socio-economically restricted medium of television, state ownership is the predominant pattern in spite of the emergence of private broadcasting under restrictive conditions in Nigeria in the years since 1994.

In Kenya, the electronic media are largely government controlled. Specifically, they are supervised by the Ministry of Information and Broadcasting (Kareithi 1991). The picture remains broadly the same, despite the 1990 introduction of KTN-62, a commercial television service channel.

The politics of state-controlled broadcasting sometimes goes awry for joumalists, as in Tanzania, for example, where, early in 1993, broadcasters in Radio Tanzania were put under surveillance for "suppressing government news" (*New African*, April 1993, p. 41). At least one professional lost his job for allegedly giving air time to CHADEMA, one of the opposition parties.

In Nigeria, a sprinkling of private television stations and one radio station have been permitted as a complement to official broadcasting which is tepidly adulatory of the government. But even here, the furor which broke out over Raypower's relaying of BBC programs, leading to its stoppage by the authorities, points to the sensitivities and constraints of the emerging private electronic media.

Nigeria is believed to have the "largest active press community on the continent" (Parker 1993:1) followed by South Africa and Kenya. One of the interesting features of the last few years is the explosion in the Kenyan media scene, a fact underlined by the suggestive headline of an article in the February 1995 edition of the London-based *New African* Magazine, "Kenya's Booming Media."

Nigeria's leading newspapers include *The Guardian* (recently re-launched after a twelve-month proscription by the government), *The Daily Times* (in which government holds majority shares), *The National Concord* (which also suffered a recent twelve-month proscription), *The New Nigerian* (wholly government-owned) as well as *The Vanguard* and *The Champion*. Although there is a lively tradition of independent press ownership in Nigeria, there is no exact correlation between ownership and political postures. The state has successfully penetrated some nominally independent newspapers while this writer has been able to address burning socio-political issues from an independent position in *The Daily Times,* of which government holds sixty percent of the shares.

Kenya's major newspapers and magazines include *The Daily Nation* and *The Sunday Nation*, an influential group in which Aga Khan is the principal shareholder (Uwechue 1991; Kareithi 1991:200); and the Standard Group, which publishes *The Standard* and *The Sunday Standard*. There is also the *Weekly Review* and *Taifa Weekly* (Uwechue 1991:1058). Then there is the state-owned *Kenya Times* and *Sunday Times*. The Kenya News Agency (KNA) is similarly owned by the Kenyan party in power, KANU, along with Robert Maxwell, who holds minority shares. "Kenyan publishing" one journal reported last year, "is beginning to rival South Africa and Nigeria in the sheer number of titles published" (*New African,* February 1995, p. 40).

As in Nigeria, the Kenyan media market is combustible in the sense that it has a high mortality rate of publications. Some of the recent interesting additions to the newspaper and magazine scene in Kenya include *The East African* which enjoys modern technology in its production, and the recently relaunched *True* and *Drum* Magazines published by Jim Bailey, a South African. Among other politically interesting magazines are *Nduru*, devoted to human rights issues and published in English, Kiswahili, Kikuyu, and other dialects, and *The People,* which serves mainly the suburbs of Nairobi Westlands. *The Standard,* the oldest newspaper in Kenya, is owned by Consolidated Holdings Limited, and, in spite of private ownership, has tended to maintain a pro-state editorial posture (Kareithi 1991).

Uganda's major newspapers include *New Vision, The Monitor, The Weekly Topic,* and *The Citizen.* Of these, the first is owned by the National Resistance Movement, the ruling organization in the country. There are others like *The People,* owned by the UPC (an opposition party). Although the NRM daily is widely circulated, there are about 20 newspapers of varying sizes and scope (*New African,* Jan. 1993, p. 29). *The Monitor* and *Weekly Topic* are influential and played noteworthy roles in the Ugandan constitutional debates that preceded the 1996 election.

Tanzanian newspapers include *The Daily News, Uhuru, Sunday News,* and *Mzalendo*, all of which are owned by the Government. Their role has declined in recent years as new, independent media have emerged on the scene. Tanzania nowadays has a very vibrant press in both English and Swahili. Among media in English are *The Guardian* and *The Express*, while the most popular in Swahili are *Majira, Nipashe*, and *Mtanzania*. All these newspapers appear six or seven times a week. There is also a growing, but still fledgling tabloid press in Swahili, which includes papers like *Kasheshe.* One of the problems facing the newspaper publishers in Tanzania has been the shortage of newsprint. *The Daily News*, in its February 7, 1996 edition, reported the cutback in circulation by fifty percent of newspapers, including *The Daily News,* as a result of newsprint shortage arising from delays at the Southern Paper Mills at Mgololo in Mufindi district *(Daily News,* Feb. 7, 1996, p. 1). With regard to content, the Tanzanian media situation has changed quite dramatically since the privately owned radio and television stations as well as the newspapers were allowed in the early 1990s.

The Conceptual Backdrop

In this section, I clarify my use of the words "governance" and "media" and tease out inter-linkages between them in order to provide a conceptual framework for the empirical sections of the paper.

Although governance is a central concept in political science, its contemporary usage denotes a set of institutional, sociopolitical, and ideational reforms congruent with sustainable development. The prolonged economic downturn of the "lost decade" of the 1980s and the mixed record of structural adjustment reforms in African countries created renewed scholarly and policy interests in regime management, rule-based structures, and good governance (Hyden and Bratton 1992).

Beginning from its seminal study, titled *Sub-Saharan Africa: From Crisis to Sustainable Growth* published in 1989, the World Bank pioneered discussion on the imperatives of governance, or "good governance," for any meaningful effort to reverse the socio-political and economic crises in Africa. The document adumbrated that, ultimately, better governance requires political renewal. This means a concerted attack on corruption from the highest to the lowest levels. This can be done by setting a good example, by strengthening accountability, by encouraging public debate, and by nurturing a free press. It also means empowering women and the poor by supporting grassroots and non-governmental organizations (NGOs), such as farmers' associations, co-operatives, and women's groups (The World Bank 1989:6).

Based on this credo, and on capacity-building initiatives, the World Bank, the Ford Foundation, and an ensemble of international donor agencies launched governance programs of various hues to increase the accountability and democratization as well as the cost-effectiveness of their aid programs in Africa. A new word, "conditionality," referring to the insistence of donors on certain indices of governance and democratization, soon entered the political lexicon.

The drive for improved governance in Africa, defined by the World Bank as "the exercise of political power to manage a nation's affairs" (1989: 60), received scholarly impetus from the African Governance Program of the Carter Center of Emory University, where Professor Richard Joseph and other scholars linked governance to legitimation processes and sought to free the concept from the haze and fuzziness that had begun to settle around it. An important scholarly contribution in the direction of conceptual clarity and policy analysis is the pioneering book, *Governance and Politics in Africa*, edited by Goran Hyden and Michael Bratton which located the concept in comparative politics and applied it to various dimensions of state-society relations in Africa (Hyden and Bratton 1992). Defining governance as "the conscious management of regime structures with a view to enhancing the legitimacy of the public realm" (1992:7), Hyden and other contributors map out a policy and research agenda in which the possibilities and constraints of "regime-altering reforms" (Bratton 1992:270) as well as the mechanics and modalities of legitimacy-enhancing projects become central problematics. Although similarities between governance and democracy abound, there are nuanced differences between the two. Hyden (1992), for instance, enlists the ideological tenets of liberal democracy in his definition of governance, above, but the focus remains on regime management, not ideology, or even specific regime structures.

The watchdog role of the media over these regime structure is well articulated by a Nigerian journalist who argued that "the media are charged with the role of holding government accountable and to guard against the abuse of power— hence the need to raise countervailing structures of surveillance to monitor government's activities and stem an inherent disposition towards excess" (Oseni 1995:3).

In the period under study, the media advanced the ethic of open and accountable governance by stimulating debate and pushing alternatives to neopatrimonialist and authoritarian politics. They also campaigned for new legitimacy-enhancing rules. The trouble is that the media operated in a context of censors and authoritarian gags, economic depression, an occasional irresponsible strain born of a frankly commercial ethic, state co-optation of influential journalists, and the like. It is these formidable constraints to media effectiveness that make the analysis rich and the dynamics of governance and media activity complex.

Referring to the progressive and dynamic activities of the Nigerian media in an earlier period, Professor Larry Diamond argued that "These positive contributions were counterbalanced but not outweighed by some continuing tendency toward irresponsible sensationalism and the proclivity of some newspapers to reflect and accentuate the polarisations of partisan loyalties. More effectively, but at greater risk to its practitioners, the press has kept alive the commitment to democracy and sought to establish some kind of accountability during periods of authoritarian rule" (Diamond 1990:1). The weaknesses and occasional hysteria of the media in the period under study vitiate but do not outweigh their enduring contribution to governance and democratization through the creation of images and constituencies for creative politics and change.

There is a universal recognition of the roles of the media as the informant, archivist, antennae, and bard of society. Their pedagogic and socializing functions as well as their activity in shaping the collective memory of a people and the creation of alternative epistemes are also widely recognized (Connerton 1989; Robert Fatton, Jr. 1995). Postmodernist trends in media research tend to lean heavily on literary and performance studies in observing how different "narrativising strategies" help to challenge or interrupt a community's so-called "master discourses" by "indexing a group's ability to consolidate around codes of knowledge" (Zelizer 1993: 82-83; Sorlin 1994).

An inclusive conceptualization of the mass media ought to involve a discussion of the print and electronic media, popular culture, advertising, theater arts, and literature (Whetmore 1982). However, such a proposition will be quite an unwieldy and onerous one within the context of this write-up. The media are conceived of as "any agency, modern or traditional that operate for the articulation and dissemination of ideas and information generally with intent to influence or control an audience or the institutions that constitute legalized power and activity" (Omole 1995:16). Generally media theorists sketch out four models of state-media relations: social responsibility, authoritarian, libertarian and social-centralist (Siebert et al. 1956).

The libertarian model, which emphasizes free expression along the lines of the First Amendment of the American Constitution, is the one that broadly informs media practice in democratic countries. The authoritarian and social-centralist models both mandate that the press publicize the activities of regimes and be controlled by those regimes. This is another way of saying that the politics of meaning is monist and regime-determined. Neither would brook independent media ownership.

The social responsibility theory is the one subscribed to by most African regimes. It stresses the obligations of journalists to take into account social and political sensitivities and asks government to regulate the media in consonance with the dictates of nation-building and developmental programs. This sounds innocuous enough on paper, but the trouble is that regime-survival and neo-patrimonialist exigencies often define these "responsibilities" in African regimes.

In an influential formulation of state-media relations in regimes transiting from authoritarianism to democracy, Karol Jackobowicz posited that "the less democratic a state, the more it is likely to perceive all the media as playing a political role and therefore requiring strict supervision. Such a state is prone to use administrative methods and possibly coercion. The less democratic a state, the more it is predisposed to apply the methods of cultural politics to determine the meanings and definitions of reality disseminated by them" (Jackobowicz 1995:127). If a society is "democratic in so far as the public can play a meaningful role in managing their own affairs" (Chomsky 1991:12), then the media evidently have a crucial role to play in fostering healthy political debate on policy alternatives, complementing the interest-aggregation functions of parties and other groups, stimulating adversarial policy debate in order to refine the policy-making process, and creating an appetite among different publics for major socio-political reforms (Hydle 1972). Through agenda setting, the media enhance the potential for democratic change and policy innovation.

Impact on Governance and Democratization

How exactly do the media contribute to improved governance and democratization? I have already suggested that they do this by highlighting issues of accountability, by nudging governments towards a greater respect for human rights (including those of minorities and marginalized groups), by exposing corruption and rent-seeking behavior and by setting the agenda for public discourse in such a way that it captures these fundamental issues.

I shall expatiate on this theme by citing examples of media advocacy and contributions to governance. In the Ugandan constitutional debate which began in earnest in 1992, the media was in the thick of things. The Constituent Assembly Bill of 1992 marked the beginning of a process that was to culminate in the adoption of a Republican Constitution and the election of May 1996 that returned President Museveni to power under what was described as a home-grown version of democracy.

The point at issue here is that a close reading of Ugandan newspapers at the end of 1992 suggests social and political alertness and a readiness to engage the authorities in debate over the emerging model of constitutional engineering. *The People* lent its pages to criticisms of the bill and published the comments of Mrs. Cecilia Ogwal, Assistant Secretary-General of the Uganda People's Congress, who iterated "numerous loopholes" in it (*New African*, January 1993, p.18). The weight of these comments and posture is not considerably diminished by the fact that *The People* was regarded as a mouthpiece of the Uganda People's Congress.

Similarly, *The Citizen*, also regarded as evincing sympathy for one of the emergent parties, complained of specific provisions in the bill which empowered the President to nominate fifteen delegates to the Constituent Assembly (*New African*, January 1993, p.18). Other publications, including *The Monitor* and *The Weekly Topic,* also took critical positions regarding the bill. As a result of the hail of critical responses, Mr. Sam Njuba, Minister of State for Constitutional Affairs, said at a press conference that the bill was subject to debate. The point here is that the media acted as a receptacle and antennae of an emerging process of democratic engineering. A healthy, if guarded pluralism was and remains a marked feature of the Ugandan media. Both *The Monitor* and *The Weekly Topic* evince sympathies for the opposition while *New Vision* tends to be more supportive of the positions taken by the National Resistance Movement, although it has at times taken a critical stance vis-a-vis the government.

Similarly, in Tanzania the ebbs and flows of multiparty politics impacted on the media just as the media also shaped the process. The banning of *Michapo* (Palaver) in February 1993 by the government under the 1976 law may not have been due to the fact alone that the paper was carrying abusive and salacious stories but perhaps because it published a "scoop" about "Operation Crush," a secret instruction to security agencies to rein in outspoken and opposition media. Indeed, the media acted as the whetstone of the emergent pluralism in Tanzania in the three or four years before the elections that were held towards the end of 1995. For example, an irked President Mwinyi, complained in February 1993 that "All the private newspapers are against us. They have been calling us names, till they have exhausted their bad vocabulary. We won't tolerate further invective" (quoted in *New African,* April 1993, p.41). Such statements notwithstanding, the government has been unable to muzzle the media to such an extent that they can no longer openly criticize officials and their policies. In fact, in the latter part of the 1990s, Tanzania has emerged as one of the more promising places for media freedom in Africa, although Zanzibar, as discussed by Kakwenzire in Chapter Three, is an exception.

In Kenya, the pluralism and boisterous diversity of titles ensure that democratic issues and policy reform get good airing. The human rights magazine *Nduru* is owned by Paul Muite, a courageous and outspoken member of parliament. Similarly, the articulate public in Kenya have a healthy regard for the authoritative and influential editorial opinion of *The Daily Nation* (Interviews in Nairobi, May 18, 1996). On the eve of the 1992 multiparty elections, for example, it warned against an incipient anarchism by noting that Kenya faces the prospect of becoming "a madhouse in which everyone is shouting to be heard and no one is willing to listen" (*Newsweek,* December 16, 1991, p. 18).

In Nigeria, a tradition of heroic defense of civil liberties dating back to the colonial days inform media practice (Omu 1978; Dare 1996). In March 1993, when a motley of individuals close to President Babangida started a campaign for the scuttling of the transition to democracy and an indefinite perpetuation of military rule, I argued in my *Sunday Times* column of March 14th that: "Since democracy offers opportunities for frankly discussing differences and conciliating opposed perspectives, since it prescribes a decent format for changing power, the transition to democracy should be concluded in August this year as scheduled by the military leaders. By the same token, any sermons or campaigns asking the military to extend its stay beyond the promised date should be seen as misguided, diversionary and scornful of our sovereignty" (*Sunday Times,* March 14, 1993, p. 4). Unconvinced that the issue had been laid to rest, I returned to it in my May 2, 1993, column of the *Sunday Times*, (p. 17) titled "The antidemocratic lobby and its agenda." After discussing the various reasons given by the lobby for its anti-democratic posture, I averred that "surely as President Babangida had repeatedly told other African leaders, there is no substitute for organizing and furnishing democratic systems that endure on the continent. We have a right to be disdainful of the anti-democratic campaign whether in its raucous banner-waving versions or in the sophisticated, sly advocacy of its theoreticians." What I said in somewhat measured cadence was yelled by opposition journals like *The News* and *Tell* Magazine, which warned apocalyptically of dire consequences if the transition was aborted (*The News*, May 24, 1953). Of course, as we now know, the warnings fell on deaf ears, but civil society had been sufficiently "mobilized" to protest deafeningly the annulment of the June 1993 elections, a process which culminated in the ousting of General Babangida from office.

Nineteen-ninety-four was a difficult year for the Nigerian media. A number of journalists were detained and several newspapers closed down in the wake of civil demands and agitation for a "revalidation of the June 12, 1993, elections." It was also a year to observe the media in the throes of democratic struggle. One of the newspapers in the vanguard of the crusade for a reversal of the annulment was *The Guardian*, an independent newspaper owned by Chief Alex Ibru, a businessman from Delta State in Southern Nigeria. On June 11, 1994, *The Guardian* criticized the arrest of political leaders who led the democratic agitation. The paper argued on its editorial page under the heading "An Unacceptable Response" that "The majority of those arrested have not been charged at all with any offense. Their detention appears not to be backed by any law known to the public, and they are being held in degrading conditions. And all this for demanding an immediate transition to government based on the consent of the people—it is a great insult not only to the exalted persons but to all Nigerians that founding fathers such as Chief Enahoro, Chief A. M. Ajasin and others of stature are arrested, detained and officially harassed for what is, at bottom, political activity designed to restore sovereignty to the people."

In the same vein, I argued in my *Sunday Times* observatory of July 10, 1994 (p. 9), that "A number of issues are thrown up by the rending account of shabby treatment given to Chief Abiola. The first is the perennial one of whether our conception of human rights extends to those who are awaiting trial or serving jail terms. Bashorun Abiola has tried in his own way to speak up and protest a grave electoral injustice—national reconciliation based on genuine desire to forge ahead requires the release at least on bail of Chief Abiola and others still being held so that they can contribute their quota to national development." Clearly, the media are often on the cutting edge of the empowerment and democratization drive in Africa. For this they pay a high price, as I have already indicated. Imprisonment, job losses, detention, closure of newspapers, and denial of an economic life-line in the form of advertising revenue are some of the costs of advocacy.

Inventive strategies for reining-in the media include the burning of newspaper houses, assassination attempts on the life of publishers (such as Chief Alex Ibru of Nigeria), stiff registration laws, the publication of fake editions of opposition journals, and subtle and unsubtle forms of censorship.

In Tanzania, there has been an ongoing controversy over an alleged plan by the state to use the instrument of a Press Council to gag independent journalists, but it was eventually resolved in favor of establishing an independent Media Council, made up of representatives both from the media and other institutions in society, which would serve the purpose of hearing complaints raised against media representatives or institutions. Developments in Nigeria in the 1990s during the Abacha regime went in the opposite direction. Government resurrected the Newspaper Registration Act, which sets stiff conditions for newspaper registration and practice. The Nigerian Union of Journalists is fighting a legal battle to get the decree withdrawn. In all the countries under discussion, journalism remains a high-risk profession, as harassment, intimidation, and state policy remain potent instruments of media control.

The next section looks at the harsh economics of media practice, which has occasioned a high mortality rate of publications, while the succeeding section takes up antinomies of media effectiveness like ethnicity, ownership patterns, and the strain of recklessness in journalism practice.

Harsh Economics: Publish and Perish?

One other crucial blind spot in a majority of books and monographs on the African media is the economics of production and how this impacts on the viability and capacity of the media. For example, neither Adeyinka Adeyemi's monograph on the Nigerian press (Adeyemi 1995), Adigun Agbaje's otherwise insightful book (Agbaje 1992), or Tale Omole's research report (Omole 1995) explore this dimension of the media. As already indicated, newspapers and magazines have a high mortality rate all over Africa, principally due to the impact of adjustment policies and the turbulent economic milieu, marked by double-digit inflation and diminishing purchasing power.

Before going into specifics, it should be noted that the economic vicissitudes of media are a global trend. The corporate mergers, and the industrial agglomeration of the 1980s and 1990s, were reflected in the media in the shape of acquisitions, joint ventures, and alliances. The demise, mostly through absorption into larger publications of a number of well-known afternoon dailies such as *Minneapolis Star*, *Cleveland Press*, *Washington Star,* and *Oregon Journal* in the 1980s, is well documented (Dennis et al. 1984:62). Similarly, one scholar estimates that "American firms made a record $22 billion worth of multimedia mergers and acquisitions in the first half of 1995" (Hans d'Orville 1995:194). This trend has in fact become the hallmark of the "informatics" age, with the prominence and global reach of several conglomerates offering a wide array of services ranging from electronic publishing through telecommunications and computers to cable, entertainment, and movie production (Hans d'Orville 1995). In Africa, however, the demise, occasional resurrection, and general turbulence of media is not predominantly due to globalization or the expansionist drives of emergent or established conglomerates. It is rather explained more by the fact that most of the input into newspaper and magazine production such as black ink, printing film, newsprint, plates, and other infrastructural material are imported and are therefore subject to such problems as devaluation of the local currencies, import duties, and a battery of taxes such as Value Added Tax (VAT) and others. The familiar repertoire of survivalist stratagems, such as increases in cover prices and advertising rates, sensationalism and scandal-mongering by tabloids, have already been deployed to the point of exhaustion. They no longer stave off media collapse.

In Kenya, one report says that the demise of magazines and takeover of ailing publications is "as common as cars on Uhuru Highway" (*New African*, Feb. 1995, p. 40). Similarly, a number of the newspapers that mushroomed on the eve of the 1992 election did not survive the economic doldrums of that season. One economic journal which died in the slump of those years is the *Weekend Mail,* an event which helped the recent rise and success of the respected *Economic Review* (*New African*, February 1995). One related feature of the Kenya media scene is the keen competition, especially in the magazine sector, a fact which ensures that only the fittest do survive. A situation where close to two hundred periodicals compete for attention in a country of twenty-seven million (a majority of whom live in the rural areas) underlines the competitive angle of Kenyan publishing.

Related too to the unstable media topography is the rapid movement of personnel across jobs. The career of Joseph Odindu, who was fired by the *Nation* group in 1988 but invited six years ago to be managing director of *The East African,* is symptomatic of the sort of rapid personnel changes, firing, and possible re-absorption that one finds all over the continent. I have already mentioned the cutback by fifty percent of print runs of major newspapers in Tanzania, including the influential *Daily News,* in view of the critical shortage of newsprint, a fact occasioned by the closure of the paper mill at Mgololo.

In Nigeria, more than twenty-eight publications perished in the two years between 1993 and 1995. So harsh is the inflationary regime that those newspapers and broadcast media which have survived have had to "downsize" their labor force, reduce the number of titles, or introduce commercial strategies and incentives to keep afloat.

Table 1: Retired Publications in Nigeria (1995-96).

A.M. News	*Link Football*
Abuja Newsday	*Mail*
Business Champion	*Mastersports*
Citizen	*Money Matters*
City News	*New Agenda*
City Sports	*Nigerian Herald*
Corporate	*Poise*
Daily Satellite	*Quality*
Economist	*Razor*
Eko	*Sports International*
Evening Times	*Sports Star*
Financial Post	*The Republic*
Gbohungbohun	*The Voice*
Isokan	*Timesweek*
Lagos Life	*Viva*
Lagos Weekend	

Source: *Newswatch,* Nov. 6, 1995, and author's research notes.

The titles in Table I have all been retired because of the crunch. The list does not include titles such as *The New Nigerian,* which suspended publication in 1995 but was restored some months later by the federal government, its proprietor, under a new engagement. One of the most recent casualties on the Nigerian newspaper scene is *A. M. News*, a spiky opposition newspaper produced by a group of intellectuals, the most prominent of which have been detained several times by the authorities. The newspaper announced its own obituary two months ago. Newsprint, which is perhaps the major commodity in publishing, is imported. The only local source, the Nigerian Newsprint Manufacturing Company at Oku Iboku in southern Nigeria, is self-closed as a result of production problems. The price of newsprint rose from N17,000 per ton in 1992 to N88,000 per ton in 1995 and then to N120,000 per ton in 1996. Newsprint accounts for sixty-five percent of the cost of producing newspapers. A ton of newsprint can produce only twelve thousand copies of a twenty-four page newspaper depending on its quality and infrastructural efficiency (Egochukwu 1996).

How then does this array of problems impact on media viability and their capacity to advance governance-related agendas? As I have observed elsewhere (Dele Olowu et al. 1999), one economic law that works against opposition newspapers is that most advertisers do not patronize them for fear of being blacklisted by government. Co-optation of radical or influential journalists is a distinct strategy employed by neopatrimonialist regimes, which come close to constructing incorporationist alliances in the bid to create nationwide platforms (Agbaje 1992; Adeyemi 1995).

Opposition media have to fight against more economic odds, which makes democratic struggles more of a tall order. Second, the dizzying rise and fall of newspapers and magazines creates a climate of job instability for professionals and makes it easy for employers to breathe down their necks. Third, and related to the above point, there is a drop in professionalism as journalists employ dubious survival methods, battle with poor and irregular pay, and have to cope with what is often described as the "subversive generosity" of state officials. Finally, following the global trend, newspaper readership in Nigeria has declined with the rise of television, radio, and cable (Ben 1990). Harsh economics of production is one variable that constrains the capacity of media professionals to advance governance and democratic objectives, although they continue to struggle at the limits.

Antinomies: Ethnicity and Tabloid Excesses

In this section, I examine antinomies to media effectiveness posed by ethnicity or alleged monopolies created by locational concentration of media as well as questions of balance and responsibility. For if the media, as is sometimes said, are the cutting edge of democratization, then we must probe their outlook, inner-life, and tendencies in order to understand the nexus of ideational, sociological, and psychological factors which affect their performance and potential.

Although conventional typologies dichotomize publicly and privately owned media, I agree with Adigun Agbaje, who, in a study of the Nigerian press, argued that "Private ownership does not automatically translate into more press autonomy" (1992:97). This can be fairly generalized across the continent. I have already alluded to the prostrate editorial posture of the independent *Standard* in Kenya. In Nigeria, some newspapers—like *The Champion*, owned by the Igbo businessman, Emmanuel Iwuanyanwu, as well as *The Democrat, The Reporter,* and the defunct *Citizen* Magazine, all owned by Northern Proprietors have adopted pro-state editorial postures. Conversely, as I have already demonstrated, *The Daily Times* has often offered its pages to views which, to say the least, were bound to irritate the government, its principal shareholder.

To give one curious example of these antinomies, some Northern newspapers in Nigeria actually called on the government to "restrain" newspapers like *The Guardian* for "propagating a sectional agenda" (*Democrat* editorial, July 14, 1996).

In other words, the geo-ethnic fault-lines in Nigeria and other African states are reflected in the media. For this reason at least, a simplistic typology of "private vs. public media" or "state vs. the media" is inadequate to capture the complexity of the African political matrix. As Robert Fatton, has insightfully remarked in a recent article on Africa: "civil society does not always embody the peaceful harmony of associational pluralism. In fact, civil society is conflict ridden and prone to Hobbesian wars of all against all. It is the prime repository of 'invented' ethnic hierarchies, conflicting class visions, patriarchal domination and irredentist identities fueling deadly conflicts" (1995:67).

The media are criss-crossed by class, ethnic, and other divisions that affect civil society, a factor which has made sections of them vulnerable to co-optation by "incorporationist' political or military leaders who exploit these divisions. The question now is: Does this factor render the media incapable of advancing socially alert and trans-ethnic concerns? I do not think so. In the Nigerian crisis of 1993, an editor of the northern-based *New Nigerian* resigned his job rather than bow to pressures to lower professional standards for expedient political considerations. Similarly, the media preponderantly located in Southwestern Nigeria spurned Chief Ernest Shonekan, a Yoruba who was imposed on the Nigerian populace by the departing dictator as a subterfuge to legitimize his annulment of presidential elections. In other words, an ethnicist view of the media in Africa is a false one, just as it would be idle to pretend that ethnicity plays no role in the turbulent dynamics of state-society relations.

Again, it should be noted that the media coverage of ethnic conflicts, for instance, is of international salience. A recent report by an international organization observes that the media is the "third force" in ethnic conflicts and goes on to discuss the challenges of professionalism in polarized situations and how media can exacerbate or mitigate ethnic conflicts (*Daily Times*, December 18, 1995, p. 6). It should not be altogether surprising, therefore, that the relatively "low-intensity" conflicts within African nations lead to differences in perspective, standards of reporting, and editorial coverage.

The dominance of the media by the Southwest axis, historically determined by the early exposure of this region to Western education and to newspapers in the mid-nineteenth century, have featured often in the debate on media pluralism. Mr. Peter Enahoro, chairman of the Nigerian Broadcasting Commission argued recently that "many of today's so called national newspapers emanating from the Southwest are in fact regional publications whose loyalties are to the personalities and causes espoused by the apparent majority of the people of that area . . . it is tantamount to a monopoly of a vital resource with a crucial bearing on the democratic process" (Enahoro 1995:121).

I have already suggested that the picture drawn by Enahoro and other critics is a facile one. Quite often the media have risen heroically to advance national causes which transcend partisan and primordial concerns. Second, a close examination of ownership patterns reveals that prominent newspapers located in the Southwest—such as the influential *The Guardian, The Vanguard,* and *The Champion*—are owned by Nigerians who are not from the Yoruba tribe of the Southwest. The proponents of the ethnicist or regional bias in Nigeria and elsewhere may have made too much of it.

Another popular debate revolves around the ethical profile, responsibility, and even patriotism of the media. State officials in Tanzania, Kenya, Uganda, and Nigeria frequently chide the press for exceeding the boundaries of decency and responsibility. Sometimes punitive actions are meted out to the media on account of their alleged irresponsible tenor. In Uganda, tabloid excesses constitute a subject of legitimate concern among the articulate public (Discussion with an Ugandan academic, in Nairobi, May 18, 1996).

In Tanzania, Dr. Shija justified the banning of two newspapers in 1993 on the grounds that they "carried abusive stories bent on shaming our society". He added ominously: "This is only the start. We will stretch further to deal with irresponsible media" (in "Curbing the Press," *New African*, April 1993, p. 41). His scare tactics, however, never had the effect of intimidating the press and shortly after these pompous statements he was moved to another ministry. The result was a much more constructive approach to the issue of how the media and the government could agree on a formula for retaining press freedom while at the same time encourage discipline and responsible reporting.

There are at least two kinds of publications that raise these hackles. The first is the political underground press which emerged in countries like Nigeria as a response to authoritarian curbs of the formal media from about 1992 onwards. Operating with mobile logistics, their casual profile makes it easy for them to evade the censor. They feature a cheeky and robust temper. As I observed in my *Sunday Times* column of April 3, 1994 "The phenomenon of the underground political press, some of which have been described as the suicide squad variety is partly a response to the abnormal tensions generated by the collapse of General Babangida's abortive Caesarism. In response to the swagger, double-dealing and government-by-ruse strategy of the terminal years of Babangida's government, an unconventional media emerged to arrest the threat and to try to restore civil will. Consequent upon the annulment of the June 12 elections, civil society rose up in arms against the dictator and the underground press played a heroic role in this struggle" ("The Reporter as Ombudsman," *Sunday Times,* April 3, 1994, p. 9).

Authorities in Nigeria and elsewhere have found it difficult to cope with or suppress this media genre, as a number of them have shown remarkable resilience. This genre in some countries overlaps with the junk variety described in the article cited above as "prodigally unethical, abusive, crude, and vagrant. An arm of an emergent anomie in society, they operate at the borders of the law and of decency." This latter group specializes in salacious and juicy stories on the private lives of the high and mighty. Interestingly, most of them have succumbed to the rigorous laws of economics and have disappeared, at least in Nigeria.

The way to deal with media of this kind is to make them face the consequences of their bravado and voyeurism in court rather than use their excesses as pretexts to rein in the media as a whole. Again, the political underground press may likely disappear once a return is made to a democratic and salutary keel in most African countries.

In the next section, I highlight the role of the international media, while a final section makes policy recommendations and attempts a brief prognosis.

The International and Alternative Media

If media studies have spawned a "research tradition which sup-
plies instead of answers a plethora of relevant, but inconclusive, and at times seemingly contradictory findings" (Klapper
1982:30), it is partly because their object of study, the media are
in a state of rapid flux and reflect the oscillating pace of contemporary history. One hitherto little studied area is the dynamic
impact of both the international media and the underground press
on the trajectories of democratization and regime-altering
reforms in Africa (Hyden 1992). Specifically, studies that address
the seminal influence of these two media in the current phase of
democratization are few and far between.

Not only in Nigeria, but all over Africa there is a growing
impact on domestic politics by the international media. The CNN
and various international services of the BBC, including those in
local vernaculars, are important here. These developments have
been given impetus by emerging trends in the communications
industry which have virtually reduced the world to a global village or microchip. As Hans d'Orville (1995:195) argues: with the
rise of satellite-based broadcasting, the smooth line dividing
"domestic" from "international" coverage has been irrevocably
blurred: CNN is now seen in more than 140 countries and every
month brings announcements of new regional systems, satellites,
channels, and programs that consolidate, fill in, and expand this
vast new global network. Interestingly, the impact of this explosion in communications media and their transnationalization is
still being debated, even in older democracies where complaints
are being made about the effect of CNN on policy-making, and
an emergent media pervasiveness with its ambiguous consequences for statecraft. There is no doubt, however, that we are on
the threshold of an information revolution which challenges the
very foundation of the Westphalian nation-state.

In Africa, the influence of international media tends to rise in
times of crisis, when domestic media are put under the thumb of the

state. People could be seen congregating around small transistor radios even in the rural areas or glued to CNN news programs in the cities as they await bits and pieces of information on unfolding situations. As a result of their ubiquity, state officials have become quite jittery about the impact of this variety of media, as the expulsion of the CNN crew from Nigeria in August 1994 for a few weeks illustrates. The weaknesses in capacity of the African media also spawn an excessive dependence on international news agencies, with the result that much of what is published domestically in fact derives from external sources. In Nairobi and Lagos, for examples, elites tend to show preference for international media in view of their richer content and frank reportorial styles.

The months preceding the multiparty elections in Kenya in December 1991 witnessed a sharp focus on Kenya by the international media. Indeed, as I shall shortly show, this focus, which is a form of agenda-setting, constitutes one of the factors and forces which whittled down President Moi's well-known resistance to multipartyism. *The Economist* (of London) and *Newsweek* can be taken as representative of the international print media, with respectable circulation figures in most African capitals. Neither of them has an African section, but Africa is reported under their international sections along with Latin America and the Middle East. Considering this factor, their repeated zeroing-in on the ferment and convulsions associated with democratization and governance demands in Kenya can be regarded as exceptional. The London *Economist* (October 5, 1991, p. 57) carried an article entitled "Something Rotten in Kenya." The piece chronicled such things as "the unsolved murder of the foreign minister," the escalating incidences of corrupt practices, as well as growing demands for reform by Kenyan lawyers and active sectors of civil society. In its November 23, 1991 (p. 61) issue, *The Economist* became emphatic with its article titled "On The Brink." It described the running battle between Smith Hempstone, then American Ambassador, and the Moi government over human rights issues and dubbed Kenya's "single party autocracy" as "obdurate" and repressive of democratic demands.

The Economist got a helping hand from *Newsweek* when, on November 25, 1991, it captured "The Wrath of an Autocrat," in an incisive write-up lamenting that "Moi's crackdown on proponents of democracy promises to make a bad situation worse." Hinting darkly at other forms of diplomatic pressure, *Newsweek* noted that the Paris Club was going to hold a meeting of Kenya's creditors the following week. It accurately predicted that Kenya's human rights posture and resistance to multipartyism would affect the possibility of getting aid allocations and concessions.

On December 9, 1991, a remarkable article (p. 20) in *Newsweek* titled "Let Freedom Ring," a paean to the emergent wave of democratization and reforms, returned to the Kenyan issue, among others. Written by Jeffrey Bartholet, the article traced the trajectory of democratization in Africa and lambasted "Africa's modern day despots." The article gave President Moi a pat on the back for "ordering the arrest of several officials implicated in the murder of Ouko."

By the time *Newsweek* returned to the Kenyan scene on December 16, 1991, President Moi had bowed to pressure for multiparty elections. This was a direct result of the combined activities of the Kenyan civil society, the donor community, and the international media.

As the London *Economist* reported in its issue of February 22 (p. 19), twelve donor governments and international aid agencies had actually embargoed new aid for a period of six months in order to reinforce their demand for the "early implementation of political reform." The *Economist* took a look at Tanzania in the same write-up and observed, with satisfaction, that president Ali Mwinyi had taken a cue from developments in Kenya and scheduled multiparty elections for 1995. In this way, the international media played a decisive role in bringing about the switch to multipartyism in Tanzania and, arguably, in Kenya, as announced on December 3, 1991 by President Moi.

Apart from the influence of these write-ups in emboldening civil society, the media helped to mirror as well as crystallize an international perspective on the Kenyan situation. Insistence on multipartyism aside, the articles broadly purveyed a reform agenda encapsulating such things as accountability, open government, and respect for public opinion. Similarly, the outrage conveyed in the international media, especially those in the United States, was one factor which accelerated the forced departure, in August 1993, of President Babangida after he annulled the June 1993 elections.

Editorials on Nigeria's political change appeared in such papers as *The Christian Science Monitor* and *The Washington Post* urging the United States to take strong action against Nigeria and Babangida (Adeyemi 1995:14-15). In an influential commentary reproduced in the *Guardian* (Lagos, July 19, 1993, p. 6), *The London Economist,* under the heading "Nonsense in Nigeria" averred that "The rest of the world regards Zaire as a bad joke, because the man at the top there had made it one. Do Nigerians want to go the same way?"

The Washington Post editorial on the crisis reproduced in the *Guardian* of the same edition (p. 7), thundered: "General Babangida has shown contempt for the ballot box and civilian rule. Fortunately, because Nigerians are not content to leave their future in the hands of soldiers, the day is slipping away in which strongmen can act with impunity." Needless to say, these reactions and sustained output helped to shape and hone international and domestic opinion which made the dictator's exit inevitable. Nigeria in particular has continued to attract the attention of the international media. In 1995, according to one estimate by a United States-based research group, 3,574 stories on Nigeria were published by American newspapers, an increase of forty-eight percent over 1994 figures (*Champion*, January 4, 1996, p. 3). The spate of mostly bad publicity on Nigeria has led to frantic image refurbishing activities by the government.

There is a rediscovery of the potential and prospects of alternatives to mass media in the wake of censorious and severely restrictive media policies. Some of the more prominent mechanisms in vogue include folk drama, festivals, music concerts, pamphleteering, wall posters, and oratorio. Others include communal gatherings and commuting in rural areas to spread word about impending activities which may include civil disobedience. One scholar argues that "such modes of expression have an authority which allows the emerging civil society to free itself from the shackles of official propaganda and to define the image of its own evolution" (Monga 1995:368). Alternative media, which were deployed to telling effect in Nigeria during the democratic struggles of 1993 in the shape of highly acerbic indigenous best-selling lyrics, wall posters, and denunciatory festivals, come into their own in times of crisis when repression virtually subdues the regular media. They represent a vocabulary and episteme of subordinated social groups who employ it to announce their divorce from predatory and oppressive regimes (Fatton 1995:68).

There is also, quite often, an interfacing of modes and media as groups and constituencies deploy vernacular forms and images in the context of the regular media to sharpen their messages and create audience effect. Sometimes, alternative media agencies take their cue from something published, but dilute or compress it, using their peculiar instruments to give it bite.

Conclusions

I have tried to show that the media were and remain in the vanguard of governance reforms and democratization in Nigeria and East Africa since1990. Obviously, their effectiveness in each country is a function of previous legacies of media advocacy, the capacity of the particular media, and the constitutional and political contexts under which they operate. Backed by the international media and sections of civil society, the domestic media recorded striking successes in Kenya in 1992 and in Nigeria in 1993 in the face of official persecution and resistance to reforms. In Uganda and Tanzania, the media were in the forefront of multiparty advocacy and new governance regimes.

As we have shown, constraints on media effectiveness go beyond political intimidation by civilian or military autocracies. They include economic pressure, obsolete technology, and a certain irresponsible tenor born of frank commercialism, ethnicity, and opportunism. It is argued that these constraints weaken media power but do not cancel out the often heroic role that journalists play in stimulating changes in political attitudes and in exposing rent-seeking behavior or neopatrimonialism.

Criticism of media conduct is not confined to Africa. Joan Konner, Dean of the influential Columbia University Graduate School of Journalism, was reported to have said at the Andrew Cecil lectures on November 10, 1992, that "most of journalism—about 80 per cent—has always been vulgar and about five per cent has been outstanding" (Agbese 1995:2). This may be a slight exaggeration, but it underlines the strain of withering criticism in older democracies about media performance. In Nigeria and Kenya especially, journalists continue to subject governmental conduct and posture to searing criticism, pointing up policy alternatives and articulating a vision of governance that differs from establishment perspectives.

To make the media more responsible and responsive, more attention ought to be paid to professional training and rigor. Professional associations of media workers should put teeth into their regulatory functions with a view to upgrading the ethical profile and comportment of journalists. There should be better linkages between international organizations, especially NGOs and embattled media institutions. If the future of governance in Africa is partly dependent on the activities of vibrant, independent media, then something should be done to stave off the frequent collapse of pro-democracy journals and newspapers.

The future of democracy in Africa appears uncertain as, for example, events in Burundi and Niger—where fledgling democracies have been thwarted by soldiers—illustrate. The gains of the democratization wave in its current phase can only be preserved by a vigilant civil society featuring an active and responsible media.

Democracies, however immature, provide guarantees of press freedom; military rule denies them routinely. In struggling for improved and open governance, therefore, media are advancing their professional interests. The liberal imagination is likely to expand in East Africa as civil society rediscovers its strength and engages officialdom in keen and sustained dialogue over the widening of democratic space.

In Nigeria, where the media have kept vigil over the ongoing re-democratization process, we are likely to see a deepening of the content and thrust of media advocacy for reforms precisely because recent history cautions against a "laid back" or somnolent approach. Which is to say that the travails of the media and civil society in Africa may, ironically, foster lively awareness of the need to create and sustain safeguards against official despotism and excesses.

An African perspective on governance and the media, as this chapter has hopefully illustrated, is not necessarily different from that of other regions of the world. Africans, like media people elsewhere, have to struggle for their rights and their significance lies precisely in the fact that these struggles also have the effect of improving governance. The media in Africa, while still anxious to gain full respect by the authorities, are nonetheless more than any other set of institutions, responsible for enhancing the public accountability of state officials. The role of the media, therefore, deserves continued attention by researchers and practitioners alike.

Works Cited

Adeyemi, A. "The Nigerian Press Under the Military: Persecution, Resilience and Political Crisis." Discussion Paper Presented at the Joan Shorenstein Center, John F. Kennedy School of Government, Harvard University, May 1995.

Agbaje, Adigun. *The Nigerian Press, Hegemony and the Social Construction of Legitimacy 1960–1983.* New York: Edwin Mellen Press, 1992.

Agbese, Dan. Paper presented at a Workshop on News Judgement and Management. Organized by the Nigerian Press Council, Gateway Hotel, Ota, Nigeria, June 22–24, 1995.

Ben, A. *The Decline of Discourse, Reading, Writing and Resistance in Post Modern Capitalism.* New York: The Falmer Press, 1990.

Bratton, Michael, and Donald Rothchild. "The Institutional Bases of Govemance in Africa." In Goran Hyden and Michael Bratton, eds. *Governance and Politics in Africa.* Boulder, Colo.: Lynne Rienner

Publishers, 1992.

Chomsky, Noam. "The Struggle for Democracy in a Charged World." *Review of African Political Economy* 50 (March 1991):12–20.

Clark, T. J. *The Painting of Modern Life*. New York: Knopf Publishers, 1984.

Connerton, P. *How Societies Remember*. London: Cambridge University Press, 1989.

Dare, Olatunji. "Press and Politics in Nigeria Since 1960." Paper Presented at the Friedrich Ebert Foundation Seminar on Art and the Development of Civil Society, Ijebu Ode, May 13–15, 1996.

Dennis, E. E. and John Merrill. *Basic Issues in Mass Communication*. New York: Macmillan, 1984.

Diamond, L. "The Accountability Gap in the Transition to Democracy in Nigeria." Paper for Presentation at the 33rd Annual Meeting of the African Studies Association, Baltimore, November 1–4, 1990.

d' Orville, Hans. "The New Challenge of Global Communication." In Hans d'Orville, ed. *Leadership for Africa: In Honour of Olusegun Obasanjo on the Occasion of His 60th Birthday*. New York: African Leadership Foundation, 1995.

Egochukwu, S. "Marketing Press out of Distress." *Media Review* (March/April 1966).

Fatton Jr., Robert. "Africa in the Age of Democratization: The Civil Limitations of Civil Society." *African Studies Review* 38, 2 (1995):67–99.

Herbert, S. "History, Philosophy and Public Opinion Research." *Journal of Communication* 43 (1993):141–145.

Hyden, Goran, and Michael Bratton, eds. *Governance and Politics in Africa*. Boulder, Colo.: Lynne Rienner Publishers, 1992.

Hydle H. L. *The Press and Politics in Nigeria*. Dissertation Submitted for the Degree of Doctor of Philosophy, Dept. of Political Science, Columbia University, 1972.

Jackobowicz, K. "Media Within and Without the State: Press Freedom in Eastern Europe." *Journal of Communication* 45 (1995):125–139.

Kareithi, P. J. "Multinationals and Foreign-Owned Media in Developing Countries: Lonrho and the Standard Newspapers in Kenya." *Crime, Law and Social Change* 16 (1991):199–212.

Klapper, J. As quoted in: Edward Whetmore. *Mediamerica: Form, Content, and Consequence of Mass Communication*. Belmont, Calif.: Wadsworth, Inc., 1987.

Monga, C. "Civil Society and Democratization in Africa." *Journal of*

Modern African Studies 33, 3 (1995): 359–379.

Olowu, Dele, Kayode Soremekun, and Adebayo Williams, eds. *Governance and Democratization in Nigeria.* Ibadan, Nigeria: Spectrum Books, 1995.

Olowu, Dele, Kayode Soremekun, and Adebayo Williams, eds. *Governance and Democratization in West Africa.* Dakar, Senegal: CODESRIA Press, 1999.

Omole, Tale. "Handcuffing the Media: A Study of an Aspect of Governance Without Democracy in Nigeria's Transition to Civil Rule Under the Military." Research Report Presented to the Governance and Democratization Workshop in Nigeria, Ife, Feb. 20–24, 1995.

Omu, Fred. *Press and Politics in Nigeria, 1880-1937.* London: Longman Press, 1978.

Oseni Tunji. "Government-Media Relations: A Case of Mutual Exclusivity?" Lecture Delivered to the Quarterly Forum of the NTA, Ibadan, Nigeria, July 27, 1995.

Parker, R. Preface to *The Nigerian Press Under the Military: Persecution, Resilience and Political crisis; 1983–1993* by A. Adeyemi. Discussion Paper Presented at the Joan Shorenstein Center, John F. Kennedy School of Government, Harvard University, May 1995.

Siebert, Fied. *Four Theories of the Press.* Champaign-Urbana, Ill.: University of Illinois Press, 1956.

Sorlin Pierre. *Mass Media.* London: Routledge, 1994.

Switzer, Les. "The Growth of the Media in the Third World: African Failures, Asian Successes." Book review, *African Studies Review* 38, 2 (September 1995):132.

Whetmore, E. J. *Mediamerica: Form, Content and Consequence of Mass Communication.* Belmont, Calif.: Wadsworth Inc., 1982.

World Bank. *Sub-Saharan Africa: From Crisis to Sustainable Growth.* Washington D.C.: The World Bank, 1989.

Zelizer, Barbie. "Has Communication Explained Journalism?" *Journal of Communication* 43, 4 (Fall 1993):80–88.

5

Governance and the Ethnic Factor

Rotimi Suberu

Introduction

This essay is concerned with the ramifications and implications of ethnicity for governance in Africa. Ethnicity is not only a contentious and often ruinous political phenomenon, but also an analytically amorphous and onerous concept. In Africa and beyond, ethnic (as well as religious and regional) identity conflicts have hobbled the capacity and legitimacy of governments, drained the integrity and unity of states, and ravaged the cohesion and coherence of civil societies. Although these conflicts have long been a feature of the African political landscape, they have recently acquired a new visibility and stridency owing largely to the declining capacity and viability of the centralized African state, the collapse of the continent's economies, the demonstration effect from the explosion of ethnic nationality passions in the former communist states, and growing external (donor) pressures for economic and political liberalization. The genocidal Hutu-Tutsi conflicts in Rwanda and Burundi, the secession of Eritrea and Somaliland from Ethiopia and Somalia, respectively, the Ogoni crisis in Nigeria, the ethnic clashes in the Kenyan Rift Valley, the resurgence of Zanzibari separatism in Tanzania, and the continuing insurgency in Liberia, Sudan, Angola, and Uganda represent only a few of the flashpoints of ethnic, regional, or religious turbulence and intransigence in Africa. Outside the continent, identity issues have also convulsed or sorely strained the cohesion of countries as diverse as India, Canada, Northern Ireland, the former Yugoslavia, and the former Soviet Union.

At the analytical level, the huge and growing literature on ethnicity has often faltered and foundered in the face of the sheer ambiguity, ubiquity, fluidity and seeming inscrutability and intractability of the ethnic phenomenon. Indeed, there is little clarity and much confusion about the very meaning of ethnicity and its relationship with such analogous collective-identity categories as race, religion, region, nationalism, and class. Yet, in the words of one observer, "without minimal theoretical clarity and consistency, practical attempts at ethnic conflict resolution would appear to be foredoomed" (Ra'anan 1989:19).

Some of the analytical confusion besetting ethnic studies may be avoided by making distinctions among ethnic group, ethnic pluralism, and ethnicity. Essentially, an ethnic group is an ascriptive social collectivity whose members not only share such objective characteristics as group name, core territory, language, ancestral myths, culture, religion, and/or political organization, but also possess some subjective consciousness or perception of common identity or descent. Such sense of common identity is, however, invariably developed only under conditions of ethnic pluralism, that is, under situations involving contact or interaction between two or more ethnic groups. Ethnic pluralism is a necessary, but not sufficient, condition for ethnicity. Consequently, most analysts use the term "ethnicity" to refer specifically to the mobilization and politicization of ethnic-group identity in situations of competitive or conflictual pluralism.

If governance is broadly understood to mean the creative exercise of political authority to promote the ends of good government, then a governance approach to ethnicity would seek to identify and create rules and institutions that may promote equity and amity in inter-ethnic and/or state-ethnic relations and generally channel ethnicity along constructive, rather than oppressive or destructive lines. (Hyden 1990, 1992). In attempting to explore the nexus between governance and ethnicity in Africa, the rest of this paper will be devoted to an explication of the dynamics of ethnicity as currently conceptualized in theory and policy analysis, the basic contours of the African experience with ethnic conflicts and their management, the specific trajectory of ethnic governance in Nigeria (Africa's most populous state), and the general implications of all this for governance prospects and processes in Africa.

Ethnicity in Theory and Policy Analysis

For a long time theorization about ethnicity was dominated by the polarization between primordialists and situationalists. Succinctly, "primordialists" portrayed ethnicity as a transcendental behavior which is driven by the biological and cultural "givers" of ethnic identity and concerned with the promotion of such identity as an end in itself rather than as a means to other interests. Situationalists on the other hand see ethnicity as transactional or instrumental action; a contingent malleable or pliable self-classification that is often contrived by elites and their constituents to obtain economic or other non-ethnic rewards (Mitra 1995:60–61). Although many analysts concede that most cases of ethnic conflicts combine primordial and instrumental impulses in a complex repertoire, the situationalist perspective has enjoyed paradigmatic hegemony in Africa where, according to James Scarritt (1993:286) "politicized communal contention over economic distribution issues is the prevalent form of politically relevant ethnicity." Yet, while the situationalist perspective is valid in its characterization of much of ethnic politics as basically rational and elite-driven, the primordialist or "consummatory" perspective is invaluable because it directs attention to the non-instrumental emotions and motivations—e.g., the struggle for individual esteem and group worth, the quest for symbolic dignity, or the deep psychological impulses and anxieties that inspire many instances of mass-based pathological ethnic conflicts. Both perspectives may be profitably utilized or synthesized in a "constructivist" paradigm that seeks to explain the complex and contradictory processes involved in the creation, appropriation, reproduction, and reconstruction of ethnic consciousness (Young 1994:79–80).

An underlying theme in much of the literature on ethnicity concerns the role of the state as the "organizing principle" that animates, defines, and frames ethnic behavior. Indeed, as scholars like Donald Horowitz (1989:453) and Crawford Young (1982:72) have surmised, one of the features common to modern ethnicity is its highly focused relation to the state, which is the pre-eminent theater for social intercourse and collective conflict. This suggests that the dynamics of ethnicity may be more fruitfully and fully comprehended by interrogating the structure and conduct of the state: its ethno-demographic configuration or composition, socio-economic structure, historical evolution over time, political institutions and processes, and the general struggle to control, constrain, or exit from it.

Regarding the ethnic composition of the state, it should be obvious that very few states in the contemporary global system are "nation-states" or truly ethnically or culturally homogeneous and discontinuous. On the contrary, in most cases the state is larger than the ethnic group or the latter is distributed across two or more states. Moreover, as the example of Somalia poignantly illustrates, even apparently culturally homogeneous states may come to embody or develop disruptive and potentially disintegrative sub-national divisions and tensions of an essentially "ethnic" or sectional nature.

Despite their general heterogeneity, however, states do differ in the structural specificities and institutional contexts of their ethnic configuration. One important structural variable involves the distinction between states with ranked ethnic groups and those with an unranked ethnic structure. Ranked ethnic groups are stratified or hierarchically ordered in socio-economic terms, while unranked ethnic structures are marked by the absence of any such coincidence between ethnic and socio-economic (class) boundaries (Horowitz 1985:22). There are obviously no pure examples of ranked or unranked ethnicity. However, the ethnic systems of Rwanda, Burundi, Apartheid South Africa, pre-revolutionary Zanzibar, and perhaps Sudan approximate the model of ranked ethnicity while most other African countries are populated mainly by unranked or parallel ethnic groups. Ranked ethnic systems tend to be more ideologically and socially entrenched and less politically competitive than unranked systems. However, as the Tutsi-Hutu struggles in Burundi and Rwanda illustrate, such ranked systems are also vulnerable to the violent conflagrations that develop when entrenched inequalities are challenged by subordinate groups.

It is also possible to distinguish between states with centralized ethnic systems and those with dispersed ethnic structures. Ethnically centralized states are demographically dominated by a few large ethnic and/or regional groups whose interactions and frictions invariably come to permeate or polarize virtually all aspects of national politics (Horowitz 1985:37). Rwanda, Burundi, Zimbabwe, Nigeria, and (to a considerably lesser degree) Kenya and Uganda have relatively centralized and thus politically salient and incandescent ethnic or ethno-regional diversities. Mainland Tanzania with its estimated 100-odd linguistic groups, none of which enjoys demographic or socio-economic predominance over the others, is perhaps the paradigmatic African case of dispersed ethnicity. Not surprisingly, Tanzania has not experienced the ethnic tensions over land, jobs and other benefits so characteristic of Kenya and Uganda, Tanzania's northern neighbors (Glickman 1995:289). A further distinction can be made between states with geographically concentrated ethnic groups and those with territorially intermixed groups. Most African states encapsulate geographically concentrated ethnic populations, although such concentration has been progressively diluted by the countervailing forces of migration and urbanization. It is broadly recognized that geographically concentrated ethnic structures are relatively more conducive to inter-ethnic peace, not only because inter-ethnic intercourse and friction are less socially prevalent in such contexts but also because the geographical concentration of identity groups facilitates the implementation of federalist and other territorial formulas of ethnic conflict-management (Lijphart 1977:87–99). Thus, Nigerian federalism has been animated and sustained by the desire to grant some autonomy to relatively discrete ethno-territorial segments, while the federalist debate in South Africa has been constrained by the absence of any definitive congruence between ethnic or racial divisions and provincial or regional boundaries. Similarly proposals for the establishment of a separate Tutsiland and Hutuland as a way out of the savage Hutu-Tutsi clashes in Rwanda and Burundi have appeared impracticable and even "appalling" because of the geographical intermixture of the two groups *(West Africa,* May 8–14, 1995, p. 692).

We may also distinguish between ethnically plural states in which the overall socioeconomic structure is so complex that "ethnic loyalties tend to compete with and are often crosscut (and defused) by numerous other identities" and states in which ethnicity constitutes the primary singularly explosive axis of sociopolitical conflict (Diamond 1987:117). Reflecting the limited elaboration of their socio-economic structures, most African countries lack the complex crosscutting patterns of loyalties found in the industrially advanced "First World." Rather, in these countries, "community loyalties are still very strong and reinforced by other factors," such as non-ascriptive civic and functional economic ties (Hyden 1992:17). Related features of the multi-ethnic African State are the structural primacy and economic centrality of the political arena, and the relative absence of non-state routes to socioeconomic advancement. As Larry Diamond (1988:21–22) has shown, this statism has exacerbated ethnicity in at least two ways:

> First, it is widely recognized that the growth and concentration of resources in the state has increased the salience of state control for ethnic groups as much as for individuals and, hence, has produced a zero sum ethnic struggle for political power. Second, with the whole process of class formation and consolidation at stake for the political class, politicians have been prone

to manipulate ethnic attachments and tears as a means both for mobilizing electoral support and for diverting attention from their own corrupt accumulation and abuse of power.

What is more, the overbearing (and essentially inefficient and predatory) role of the state in economic life has been an important source of Africa's dismal economic performance. Given the "centripetal influences of economic progress and the centrifugal influences of economic decay", it is not surprising that the economic crisis of the African state has promoted ethnic parochialism and nationalism (Adamolekun and Kincaid 1991:185). Thus, for example, the rise of Zanzibari separatist nationalism since the 1980s has been linked to the fiscal crisis of the Tanzanian state, and the expectation of Zanzibari politicians that the weakening or dissolution of the union with mainland Tanzania (Tanganyika) would open up more economic opportunities and benefits for Zanzibar (McHenry 1995:12). A final "structural" variable shaping ethnic outcomes relates to the historical evolution of ethnic political conflict. It is broadly recognized that once a serious outbreak of ethnic contention occurs, it creates a legacy of conflict that may come to shape, constrain, foreclose, or reinforce subsequent ethnic outcomes. Consequently, ethnic policy analysts like Horowitz (1985, 1989) and Okwudiba Nnoli (1994) have emphasized the need for early or timely solutions to contain ethnic conflicts before they reach the threshold of intractability or irreversibility.

Ethnicity is not simply a function of structural and historical factors or what Horowitz has labeled "raw conflict conditions" (Horowitz 1989:451). On the contrary, ethnicity is also significantly shaped by the political institutions that have been put in place to mediate or regulate ethnic conflicts. Generally ethnically turbulent or polarized states are often implicated in the political exclusion or repression of their ethnic segments, while relatively ethnically quiescent or peaceable plural states are characterized by the establishment of political agreements and institutional arrangements that address ethnic concerns democratically, humanely, and constructively.

The major institutional mechanisms for containing ethnic conflicts range from such repressive and/or counterproductive "solutions" as extermination, expulsion, subjection (control), assimilation, and "integration" to such relatively more creative and effective techniques as democracy, autonomy, proportionality, minority rights, and the broad ethos and values of multiculturalism (Rothchild and Olorunsola 1983; Zartman 1989; Gurr 1993). Some of these strategies have featured prominently in various combinations and permutations in the ethnic conflict-management practices of African states.

The (Mis)Management of Ethnicity in Africa

The student of comparative ethnicity is immediately confronted with the irony that while Africa contains some of the most deeply divided countries on earth, the continent appears to be the least creative, innovative, or responsive in developing institutional solutions to ethnicity. As Ted Gurr and his collaborators have confirmed, owing to the extreme arbitrariness and artificiality of colonial era territorial demarcations and manipulations in Africa, the continent has the largest concentration of ethno-political minorities at risk in the world followed by Eastern Europe, Asia, the Western democracies, and Latin America in that order (Gurr 1993:315). Yet, even a cursory examination of political processes in the typical multi-ethnic African state immediately reveals an overriding tendency towards the repression or manipulation rather than accommodation and mediation of ethnic divisions and tensions.

Borrowing from the influential work of Donald Rothchild (1985, 1986, 1991), it is possible to distinguish among three broad institutional paradigms of state responses to ethnicity in Africa, namely, hegemonic repression, hegemonic exchange, and polyarchical or non-hegemonic exchange.

Hegemonic Repression

A commonplace development in the immediate post-colonial era in Africa was the dismantling of the liberal democratic constitutional regimes that were hastily and often crudely constructed in the late colonial era and their replacement with hegemonic one-party or military regimes. In a number of countries, one major consequence of this constitutional decline was the progressive militarization, centralization, personalization, and ethnicization of state power and the corresponding repression of individuals, groups, and ethnic communities opposed to this hegemonist project. Some of the more notorious instances of repression have occurred in such countries as Uganda, Liberia, Somalia, Ethiopia, and Sudan.

In Uganda, the dismantling of the country's quasi-federal constitution and traditional (Kabaka) monarchy in 1966 ushered in two decades of ethnic repression under two dictators, Milton Obote and Idi Amin. In seeking to consolidate their personal rule, both dictators turned the northern-dominated Ugandan military into an ethnic apparatus not only for the persecution and suppression of the restive (and relatively more modernized) southern population, but also for the annihilation of rival northern elements and groups. Repression left over one-half million Ugandans dead, provoked armed resistance to the Obote and Amin regimes, and culminated in the eventual implosion of the Ugandan State. Despite the remarkable measures that have been taken to reconstruct the Ugandan state under the leadership of Yoweri Museveni since 1986, the legacy of ethno-regional alienation, contention, and rebellion has not been completely overcome (Khadiagala 1995; Rupesinghe 1989; Kokole and Mazrui 1988; *West Africa,* February 26–March 3, 1996, p. 313-314).

In Liberia, Sergeant Samuel Doe sacked the civilian administration of William Tolbert in 1980 in a popular coup that ostensibly would end the politico-economic hegemony of the Americo-Liberian oligarchy and expand opportunities for the diverse Liberian ethnic groups. Doe's subsequent personalization of power led to the corruption of the electoral process, brazen favoritism to

Doe's Krahn ethnic compatriots in the military power structure, and the alienation, opposition and attendant state-sponsored repression of Liberia's non-Krahn ethnic groups, especially the Gio. Since the bloody overthrow of Doe in 1990, Liberia has descended deeper into a destructive, protracted, and seemingly unresolvable internal war that has claimed the lives of about five percent of the population and forced the dislocation of most of the remainder. The attendant collapse of the Liberian state has elicited a major international peace-keeping operation in the country and provoked several international talks to negotiate the demobilization and reconciliation of its contending armed fictions and warlords (Ellis 1995; Lowenkopf 1995; *West Africa*, September 4–10, 1995, p. 14–24).

The political manipulation and military repression of clan-sections were also a primary source of destructive internal conflict and warlordism, economic and demographic dislocation, international intervention, and political disintegration in Somalia. During his long personal rule from 1969 to 1990, Somalia's military dictator, Mohammed Siyad Barre, progressively came to rely, for political survival, on a cynical and cruel strategy that involved the promotion of the political and military hegemony of his own Marehan clan of the Darod clan-family, the brutal manipulation and intensification of inter-clan divisions as a strategy of divide-and-rule, and the intimidation, persecution, and elimination of elements—and whole populations—associated with opposing clan-families, including the Iraq in the North (current Northern Somaliland) and the Hawiye in the South (Adam 1995a, 1995b).

Few African countries have experienced greater ethno-nationalist pressures than the multinational state of Ethiopia. Under the regimes of Emperor Haile Selassie (1941–1974) and President Mengistu Mariam (1974–1991), the Ethiopian state sought to contain its Eritrean, Somalian, Oromo, and Tigrean national minorities by assimilation into the dominant Amharic culture if possible, and by manipulation and coercion if necessary (Scarritt 1993:280). The predictable result was violent rebellion by these minorities. With the overthrow of Mengistu's brutal regime in 1991 and the secession of Eritrea in 1993, the new

Ethiopian leaders have sought to give greater recognition to ethnic nationality rights and to reconstruct the Ethiopian State along federalist lines.

In equally divided Sudan, however, the Islamicist, Arab-dominated central government continues both to resist the establishment of a multicultural and secular state and to prosecute a brutal but apparently unwinnable war against rebel movements in the predominantly non-Muslim black African south *(West Africa,* 28 March–3 April 1994, p. 534; Deng 1995). The pattern in all these instances of hegemonic repression is clear. The appropriation and monopolization of power by a narrowly based political clique or dictator engenders alienation and provokes opposition among the excluded elements and groups. The brutal repression of this opposition leads to full-scale armed rebellion or resistance, which eventually degenerates into a protracted, seemingly intractable civil war and/or culminates in the implosion of the state and subsequent need to reconstruct it. Often the crisis unleashed by hegemonic repression cannot be contained without substantial international intervention and arbitration.

Hegemonic Exchange

Rothchild (1985) regards this as the model paradigm of ethnic conflict-management in middle Africa. Hegemonic exchange regimes combine some form of authoritarian bureaucratic (single-party or military) and/or personal rule with policies and practices designed to accommodate or conciliate diverse ethnic segments. Like systems of hegemonic repression, hegemonic exchange regimes are characterized by the abrogation or restriction of conventional pluralist democratic institutions and processes. Unlike fully repressive systems, however, hegemonic exchange regimes are usually not implicated in the systematic and sustained coercion or repression of their component ethnic communities. On the contrary, these regimes devote considerable energy to the elaboration and implementation of strategies designed to ensure some equity, reciprocity, and stability in state-ethnic and interethnic relations.

Most of such hegemonic-exchange strategies revolve around a policy and practice of proportionality, according to which appointments to cabinet or ministerial positions, recruitment into the bureaucracy, allocation of state expenditures, and other distributive decisions are consciously governed by the need to benefit all major ethnic groups or interests in rough proportion to their relative numbers in the population. Although hegemonic exchange practices were a feature of some of Africa's more liberal military regimes, in countries like Ghana and Nigeria, the one-party systems of Cote d'Ivoire and Kenya under Felix Houphouet-Boigny and Jomo Kenyatta, respectively, provide the most outstanding experiments in hegemonic exchange in Africa.

During his long term of office from 1960, when he led Cote d'Ivoire to independence, until his death in 1993, Houphouet-Boigny demonstrated great astuteness in reconciling and balancing the country's diverse ethnic and regional forces. This balancing act was achieved and sustained by such strategies as the incorporation of all major regional elites into the organs or branches of the sole ruling *Parti Democratique de Cote d'Ivoire* (PDCI), the National Assembly, and the cabinet, the broad application of the proportionality rule in distributing developmental resources to the various ethnic regions, the cultivation of a largely independent role for Houphouet-Boigny as a mediator of competing sectional and factional interests, the development of a technocratic civil bureaucracy as a buffer against the elaborate system of ethnic patronage or patrimonialism prevailing in the political realm, and the explicit discouragement or stigmatization of aggressive dysfunctional or extra-systemic ethnic mobilization (Rothchild 1985:79–80; Crook 1990).

In Kenya, Kenyatta similarly displayed remarkable acumen in striking a balance between his roles as the foremost leader of the Kenyan nation and the paramount patron of the Kikuyu ethnic group. Despite the periodic ferocity and abiding uncertainty of interethnic political competition in Kenya, Kenyatta made concerted efforts to ensure that no major ethno-regional group was permanently or completely excluded from power or the sole ruling party, the Kenyan African National Union (KANU). Considerable reciprocity in state-ethnic relations was also achieved under Kenyatta through the promotion of significant participation and competition with KANU, the strategic proliferation and distribution of patronage political appointments (mainly ministerial and assistant ministerial positions) to local bosses and notables in return for their mobilization of grassroots support for the party, the institutionalization of provincial-level administration, the encouragement of community development or ethnic welfare associations, and the protection of the relative autonomy of the judiciary and the bureaucracy (Barkan and Chege 1989; Barkan 1992; Mugai 1995).

If Cote d'Ivoire and Kenya represent relatively successful examples of hegemonic exchange regimes in Africa, the experiences of these countries also underscore the profound limitations of such regimes. First, as a hybrid of control or hegemonic and conciliar or polyarchical mechanisms of ethnic management, hegemonic exchange regimes are inherently ambivalent and actually tend to rely periodically on practices of manipulation, domination, exclusion, or repression. The numerous instances of sectional provocation, including fears of Boule or Kikuyu domination under the regimes of Houphouet-Boigny and Kenyatta, well underscore this point. Moreover, under both leaders the predominant tendency seemed to be not the management of ethnicity in any creative and ordered fashion, but its manipulation and appropriation in order to secure the survival of the personal ruler and the hegemony and stability of the single party.

Second, because they are ultimately based on informal, personal, or ethnoclientelistic networks and linkages rather than on formal or constitutional rules, hegemonic exchange processes are vulnerable to manipulation or even destruction by new political coalitions, elites, or personal rulers. Thus both Henri Konan Bedie and Daniel arap Moi, the successors to Houphouet-Boigny and Kenyatta, respectively, have demonstrated far less acumen than their predecessors in containing ethnic tensions and factionalism, and they appear actually to be presiding over the disintegration of the delicate multiethnic ruling political coalitions constructed by these earlier statesmen (Barkan 1992; Mugai 1995; *West Africa,* February 20–26, 1995, p. 262).

A final limitation of hegemonic exchange lies in its very close kinship with patrimonial politics. In Africa, patrimonialism has reduced politics to the competition for public resources and positions among ethno-clientelistic patronage networks. This not only inhibits the development of progressive or policy-oriented politics but also reinforces the institutionally ruinous and economically costly tendency in the continent to reduce and fragment public offices and resources into objects of personal and sectional appropriation.

Polyarchical Exchange

The term "polyarchy" was originally used by Robert Dahl (1971) to denote the regime of liberal democracy. Thus polyarchical or non-hegemonic exchange refers to the values institutions and processes of ethnic conflict-management under the liberal democratic constitutional framework. These processes often include not only a fully representative and competitive political system that is anchored in the rule of law but also revolutionary or autonomist arrangements proportionality practices, and special provisions and institutions that cater to the specific needs of vulnerable ethnic groups.

For much of the post-independence era in Africa, only Mauritius and Botswana could boast of truly polyarchical regimes on the continent. Indeed, despite its deep class, ethnic, racial, and religious divisions, Mauritius has been able to sustain a stable democratic system for virtually all of the period since Independence in 1968. This feat has been facilitated by the control of governmental power by delicately crafted inter-party coalitions by a proportional multi-member electoral system that ensures some representation and recognition for the best losers by a poly-ethnic official ideology that sees cultural diversity in itself as a virtue and by the complete demilitarization of the state (Brautigam 1995; Eriksen 1992:223).

Although considerably less heterogeneous, culturally tolerant, or democratically competitive than Mauritius, Botswana has also been remarkably successful in using liberal democratic institutions to balance the competing interests of its major Tswana sub-ethnic groups and to secure some measure of security for non-Tswana minorities like the Kalanga and the Bakalagadi (Hohn 1988; Holm and Molutsi 1992; Molutsi 1995). Even though the minorities resent cultural and politico-economic domination by the Tswana, the stable multiparty system does offer them tremendous opportunity to voice their dissent and seek redress democratically and peacefully rather than violently.

Significantly, since 1989, a wave of democratization has swept through Africa with about three-fourths of the continent's previously authoritarian regimes subjecting themselves to multiparty electoral contests (Bratton 1995). However, in over half of these democratizing countries, including Kenya and Cote d'Ivoire, the electoral contests have culminated merely in the reselection and dubious legitimization of the incumbent personal ruler or party. In several other cases of democratization, including Zambia and Benin, the election of new governing coalitions or parties did not produce significant changes in the old practices of ethnic domination, exclusion, or manipulation. Generally, Africa's new democratic states are politically fragile and vulnerable. Nevertheless, there can be little doubt that Africa's recent democratic rebirth has opened up new pressures, opportunities, and possibilities for individual and group participation that could herald a progressive move towards more liberal processes and institutions of ethnic conflict management on the continent.

Most strikingly, the holding of the first ever multiracial elections in South Africa in 1994 did transform that deeply divided racial-hegemonic state into Africa's newest experiment in the use of polyarchical institutions to manage diversity. Among the features of South Africa's interim fledgling constitution is a provision for a central government of national unity, a proportional-representation electoral system, the extensive decentralization of powers to regional provinces, and an entrenched bill of civil and political liberties (Friedman 1995; Shezi 1995). Although threatened by continuing political violence and the perverse legacy of apartheid, the South African experiment in multiracial polyarchy does hold enormous promise as a model for ethnic conflict management in Africa. The heady achievements of South Africa, however, contrast sharply and poignantly with the steady deterioration of Nigeria from Africa's most populous and promising polyarchy into one of the continent's more repressive military autocracies and democratic backsliders.

The Pathologies of 'Military Federalism' in Nigeria

Nigeria has flirted with all three of the aforementioned paradigms of ethnic conflict management in Africa. Nigeria came into independence in 1960 with several liberal democratic institutions, including strong regional parties, a federal constitution, a civilian political executive, a bicameral federal legislature, an independent judiciary, and a free press. This experiment in polyarchy was, however, gravely undermined by the deeply flawed three-region federal structure. That structure operated disastrously to promote the hegemony of the country's three principal ethnicities of Hausa-Fulani, Yoruba, and Igbo to alienate the country's numerous ethnic minority communities and to engender destructive ethno-regional or interregional suspicion and polarization.

The intervention of the military in national politics in 1960 and the attendant suspension of the country's democratic institutions almost immediately led to the escalation of ethno-regional conflict into a full-blown civil war which claimed some one million lives. Nevertheless, the first phase of military rule in Nigeria (1966-1979) was largely one of hegemonic exchange, in which authoritarian military rulers not only sought to incorporate credible and notable ethno-regional elites into their administrations, but also achieved an important political feat in reconstituting the country's lopsided and unwieldy regional structure into a more institutionally balanced federal structure of twelve and later nineteen states.

Although short-lived, Nigeria's second experiment in polyarchy (from 1979 to 1983) gave ample expression to the positive impact of the new multi-state federalism in crosscutting and diluting ethnic majority solidarity and hegemony in empowering ethnic minorities in decentralizing powers and resources to the states and localities, and in generally moderating the country's inherent ethnic divisiveness and explosiveness. However, these achievements were gravely tarnished by the financial profligacy and political excesses of the civilian political class which provided the pretext for the second intervention of the military at the end of 1983.

Compared with the first phase, the second phase of military rule has witnessed a dramatic depreciation in the moral authority and political credibility of the military via the excessive personalization of state authority by the military head of state and an increasing proclivity towards a reliance on hegemonic repression rather than hegemonic exchange in the management of state-ethnic relations. Indeed, contemporary state-ethnic dynamics in Nigeria are trapped in a ruinous spiral of overcentralization, exclusion, repression, and imminent disintegration (Olowu 1990; Suberu 1994; Diamond 1995).

Overcentralization

Nigeria's federal or decentralist political institutions have been the primary casualties of the extended political interventionism of the country's military. Although the soldiers have almost always expressed a formal commitment to the retention of the country s federal structure, the military's unified and centralized command system has cohabited uneasily with federalism. Subjected to tight and crushing central controls, the country's federal institutions have become distorted and degraded beyond recognition. The more prominent sources or instances of this distortion include: the complete subordination of constituent state administrations to the unified military power structure via the appointment and frequent redeployment by the central military authorities of relatively junior military officers as state governors or administrators; the direct intervention of the central military government in the operation, composition, and reform of local government authorities; the continued dependence of the states and localities on central funding for a disproportionate amount (about 80 percent) of their revenues; the systematic manipulation of statutory intergovernmental revenue-sharing arrangements in a manner that has reinforced the financial hegemony of the center and the fiscal emasculation of the states and localities; the complete erosion of the autonomy of the judiciary, which normally plays an important institutional role in federal systems in arbitrating constitutional and intergovernmental disputes; and the proliferation of new units of centrally-funded states and local governments as part of a strategy to consolidate central hegemony, gratify distributive sectional pressures, and promote the longevity and legitimacy of the military government.

Exclusion

Military regimes in segmented states are particularly vulnerable to the development of narrow or sectional socio-political bases that exclude (or inadequately or inequitably include) large segments of their population (Horowitz 1985:443–471). Often, such sectional bases are the outcome of the ethnically skewed military recruitment practices of former colonial masters, the conspiratorial imperatives of the coup-making process, and/or the official proscription or restriction by military regimes of such conventional institutions and processes of political representation as elections, legislatures, and political parties.

Although the Nigerian military has long been regulated by various policies that are designed to ensure that its composition and conduct reflect the country's "federal character," military governments in Nigeria, as in Uganda, have been dominated largely by Northern elements. Thus all but two of the country's seven military heads of state since the initial 1966 coup have been Northerners, and all three military heads of government since the second military coup in 1983 have been Muslims from the North. Moreover, key military and ministerial positions—including the Chief of Army Staff, the Director of National Security, the Command of Major Army Divisions, and the Ministries of Defence and Internal Affairs—have been virtually monopolized by Northerners.

The sense of alienation engendered by the ethno-regional imbalance in the composition of recent Nigerian military governments has been aggravated by acts of sectional provocation and discrimination by the state. In 1986, for instance, General Ibrahim Babangida (Nigeria's military president from 1985 to 1993) precipitated an unprecedented religious crisis when he surreptitiously and clandestinely enlisted Nigeria in the Organization of Islamic Conference (OIC). His subsequent annulment of the results of an election (in June 1993) that would have placed a southerner at the head of an elected federal government for the first time in the nation's history provoked a major ethnic, regional, and institutional crisis from which the country has yet to recover (Diamond 1995).

Repression

The repression of restive communal constituencies and elites has been the characteristic response of the soldiers to the crisis of national unity into which the military itself had almost unilaterally plunged the country. Nowhere has this repression been more systematic and traumatic than in the oil-rich southeastern region of the country—especially Ogoniland (Human Rights Watch Africa 1995; Naanen 1995; see also Chapter Three in this volume). Since 1990, the half-million Ogoni who were led by the late writer Ken Saro-Wiwa have spearheaded a vigorous campaign against the inequities, pathologies, and irregularities of the Nigerian system of federalism. In particular, they have denounced the assaults of the militarized and centralized Nigerian state on the environmental, economic, and political rights of the Ogoni and other oil-producing Southern ethnic minority communities. Consequently, they have asked for responsive policies that would promote the ecological rehabilitation, economic empowerment, and political self-determination of these communities. The government has tried to contain these pressures through such repressive tactics as the proscription of ethnic associations; the announcement of a treasonable offenses law for ethnic minority activists; the military invasion, intimidation, or destruction of ethnic minority villages and settlements; the instigation or orchestration of violent clashes between neighboring oil-producing minority communities; and the harassment, detention, and arbitrary prosecution of crusading ethnic minority elites. In November 1995, the Nigerian military government provoked considerable internal alienation as well as international repudiation and sanctions when it executed Ken Saro-Wiwa and eight other Ogoni activists for their alleged roles in the gruesome murders of four pro-government Ogoni elders during May 1994 (Suberu 1996).

Imminent Disintegration

The ruinous dynamics of overcentralization, exclusion, and repression have engendered broad cynicism and skepticism regarding the viability or survivability of the multi-ethnic Nigerian state. Many, both within and outside Nigeria, have called for the confederalization or dissolution of the country into more governable or culturally compatible units. At least one noted writer has surmised that the question is no longer whether Nigeria will break up, but when (Williams 1994:16).

Perhaps the only redeeming feature of the Nigerian crisis is the continued commitment of the military to the retention of the country's federal institutional structure—even if only in a severely distorted form—and the profusion of both official and unofficial ideas and proposals for the reform and revitalization of the federal system (Olowu 1994:29). Yet, unless the military disengages from politics and allows democratically constituted governments to mediate the country's unresolved national question, it is difficult to see how the current pressures towards the implosion or disintegration of the Nigerian state may be contained.

Concluding Observations

A frican post-colonial governments have generally proven to be poor managers of ethnic political conflict. Typically, the state in Africa has relied on the hegemonic repression or manipulation of ethnic divisions, as opposed to their mediation or management through the institutions and processes of democratic constitutionalism. Despite recent democratic openings on the continent, the legacy of authoritarian ethnic-conflict management continues to pose an important obstacle to the evolution or consummation of liberal reforms in state-ethnic relations.

This chapter has argued that, although structurally and historically rooted, Africa's ethnic problems are not inevitable or intractable. With appropriate institutions, even the most destructive ethnic conflicts can be contained or averted. Although there are no universally valid formulas for managing ethnicity, African countries can learn a lot from the political processes of other deeply divided but politically peaceable and stable countries. These processes are best denoted by the broad paradigm of "polyarchical exchange" which includes four specific mechanisms of ethnic conflict-management, namely, democracy, autonomism, proportionality, and minority rights.

Far from inexorably requiring the imposition of authoritarian, one-party, or military solutions, ethnic divisions can indeed operate to induce and enrich democratic pluralism and constitutionalism (Sithole 1994). In the same vein, by providing for the political representation of various societal interests through regular and open electoral competition, and by securing basic civil and political liberties for individuals and groups, a democratic system offers a necessary (though by no means sufficient) basis for the ordered and humane accommodation of ethnic concerns. Not surprisingly, as Horowitz (1985:xiii) has succinctly observed, the rise of ethnic conflict has gone hand-in-hand with the decline of democracy in Africa. Despite their tentativeness and limitations, current movements for re-democratization in Africa do carry some promise for the unravelling of the authoritarian tendencies that have fed ethnic conflicts on the continent in the last three decades. As the experiences of countries like Sri Lanka, Northern Ireland, Angola, and Sudan illustrate, however, simple majoritarian democracy can work to exacerbate identity conflicts in divided societies. To secure political stability and equity in segmented societies, democratic institutions ought to be tailored to protect the interests of diverse groups through provisions for group autonomy, proportionality, and minority rights.

Autonomy arrangements, which are often regarded as the territorial twin of democracy, seek to avert inter-ethnic conflict by giving distinct groups some measure of self-determination. These arrangements may take the territorial forms of regional or local decentralization within a unitary state federalism, or the grant of full sovereignty to a group through the dissolution or partition of an existing state.

Because most African states already have unitary constitutions, the most realistic path to securing relative ethnic group autonomy and security would appear to lie in the more effective decentralization of powers, resources, and electoral legitimacy to local-level units—provinces, regions, districts—that are created by and remain subordinate to the national government. However, because of its presumed capacity to strike a more authentic balance between the imperatives of "self-rule" or group autonomy and the advantages of "shared-rule" or national government, federalism may be a more appropriate solution for countries like Cameroun, Ethiopia, Sudan, Democratic Republic of Congo, and Nigeria, where strong autonomist pressures or traditions already exist.

Partition is usually regarded as a policy of last resort because it is often extremely difficult to re-divide the borders of an existing state in a way that does not produce fresh ethnic minorities or antipathies and the associated pressures for purging ethnic groups from a region or even "ethnic-cleansing". Thus, in Africa there has been some reluctance to alter the colonial territorial legacy in spite of its egregious artificiality and arbitrariness. Yet, recent experiences with ethnic nationality conflicts suggest that where implacable secessionist pressures already exist, as in the Sudan, a negotiated partition may offer a more humane political solution than the continued maintenance of a state through violence, repression, or manipulation.

While autonomy arrangements characteristically seek to grant some measure of self-governance to individual identity groups, proportionality practices aim at the equitable representation and treatment of all identity groups in the central state apparatus. As already indicated, proportionality has been extensively used and developed in many African states. However, much can still be done to institutionalize, improve, and expand proportionality practices in Africa, especially through the design of electoral systems that may secure inter-ethnic moderation, toleration, and coalition by inducing or compelling candidates and parties to seek electoral support across ethnic boundaries (Horowitz 1989; Young 1995:25).

For most multi-ethnic states, the combination of democracy, relative group autonomy, and proportionality practices would suffice to secure ethnic justice. However, some constituent ethnic groups in a state such as the lower castes in India and in America may be so historically disadvantaged and/or structurally vulnerable as to require special considerations, rights, or privileges from the state to enable them to coexist or compete equitably with other groups. Nevertheless, because of their inherently contentious or discriminatory character, such affirmative-action or ethnic-preference policies are better implemented for a fixed or specified period in order to augment social and ethnic cleavages. After this fixed or specified period of time, these policies can be reversed, allowing for unfettered competition among equal individuals in the public realm regardless of ethnic or social identification.

The broad philosophical principle guiding the polyarchical mediation of ethnicity is multiculturalism. Unlike assimilation (which promotes the incorporation of minorities into a dominant culture) or integration (which seeks to bring all ethnic segments together in a new homogeneous national culture), multiculturalism does not involve the devaluation or destruction of existing ethnic cultures or the identification of the state with a particular cultural group or ideology. Rather, multiculturalism seeks to create a state which recognizes and promotes the equal rights and dignity of all ethnic cultures and groups (Eriksen 1992; Zartman 1989:525). While a preoccupation with the pathological and conflictual dimensions of ethnic political behavior has given much of the literature on ethnicity a negative tone, multiculturalism recognizes the actual and/or potentially positive role of ethnicity as a force for regenerative social integration, political mobilization, and psycho-cultural identification.

The question is: what factors or forces may induce African governments to undertake the necessary reforms in state-ethnic relations? Because the economic centrality of the state has been a powerful force driving the pressures for the appropriation, manipulation, and ethnicization of political power in Africa, current economic reforms designed to reduce the size and role of African governments may help at least in the long run to engender a climate that is more conducive to reforms in state-ethnic relations (Ottaway 1995:247). Similarly, the competitive pressures associated with ongoing democratization processes could compel state-elites to pursue some measure of accountability and reciprocity in their relationships with diverse ethnic populations. Political liberalization and democratization would also strengthen the capacity of African civil societies generally—and autonomous ethnic and regional associations particularly—to operate as an important advocacy structure for reforms in state-ethnic relations. Such ethnic advocacy may benefit tremendously from the roles of interested academics and arbitrators in providing independent standards for evaluating specific assertions made by ethnic groups. Finally, the international community—including the Organization of African Unity (OAU), the relevant agencies of the United Nations Organisation (UNO), the European Union (EU), and international non-governmental bodies—has an important humanitarian, cultural, and material role to play in stimulating, supporting, and sustaining more equitable and peaceable processes of ethnic conflict management in Africa.

This chapter has tried to indicate what the principal issues are with regard to how African countries may more effectively deal with the ethnic factor in the context of political governance. As can be deduced from this account, the issues facing African governments are very similar to those encountered in other regions of the world where the ethnic factor is significant. The problem in Africa so far has been the little interest that the continent's political leaders have shown in dealing with ethnicity in terms of constitutional and legal provisions that enable people to feel secure and governments able to manage this set of issues in a manner constructive to both itself and its citizens. African scholars can make an important contribution toward raising greater awareness of how ethnicity may be politically managed in more effective ways by continuing research in this area and disseminating results to representatives of states and civil society alike.

Works Cited

Adam, H. M. (a) "Somalia: A Terrible Beauty Being Born?" in I. W. Zartman, ed. *Collapsed States: The Disintegration and Restoration of Legitimate Authority.* Boulder, Colo.: Lynne Rienner Publishers (1995):69–89.

Adam, H. M. (b) "Clan Conflicts and Democratization in Somalia," in H. Glickman, ed. *Ethnic Conflict and Democratization in Africa.* Atlanta, Ga.: African Studies Association Press (1995):197–226.

Adamolekun, L., and J. Kincaid. "The Federal Solution: Assessment and Prognosis for Nigeria and Africa." *Publius: the Journal of Federalism* 21, 4 (1991):173–188.

Barkan, J. "The Rise and Fall of a Governance Realm in Kenya," in G. Hyden and M. Bratton, eds. *Governance and Politics in Africa.* Boulder Colo.: Lynne Rienner Publishers, 1992.

Barkan, J., with M. Chege. "Decentralising the State: District Focus and the Politics of Reallocation in Kenya," *Journal of Modern African Studies* 27, 3 (1989):431–453.

Bratton, M. "Are Competitive Elections Enough?" *Africa Demos* 3, 4 (1995):7–8.

Brautigam, D. "The Paradoxes of Democratization in Mauritus," *Africa Demos* 3,4 (1995):18–19.

Crook, R. "State, Society and Political Institutions in Cote d'lvoire and Ghana," *IDS Bulletin* 21, 4 (1990):24–34.

Dahl, R. *Polyarchy: Participation and Opposition.* New Haven: Yale

University Press, 1971.

Deng, F. M. "The Sudan: Stop the Carnage," in F. J. Ramsay, ed. *Global Studies Africa*. Guilford: Dushkin/Brown and Benchmark, 1995.

Diamond, L. "Ethnicity and Ethnic Conflict," *The Journal of Modern African Studies* 25, 1 (1987):117–128.

Diamond, L. "Introduction: Roots of Failure, Seeds of Hope," in L. Diamond, J. Linz, and S. M. Lipset, eds. *Democracy in Developing Countries: Africa*. Boulder, Colo.: Lynne Rienner Publishers, 1988.

Diamond, L. "Nigeria: The Uncivic Society and the Descent into Praetorianism," in L. Diamond, J. Linz, and S. M. Lipset, eds. *Politics in Developing Countries. Comparing Experiences with Democracy*. Boulder, Colo.: Lynne Rienner Publishers, 1995.

Doornbos, M. "Linking the Future to the Past: Ethnicity and Pluralism," *Review of African Political Economy* 52 (1991):53–65.

Ellis, S. "Liberia, 1989–1994: A Study of Ethnic and Spiritual Violence," *African Affairs* 94, 375 (1995):165–197.

Eriksen, T. H. "Ethnicity and Nationalism: Definitions and Critical Reflections," *Bulletin of Peace Proposals* 23, 2 (1992):219–224.

Friedman, S. "South Africa: Divided In a Special Way?" in L. Diamond, J. Linz, and S. M. Lipset, eds. *Politics in Developing Countries: Comparing Experiences with Democracy*. Boulder, Colo.: Lynne Rienner Publishers, 1995.

Glickman, H. "The Management of Ethnic Politics and Democratization in Tanzania," in H. Glickman, ed. *Ethnic Conflict and Democratization in Africa*. Atlanta, Ga.: African Studies Association Press, 1995.

Gurr, T. *Minorities at Risk: A Global view of Ethnopolitical Conflicts*. Washington, D.C.: United States Institute of Peace, 1993.

Holm. J. D. "Botswana: A Paternalistic Democracy," in L. Diamond, J. Linz, and S. M. Lipset, eds. *Democracy in Developing Countries: Africa*. Boulder, Colo.: Lynne Rienner Publishers, 1988.

Holm, J. D., and P. P. Molutsi. "State-Society Relations in Botswana: Beginning Liberalization," in G. Hyden and M. Bratton, eds. *Governance and Politics in Africa*. Boulder, Colo.: Lynne Rienner Publishers, 1992.

Horowitz, D. L. *Ethnic Groups in Conflict*. Berkeley: University of California Press, 1985.

Horowitz, D. L. "Making Moderation Pay: The Comparative Politics of Ethnic Conflict Management," in J. V. Montville, ed. *Conflict and Peacemaking in Multiethnic Societies*. Lexington: Lexington Books, 1989.

Human Rights Watch Africa. *Nigeria: The Ogoni Crisis: A Case-Study of Military Repression In. South-Eastern Nigeria.* New York. Human Rights Watch 7, 5 (1995).

Hyden, G. "Reciprocity and Governance in Africa," in J. S. Wunsch and D. Olowu, eds. *The Failure of the Centralized State: Institutions and Self-Governance in Africa.* Boulder, Colo.: Westview Press, 1992.

Hyden, G. "Governance and the Study of Politics," in G. Hyden and M. Bratton, eds. *Governance and Politics in Africa.* Boulder, Colo.: Lynne Rienner Publishers, 1992.

Keller, E. "Remaking the Ethiopian State," in I. W. Zartman, ed. *Collapsed States.* Boulder, Colo.: Lynne Rienner Publishers, 1995.

Khadiagala, G. M. "State Collapse and Reconstruction in Uganda," in I. W. Zartman, ed. *Collapsed States.* Boulder Colo.: Lynne Rienner Publishers, 1995

Kokole, O. H. and A. A. Mazrui. "Uganda: The Dual Polity and the Plural Society," in L. Diamond, J. Linz, and S. M. Lipset, eds. *Democracy in Developing Countries: Africa.* Boulder, Colo.: Lynne Rienner Publishers, 1988.

Lijphart, A. *Democracy in Plural Societies: A Comparative Exploration.* New Haven and London: Yale University Press, 1977.

Lowenkopf, M. "Liberia: Putting the State Back Together," in I. W. Zartman, ed. *Collapsed States.* Boulder, Colo.: Lynne Rienner Publishers, 1995.

McHenry, D. "The Transition from the Demand for a Separate Identity to a Demand for a Separate Polity: A Comparison of the Political Uses of Zulu and Zanzibari Subnationalism." Paper for the Annual Meeting of the African Studies Association. Orlando, FL. November 3–6, 1995.

Mitra, S. K. "The Rational Politics of Cultural Nationalism: Subnational Movements in South Asia," *British Journal of Political Science* 25, 1 (1995):57–77.

Molutsi, P. "Botswana's Democracy: Past and Future Strategies," *Africa Demos* 3, 4 (1995):16–17.

Mugai, G. "Ethnicity and the Renewal of Competitive Politics in Kenya," in H. Glickman, ed. *Ethnic Conflict and Democratization in Africa.* Atlanta, Ga.: African Studies Association Press, 1995.

Naanen, B. "Oil-Producing Minorities and the Restructuring of Nigerian Federalism: The Case of the Ogoni People," *Journal of Commonwealth and Comparative Politics* 33, 1 (1995):46–78.

Nnoli, O. "Ethnicity and Democracy in Africa: Intervening Variables," *Occasional Monograph Series.* Port Harcourt, Nigeria: Centre for

Advanced Social Sciences, 1994.

Olowu, D. "Centralization, Self-Governance and Development in Nigeria," in J. Wunsch and D. Olowu, eds. *The Failure of the Centralized State*. Boulder, Colo.: Westview Press, 1990.

Olowu, D. "The Future of the (Nigerian) Federal System," *The Guardian*, (March 4, 1994).

Ottaway, M. "Democratization in Collapsed States," in I. W. Zartman, ed. *Collapsed States*. Boulder, Colo.: Lynne Rienner Publishers, 1995.

Ra'anan, U. "The Nation-State Fallacy," in J. V. Montville, ed. Conflict and Peacemaking in Multiethnic Societies. Lexington: Lexington Books, 1989.

Rothchild, D. "State-Ethnic Relations in Middle Africa," in G. W. Carter and P. O'Meara, eds. *African Independence: The First Twenty Five Years*. Bloomington, Ind.: Indiana University Press, 1985.

Rothchild, D. "Inter-Ethnic Conflict and Policy Analysis in Africa," *Ethnic and Racial Studies* 9, 1 (1986):66–86.

Rothchild, D. "An Interactive Model for State-Ethnic Relations," in F. M. Deng and I. W. Zartman, eds. *Conflict Resolution in Africa*. Washington, D.C.: The Brookings Institution, 1991.

Rothchild, D., and V. Olorunsola, eds. *State Versus Ethnic Claims: African Policy Dilemmas*. Boulder, Colo.: Westview Press, 1983.

Rupesinghe, K., ed. *Conflict Resolution in Uganda*. Oslo: International Peace Research Institute, 1989.

Scarritt, J. R. "Communal Conflict and Contention for Power in Africa South of the Sahara," in T. Gurr, ed. *Minorities at Risk: A Global View of Ethnopolitics*. Washington D.C.: United States Institute of Peace (252–289).

Shezi, S. "South Africa: State Transition and the Management of Collapse," in I. W. Zartman, ed. *Collapsed States*. Boulder, Colo.: Lynne Rienner Publishers, 1995.

Sithole, M. "Is Multiparty Democracy Possible in Multiethnic African States?" in U. Himmelstrand, K. Kinyanjui, and G. Mburugu, eds. *African. Perspectives on. Development*. London: James Currey, 1994.

Suberu, R. T. "The Travails of Federalism in Nigeria," in L. Diamond and M. F. Plattner, eds. *Nationalism, Ethnic Conflict and Democracy*. Baltimore, Md.: Johns Hopkins University Press, 1994.

Suberu, R. T. *Ethnic Minority Conflicts and Governance in Nigeria*. Ibadan, Nigeria: Spectrum Books, 1996

Williams, A. "An Arewa Liaison," *The News* (February 21, 1996).

Young, C. "Patterns of Social Conflict: State, Class and Ethnicity," *Daedalus* 8, 2 (1982):71–98.

Young, C. "Evolving Modes of Consciousness and ideology: Nationalism and Ethnicity," in D. E. Apter and C. G. Roseberg, eds. *Political Development and the New Realism in Sub-Saharan Africa.* Charlottesville, Va. and London: University Press of Virginia, 1994.

Young, C. "Ethnic Dilemmas: Democracy and the Ethnic Question," *Africa Demos* 3, 4 (1995):24–25.

Zartman, I. W. "Negotiations, and Prenegotiations in Ethnic Conflict: The Beginning, The Middle and the Ends," in J. V. Montiville, ed. *Conflict and Peacemaking in Multiethnic Societies.* Lexington: Lexington Books, 1989.

6

Bureaucracy and Democratic Reform

Dele Olowu

Introduction

Democracy is constrained in post-colonial African states by
such factors as poverty, low levels of education, deep ethnic
and religious divisions, as well as weak civil society structures
(Hyden and Bratton 1992; Ake 1995). Africa's colonial and post-
colonial public bureaucracies were considered crucial for formulating and implementing programs aimed at radically transforming
economic and social conditions in African countries within a short
period of time. Most observers at the time thought that improved
socio-economic conditions were the necessary preconditions for
the attainment of democratic governance.

As Africans struggle to transform their governance systems from autocracies into democracies in the 1990s, it is becoming ever more apparent that bureaucracies—whether of civil, military, or partisan variety—may constitute òne of the most serious,
if not the most serious, obstacle to the realization of the collective goals of the African people: economic growth, national integration, and democratization. African public bureaucracies have
over the years become ready instruments of despots and patrimo-

nial rulers and—in a few extreme cases, such as is being witnessed in Nigeria and other countries in the West African subregion (Ghana and the Gambia)—the military wing of the public bureaucracy has seized political power by force of arms and is increasingly legitimizing its near-permanent hold on power.

Several observers have highlighted the fragility of the African democratic impetus of the 1990s (Rasheed 1995). This article goes further to argue that democratic governance is not likely to make much progress unless public bureaucracies are transformed from the monocracies which serve the whims of those who control the executive branch of government in Africa to polycentric institutions whose primary concern is to serve the ordinary people of Africa efficiently, accountably and responsively. The magnitude of the change this transformation requires calls for a virtual reinvention of African governmental systems—a completely different paradigm of political and administrative systems.

The chapter begins with a conceptual statement of the relationship between democratic governance and bureaucracy before looking briefly and analytically at the experiences of the English-speaking countries in the eastern and western African sub-regions.

A Conceptual Framework

Democratic governance is here defined as a system that is characterized as a "political or constitutional democracy" (Buijtenhuijse and Rijnierse 1992; Hadenius 1992; Nwabueze 1985). The forms of political or constitutional democracy may differ from one culture to another but its essential principles are universal (Cohen 1995; Hyden and Bratton 1992).

The two most important of these universal principles are institutional pluralism and political equality (Dahl 1971; Ostrom 1995; Huntington 1992; ECPDM 1992; Buijtenhuijse and Rijnierse 1992). Democracy exists in a country when there is institutional pluralism or when there is a polycentric political order in which state and society organs are allowed to freely interact with one another (Ostrom 1990; Olowu 1995a). The emphasis is not only the equality of political actors but the legal and relative equality of all state and society institutions, including such political institutions as political parties, independent legislatures, electoral systems and jurisprudence, and active watchdog, research, and policy analysis organs and pressure groups. All of these ensure that the critical norms of good governance—efficient delivery of services, account-ability and responsiveness of public institutions, rule of law, and policy pluralism—are realized. (Sartori 1987; Hadenius 1992; Saward 1994; World Bank 1995; Beetham 1994; E. Ostrom 1993).

A recent review of the expansive literature on democracy observes that democracy refers to "a particular system of social organization of political forces in which the relationship between the rulers and the ruled is one of symmetry sustained by specific *institutions* and *attitudes* that regulate the behaviour between the ruler and the ruled and the manner in which the rules are made" (UNECA 1995:6). Similarly, Beetham (1994: 28–29), in a global review of the principles and indices of democratization, lists four major indices of a democracy: (a) popular election of the parlia-ment and the head of government; (b) continuous accountability of government—directly to the electorate through public justifi-cation for its policies and indirectly to agents acting on the peo-ple's behalf; (c) guaranteed civil and political rights; (d) a civil society which is independent and capable of influencing or checking on the exercise of governmental powers and is commit-ted to democratic values. These characterizations are similar to the ones invoked by B. O. Nwabueze (1985:1) in defining "con-stitutional democracy:" popular participation, social equality, public welfare as the object of government, and an ethic or tradi-tion of democratic behavior.

This definition of democracy or democratic governance which combines institutional and behavioral elements provides the basis for the theme of this paper: the nature of the relationship between democratic governance and modern public bureaucra-cies. Bureaucracy is the medium by which the government relates to the governed. Modern bureaucracies are expected to possess certain attributes that enable them to function in a very efficient manner. These attributes, according to Max Weber, include: a system of rational rules, specialization, precision, hierarchy, written records, routinization, separation between the public and private realms, specified delimitation of authority, a career system, meritocracy, and strict discipline and control of officials.

Even though Weber was quite pessimistic of the long-term implications of bureaucracy for democracy and emphasized the mutually reinforcing linkages between bureaucracy and economic growth, he also recognized reinforcing linkages between bureaucracy and democracy and argued that social and economic equality was one of the conditions for the emergence of a bureaucracy. Bureaucracy can promote equality by ensuring fairness and the norms of anonymity, objectivity, and neutrality to which bureaucratic officials ideally subscribe (Mccurdy 1978; Jacoby 1973).

It took another close student of bureaucracy to call attention to the instrumental nature of modern bureaucracies and the dangers inherent in the monocratic structures they nurture for democratic government. According to Vincent Ostrom (1974), the preoccupation of modern bureaucracies with monocentricity—meaning simplicity, neatness, hierarchy, and symmetry—does not necessarily result in the maximization of efficiency, measured by least-cost expenditure of time, effort, and resources, as was once generally supposed. Because bureaucracies make it possible for those who exercise political power to exploit such powers to their own advantage to the detriment of others within the same political community, bureaucratic failure can occur anywhere, even in post-industrial democracies. Ostrom therefore reasons that what a democracy requires is an administrative system that has as its defining attributes "diversity, variety and responsiveness to the preferences of the constituents"—in a word, a polycentric political/administrative order. In his words:

> Fragmentation of authority among diverse decision centers with multiple veto capabilities within any one jurisdiction and the development of multiple, overlapping jurisdictions of widely different scales are

necessary conditions for maintaining a stable political order which can advance human welfare under rapidly changing human conditions (1974:112).

The colonial state in Africa was a bureaucratic, monocratic state. It had three basic defining features. First, all governmental powers—legislative, executive, and judicial—were concentrated in the hands of appointed officials. Second, there was no participation of the governed nor accountability to them; appointed officials were solely responsible to the government of the imperial country. According to one scholar, colonial regimes were essentially elitist, centrist, and absolutist (Wunsch 1990:23). Thirdly, by imposing the bureaucratic machinery on the traditional institutions, the latter were bastardized—either by removing all the institutional mechanisms for making local chiefs accountable to their people or other chiefs or by creating "warrant chiefs" where none existed (Adamolekun 1986; Olowu 1996).

Colonial rule laid the foundation for autocratic governments in Africa. Until a few years before their hurried departure, colonial governments in most cases did not build institutions capable of constraining executive power, such as a legislature, nor did they allow political parties and independent news media and other societal organs to form. Even when these institutions were created, the period of their gestation was too short for them to be fully functional at independence. Hence, many African countries attained political independence with a qualitatively unbalanced structure of government. The bureaucratic arm was far stronger than the other civic branches of governance. The problem was not limited to Africa; a concern was expressed about governance systems in developing countries generally (Riggs 1963).

As we will show in the next section, this situation paved the way for the suspension or abolition of democratic institutions and structures and the emergence of one-party and military governments in which the bureaucracy served the interests of the ruler rather than the ruled. This hastened institutional and economic decline in the continent (Wunsch and Olowu 1990).

The Political Legacy in East and West Africa

The people in African countries were quite expectant that political independence would usher in a time of economic and social advancement. This was very much in line with the clarion call of Ghana's leader Kwame Nkrumah to seek first the political kingdom, meaning that political independence was the precondition for all other socio-economic benefits. In each country, executive power and bureaucracy became dominant after only a few years of independence. In West Africa, Ghana was the first to become politically independent, in 1958, but it was also the first to abolish its democratic constitution and substitute for it the rule of the party—the Convention Peoples Party. Sierra Leone followed suit under Dr. Stevens of the All Peoples Congress when in 1978, by a sham referendum, a one-party system was adopted. Nigeria did not have a one-party dictatorship, but was the first to come under military rule, first for thirteen years from 1966 to 1979 and then again from 1983 to the present period. Gambia is the only odd case in the West African sub-region; it was able to sustain its democratic heritage until 1994 when the soldiers mutinied and took power.

Sierra Leone has recently returned to civil government, while Ghana is currently ruled by Jerry Rawlings, a leader who originally took power using military instrumentalities and successfully transformed himself to a civilian elected leader in 1992 in an election that was shrouded in much controversy.

Similarly, three East African countries became independent with all the trappings of the Westminster model. Starting with Tanzania (which enacted a new constitution in 1962), followed by Kenya (which introduced an amendment to its constitution in 1964), and finally Uganda (which passed a new constitution in 1966), all three countries eliminated executive duality and concentrated all executive powers in one office. This was not universally welcomed. Indeed, in the case of Uganda, the President's house was attacked and the Mutesa forced into exile, where he died. In all three cases, one-party governments were introduced after the abolition of executive duality, but it was only in Uganda that the military bureaucracy took over from the party bureaucracy. In all of these countries, the democratic structures inherited at independence were eliminated within a few short years in order to pave the way for rule by chief executives who relied either on the civil or military bureaucracy or the party bureaucracy.

One of the unfortunate implications of this development has been the elimination of the principles of governmental responsiveness, accountability, transparency, and good government. Institutional structures such as legislatures and loyal oppositions and the independent civil service, judiciary, and mil military were all either suspended, abolished or radically modified to ensure they served the interests of those who exercised executive power, not the people.

For instance, under the Tanzanian Republican Constitution of 1962, the President as head of state and head of the government could dissolve Parliament and did not have to take advice from any person or institution in promulgating a bill into law. He had the power to arrest anyone. According to Mihyo (1994), the curtailments on the powers of the Tanzanian parliament were very many. The constitutions of 1962 and 1977 subordinated parliament both to the party and to the presidency and gave the presidency the right to nominate up to fifty-five percent of members of the parliament. Moreover, parliament and its members were completely dependent on the government for services both at district, regional, and national levels. Even the Speaker of the National Assembly and his/her auxiliaries were placed under control of the central establishment.

In addition, the author lists other major organizational constraints on the parliament: First, the amount of time allocated for deliberation was short. Second, parliament as well as parliamentarians lacked open and free access to information from their constituencies and from the government. They were not immune from prosecution. They were not exempt from the Official Secrets Act— government information could not be divulged to them by any official of government. Thirdly, they lacked the essential facilities and equipment. They were wholly dependent on the executive for such essentials as transport, income, political influence, information, etc. Furthermore, parliamentarians were poorly prepared for their jobs. There were no orientation seminars for parliamentarians to improve their knowledge of parliamentary procedures, supplemented by library services and regular information bulletins and newsletters. Finally, they did not even control the reports of their own activities—these were carried out by government officers. In sum, the Tanzanian parliament was a sub-unit of the state machinery rather than a separate organization capable of independent action (Mihyo 1994). The 1977 constitutional changes rendered the Tanzanian parliament "simply a committee of the ruling CCM party" (Mwakyembe 1994).

Yet the Tanzanian parliament was rated by many observers as one of the best in Africa at the time—in spite of its problems (see Tordoff 1977; Olowu 1993). The Kenyan and the Ugandan parliaments were certainly no better. An indication of the excessive powers of the executive over the legislature in the case of Uganda was the ease with which Prime Minister Milton Obote pushed through the controversial 1967 Ugandan constitution. According to Mujaju (1994: 37):

> On April 15, 1966, Dr. Obote convened an emergency meeting of parliament to which he introduced entirely new rules of the game, the revolutionary constitution which made him executive President and curbed royal privileges in kingdom areas. But what is more, there was no debate on the document; MPs voted on it without even looking at it since it was waiting for them in their pigeon-hole. They saw it after the swearing in ceremony of Dr. Obote as Executive President.

This constitution made the President completely independent of the cabinet and the parliament The President was further empowered to exercise legislative power under this decree whenever the national assembly was "in recess or had been prorogued or dissolved." The Nigerian parliaments, in both the pre-military and post-military periods, functioned in about the same manner (Adamolekun 1975).

One of the principal explanations for the surge in democratic renewal in Africa in the 1990s is that African centralized governments have not advanced public welfare—in terms of either economic growth, national integration, or democratic governance. It was thought possible that a restoration of democratic governments might advance these interests better. But the new democracies in Africa labor under a dominant executive which has the bureaucracy as its ally against other fledgling organs of the state and the society. The ruling party, for instance, remains disproportionately powerful in countries such as Ghana and the three East African states. The Kenyan bureaucracy continues to perceive itself as an agent of the ruling party, KANU, especially in the districts (Barkan and Chege 1989). In West Africa, the military has yet to accept the supremacy of civilian rule, although a wonderful turn-around in this respect has recently been experienced in Sierra Leone. In Nigeria (less so in the Gambia), military rulers continue to proclaim their capacity to fashion lasting democratic institutions despite previous failures, but in reality they continue to prepare to pursue the Rawlings option of transition from military to civilian presidents.

Besides the ease with which African bureaucracies are manipulated by those who control executive power at the center, and the relative ease with which the military wing of the public bureaucracy can usurp power due to its organizational characteristics (especially its monopoly of violence), a number of other factors militate against African public services facilitating democratic governance in Africa. Four of these are particularly critical.

First, the public sector has grown quite rapidly after independence in many African countries, whereas during the same period the institutions to make them accountable to the public were either abolished or repressed in some form. There is thus a severe imbalance between the executive and its bureaucracy on the one hand and the state and society organs that can hold these structures accountable. The subject of imbalance among political institutions received considerable attention in the 1960s, but has hardly been broached in recent writings on democratic renewal in Africa.

Second, political life in Africa as in other Third World regions is characterized by patron-client relationships. The public sector becomes an instrument for building public support for factions that are competing for power. This gives those in positions of power an advantage over the society that is expected to control them. The public sector is therefore dysfunctional in serving the public, but critical to the survival and sustenance of those who wield executive power (see Hyden 1983; Balogun 1995; Beyene and Otobo 1995). Moreover, because of the extreme concentration of wealth in the public sector and the extensive corruption and mismanagement in public life, those competing for power see the public office as the only way to social and economic improvement. According to Hadenius (1992: 136), "when so much is at stake in political life, there is no scope for the tolerance and peaceful competition which democracy requires—for the difference of result between gain and loss is so great. Politics instead assumes the nature of a relentless zero-sum game."

Third, as a result of the factors earlier enumerated, the public service lacks even the basic meritocratic features of efficiency, productivity, and other universalistic values. Many of the states in the region are characterized by a relatively swollen and systemically inefficient public sector. In fact, most of them do not measure the efficiency of their various units. Staffing within the civil service is lopsided. For instance, the Sierra Leone civil service had a total of 59,000 civil servants in 1992, but over half of this number were daily paid laborers and another ten percent were found to be "ghost," (non-existent) workers. On the other hand, the compensation levels were so low that the civil service could not attract senior executive and high level technical officers—hence the large number of vacancies at this level. The private sector enterprises paid twenty times more for these positions than the civil service paid (World Bank 1993). A similar problem exists in all seven countries in our sample.

Similarly, the military bureaucracy is large (judged by the resources invested in it relative to other sectors), but it is not a professional organization. The military, poorly paid and equipped, has become highly politicized, especially in countries that have witnessed military usurpation of political power. Military intervention in a country's political life poses three major types of problems for democratic prospects: it undermines the democratic fabric of the society—because of its unconstitutionality and the tendency to rule by exception; it increases the propensity to misgovernance and corruption, the breakdown of law and order, economic mismanagement, and ethnic and religious divisions in society, and in extreme cases war. Finally, there is a more serious problem. How will the succeeding civilian government relate to the military, and vice versa, especially in respect of past breaches of the law by the military? To prosecute these cases could lead to a backlash, with the military seizing power again; but to do nothing sets a bad precedent for the application of the rule of law.

But military rule is strongly correlated to economic underdevelopment. According to Huntington (1995:15), "countries with per-capita GNPs of $1,000 or more do not have successful coups; countries with per capita GNPs of $3,000 or more do not have coup attempts. The area between $1,000 and $3,000 per capita GNP is where unsuccessful coups occur." This completes the vicious circle: poverty was the first reason for doing away with democratic institutions, but bureaucratic rule—of which military rule is the strongest expression—has only led to bankrupt political leadership and public institutions and severe societal misery.

This brings us, then, to the fourth and final consideration: wrong-headed public sector reforms. It is possible to divide administrative reforms in Africa into two broad groups: those before 1980 and those undertaken after this date. The pre-1980 reforms sought to strengthen the hands of the executive branch through rapid indigenization of personnel, politicization of the public services, nationalization of private sector enterprises, and imposition of central controls on local governments, effectively transforming them into local administrative units. The post-1980 reforms which came during a time of preoccupation with economic and fiscal balance sought to reduce the public service rather than to redynamicize it. They completely overlooked the critical need to build capacity in the public service and neglected the political dimension to administrative reform and concerned themselves with cutting back on the public sector, with very little success (Dia 1993; World Bank 1995).

Quite clearly a different type of institutional redesign is called for if the current political reforms are to lead to a redynamization of Africa's public services. We examine the issues in greater detail in the next and final section.

Proposals for Consolidating Democracy

Four issues are key to the consolidation of democratic governance in the region under discussion: establishing a linkage between economic growth and democratization; enhancement of the capacity of civil society institutions; reinventing public sector organs; and reaffirming the critical ethical norms of the public service.

Linking Economic Growth and Democratization

The notion that some modicum of economic growth is essential for the sustenance of democracy was the major excuse for the support for authoritarianism in African countries (see Huntington 1968; Emerson 1971). Unfortunately, the African experience to date has yet to present a case of successful economic growth resulting from authoritarian governments (Anyang Nyong'o 1991:3).

After thirty years of independence, there is no convincing correlation between dictatorships or authoritarian regimes and higher levels of economic growth or development in Africa. If anything, the more repressive regimes have done much poorer than the more liberal ones. Historical experiences of some of today's industrialized nations and the recent experience of the Asian tigers may lend support to the argument for authoritarian routes to economic growth and democratic governance, but there are also examples of countries with high economic growth rates that are not democratic, the Gulf States being probably the best illustration.

The current case for democratization in Africa is thus based on the argument that economic growth is unattainable without democratic governance (Chantornvong 1988; Oakerson 1988;

Olowu and Wunsch 1990; Mkandawire 1991). Democratic institutions are likely to contribute to economic growth prospects in Africa for three important reasons.

First, they provide an opportunity to build on institutional structures that are familiar to the people—what are referred to as primordial structures and values. Some countries (e.g., Botswana, Ghana, Nigeria) have shown the possibilities of how traditional institutions may be adapted for modern uses. Studies conducted by the World Bank point in this direction (Dia 1995). Within this framework, people are able to build on the social infrastructure through linkages and reciprocity systems which can provide a framework for social progress.

Second, democratic structures help to foster institutions that hold those who exercise state power accountable. The African experience to date seems to underscore the fact that Africa has yet to produce leaders who can combine self-restraint with vision and intense patriotism in tackling state matters.

Third, democratic institutions release the peoples' social energies by emphasizing the role of the individual in society and by helping individuals to build networks across social institutions (including state and society). This sets to work a tremendous social synergy for development.

None of these possibilities are automatic, however. They are *possibilities*. Deliberate effort has to be made to ensure that these possibilities are translated into *realities* in each African country. To this end, three types of measures are required.

First, public sector organizations should be built upon the community organizations which exist in virtually every African country. The success of these groups in contrast to the massive failure of central organs indicates that they hold potential for economic growth and the democratization of political structures. If they are made the building blocks of the local government, their performance will clearly be better than the earlier structures, which were perceived primarily as state administrative organs with no local ownership.

Second, there is the need to emphasize institutional pluralism—recognizing and creating political space for the operation of five critical types of institutions: (1) political subsystem institutions, including the executive, legislature, judiciary, and quasi-judicial structures; (2) economic subsystem institutions, including both formal and informal organizations; (3) civil society subsystem institutions, including independent professional bodies, trade unions, political parties, and NGOs; (4) international subsystem institutions; and, finally (5) public administration subsystem institutions, including the civil service, public enterprises, local governments, and specialized agencies (such as police, teachers, and other decentralized organs). It is important that each of these institutions have *competence* (that is, have a clear mission recognized by other actors) that they possess sufficient independence to be *credible*, and that they have the capacity to *interact* freely with other institutional actors, whether through contestation, competition, cooperation, or conflict.

Third, actors in the public sector must be made aware through training and public education and by the public that the primary purpose of the public sector is to provide the enabling policy environment for economic growth through the following types of activities:

- support for economic and political reforms, especially in nurturing institutions for the advancement of democratization and decentralization;
- promotion of regional economic and trading opportunities;
- provision of physical, institutional, and financial infrastructure for the growth of a fledgling private sector;
- development of human resources through major investments in educational and health infrastructure;
- efficient management of key strategic industries which have backward linkages to the mass of small-scale and informal-sector opportunities; and mobilization of productive and financial resources, the stimulation of competitiveness in the global market, and reduction/elimination of waste and of the debt profile.

Enhancing Civil Society Institutions

Civil society institutions have been repressed in many countries in Africa and it is time to reverse this trend. There are three specific ways that the organs of civil society can be fostered in Africa. First, they should be granted the political space to operate as independent entities to assist the democratic process. For instance, voluntary agencies should be allowed to operate schools, health centers and hospitals, private electronic and print media, research and policy analysis centers—all of which could assist the democratic and developmental processes in several African counties. Many countries in the region drove private and voluntary agencies out of these fields in the pre-democratic era. Secondly, the capacity of these societies themselves needs to be enhanced— especially in terms of their personnel and their institutional practices such as accounting and leadership methods. Thirdly, the inputs of institutions in civil society should be sought in the governance processes, especially in the following three areas: (1) consensus building about development alternatives and plans; (2) monitoring of the activities of independent governmental agencies such as electoral commissions, watchdog organs, ombudsmen, auditors-general, civil and public service commissions, code of ethics bureaus, etc.; and (3) better management of the development process (see Rasheed and Demeke 1995, Mohiddin 1996).

Reinventing Public Sector Organs

There is a need to build public-sector organs that are controlled by the public and therefore sensitive to the public interest rather than simply to those who wield executive political power. Seven major strategies are suggested with this end in view. Due to space limitations, we shall merely mention them without discussing each in detail.

1. The capacity of the legislature to exercise oversight over the executive and the public service must be enhanced. The first step towards enhancing the capacity of the legislative branch is to assert

its constitutional position as a separate branch of the government—complete with its own personnel, infrastructure and independent information system—the most important of which is an up-to-date library and information service. Secondly, the legislatures themselves should review all laws that constrain their effectiveness—especially those which limit their power to have access to government depart ment information or to criticize government (Barkan 1979; Mohiddin 1996). Thirdly, given the relatively lower educational status of members of the legislature as compared with those in the executive branch, special centers for developing training programs and appropriate training modules for legislatures in each country should be identified and supported. Fourthly, the public account committees (PAC) should be revitalized, preferably headed by the leading member of the opposition. Audit institutions should be strengthened while the capability of the parliaments to enforce sanctions and rewards on various agencies should be enhanced.

2. The independence and effectiveness of the judiciary and critical quasi-judicial institutions must be enhanced. Specific measures in this area will include enforcing the constitutional requirement for an independent judiciary, complete with self-accounting status and independent personnel headed by the Chief Judge; reforming the judiciary in terms of access of ordinary people to legal remedies, especially in the rural areas, through the integration of formal and informal judicial systems; ensuring the independence of quasi-judicial institutions such as electoral commissions by ensuring independent funding and personnel and the representation of civil society actors on their boards.

3. Public services must be directly accountable to the public and their customers. Besides enhancing traditional accountability of the public services through the law, the legislature, and other accountable and decentralized structures, it is being proposed that the African public services should be directly accountable to the public and their customers through the adoption of citizen's charters. Under this plan, each public sector organization is required to work out what constitutes the standards of service that the public can expect of it and how it will treat its customers. This commitment to high-quality service means that performance targets will be

aligned and provide employees in these organizations a clear message of what is to be achieved. Additionally, the agency itself has a fair standard of measuring the performance of the whole agency and individual employees through its performance-monitoring system.

4. The analytical capacity of the central civil service organs and must be strengthened. Furthermore, indicators must be devised for the measuring of public service efficiency. Civil service organs should learn how to conduct information-gathering and analysis and strategic planning and review; they must learn to build a coalition with stakeholders around specific policy matters while leaving detailed execution of services to decentralized organs (see below).

While each agency would monitor its own performance, productivity units should be set up to monitor these measurements across-the-board and report periodically to the executive branch as well as the audit unit, which will render its report to the Public Accounts Committee (PAC) and the legislative committee on the public service and to the public at large.

In addition, salary levels in African PACs will have to reflect market values. Each agency and each individual's compensation should reflect the productivity as measured by independent indices within the organization, and also by the opinions of customers and users of these services. Some countries within and outside Africa are already making major changes to their compensation systems using this approach. Botswana, Zambia, Cape Verde, and Lesotho have all undertaken salary decompression schemes aimed at attracting and motivating top officials. Gambia, Lesotho, Zambia, Tanzania, and Zimbabwe are paying "scarcity" and "retention" allowances to rare professionals while the new South African government is seeking to ensure that its civil service is both meritocratic and reflects the diversity of the total population. Several other countries in the region (Ghana, Mauritania, Kenya) are undertaking other reform measures to restore a meritocratic civil service system that is able to attract and retain the best (Adedeji et al. 1995; Commonwealth Secretariat 1995; Manning 1995; Wescott 1996). Finally, a policy on training and retraining for all public officials should be in place.

5. The capacity of decentralized agencies should be strengthened. Decentralization is the single most important of the seven strategies. It encompasses enhancing the capacity of field administration agencies by providing them with the critical resources in personnel, finances, materials, and discretionary authority. Previous reforms in all the East African countries and Ghana were unsuccessful largely because of lack of sustained political commitment, the resistance from central government officials, and the tendency to confuse deconcentration with devolution. In most developed countries of the world, the majority of the civil servants actually work outside the capital cities in the regions and districts; the proportion for the United States is eighty-eight percent, the United Kingdom eighty percent, and France seventy-five percent (Smith 1985; Rowat 1990; Wunsch and Olowu 1990).

Decentralization includes delegating responsibilities horizontally within the civil service away from central coordinating organs, for example, from central ministries to line agencies. Decentralization must strengthen local governments and devolved agencies. African countries have the least developed systems of local government—in terms of both the capacity of their personnel and the level of expenditures they control. A 1982 survey of the human resource capacity of different government levels showed African local governments with a proportion of total public sector employment of only six percent as compared with twenty-one percent for Latin America, thirty-seven percent for Asia, and fifty-seven percent for OECD countries (Heller and Tait 1982; Rowat 1990). A more recent survey of expenditure decentralization showed that only seven percent of expenditures by African countries were made by local governments, much below the figures of fifteen percent for all developing countries and the thirty-five percent for the industrialized nations of the world (United Nations Development Programme 1993:69–73).

Several advantages are claimed for local governments: the stimulation of the local economy through use of local contractors, lower costs, better maintenance, closer monitoring and supervision; poverty alleviation; opportunities for various forms of *co-production* between the producers of services and the citizens;

reduction of the potential for corruption of government programs; and the mobilization of community resources to build essential infrastructures (World Bank 1989; Ake 1990; Olowu and Smoke 1992; Olowu 1992; Balogun 1993; UNDP 1993; E. Ostrom 1996). However, in Africa, these advantages remain only potentials. Local governments are usually incapacitated in performing the roles expected of them because they lack the critical resources—discretionary authority, personnel, finance, and effective systems of accountability. Virtually all African local governments are enmeshed in a vicious cycle of poor quality political and administrative personnel, low resource bases, low performance, weak accountability, public apathy, and the withdrawal of their responsibilities to other central-government-controlled agencies (Adedeji 1973; Cochrane 1984; Smith 1985; Olowu 1988; Olowu and Smoke 1992; Balogun 1993).

However, the general failure of formal local governments—with but a few exceptions (Olowu and Smoke 1992)—contrasts with the relative success of community-based *informal* local governments. One of the most important challenges for enhancing the capacity of local governments is in sychronizing these informal structures with the formal structures (Esman and Uphoff 1984, Olowu et al. 1991). Africa's growing urban centers deserve special priority as the continent is transformed from a predominantly rural to an urban population within the next quarter of a century—especially in the development of urban governance structures that can finance urban infrastructures over a sustained period of time (see Stren and White 1989; Bahl and Lin 1992; Bird 1995).

6. The critical ethical norms of the public service must be reaffirmed. Three such norms are particularly important: a meritocracy that is capable of attracting and retaining the best officers; a professional civil service with its attendant values of objectivity, political neutrality, and anonymity; and the representativeness of the various groups in the society in the public service without undermining merit. While each country certainly will differ in the manner of implementing this requirement, special attention will need to be paid to respecting the political condi-

tions for sustaining these arrangements, probably through codes of conduct for public officers, both political and administrative.

Certain political conditions are required to sustain the above-mentioned arrangements. First, a political culture of government and opposition, in which opposition parties have a good chance of competing and winning popular elections, must evolve. Second, a political culture of restrained partisanship on the part of both the government and opposition must develop. The opposition must be permitted to compete within the framework of the constitution. Third, there must be widespread adherence to a code of conduct which respects the concept of political neutrality of public servants and the idea that public servants are (junior) partners in the policy-making process. Finally, there must be adherence to the rule of law, and there must be institutions to enforce the law and codes of conduct for public officers

7. The commitment to the idea of a professional military service must be renewed, and there must be a concomitant reduction in the amount of resources devoted to defense. The elements of military professionalism include: (1) recognition by military officers of the limits of their professional competence; (2) the effective subordination of the military to civilian political leaders who make the basic decisions on foreign and military policy; (3) the recognition and acceptance by that leadership of an area of professional competence and autonomy for the military; (4) the minimization of the military in politics and of political intervention in the military (Huntington 1995:9–10). Several of the recommendations made in respect of the public services thus apply to the military bureaucracy.

More importantly, the armed forces must be demobilized and replaced by military reserves drawn from the civilian population under some form of national service for secondary school graduates trained centrally but managed and deployed at the level of community or local governments. Governments of Ethiopia, Uganda, and South Africa are already moving in these directions.

Conclusion

The program of reform enunciated above is quite ambitious. One could wonder, therefore, whether it is practicable. Some few African governments are already charting their way along these paths. Most of these efforts are relatively new, the longest being only two or three years old. The best examples are South Africa, Uganda, and, to some extent, Ethiopia. The democratic forces that brought change to these countries made the reform of the bureaucracy imperative.

For the vast majority of African countries, a combination of domestic, civil society, and external actors will be required to pressure African governments to adopt these reforms. Since the combination of these forces were essential to compel many African governments to adopt multiparty democracy, it will be necessary to have the same combinations push African governments along the path of desirable administrative reforms. It is indeed not accidental that civil service reforms in today's developed and rapidly industrializing countries have had to pass through these forms of change. Specifically, domestic pressure groups such as chambers of commerce and the professional associations of public servants and other professional groups within and outside the public service will need to adopt a reform plan which draws on the elements that have been articulated in this paper. They will need to lobby all branches of the government—especially those in the executive and legislative branches—to adopt these reforms.

The role expected of external actors will include the provision of financial support for these reforms. They could also provide specific support in two critical but related areas: research and documentation on African public services. To this end, they could help African countries by helping to create a data bank on African public services and governance institutions based at a regional center like the United Nations Economic Commission for Africa (UNECA). The main responsibility of such a data bank will be to gather and periodically disseminate information on the issues covered in this report very much along the lines that economic and socio-economic data are currently compiled by organizations such as the World Bank, the United Nations Development Programme, and UNICEF.

Each country has to make choices as to the order in which these reforms should be undertaken, but all are important. The most important consideration, however, will be a commitment to polycentric public service structures as critical attributes of democratic governance. This will require a long struggle in many countries on the continent, but it is hoped that the demonstrated gains to be had from these reforms will spur on civil society activists and other reform-minded actors and their international collaborators.

Lastly, I wish to emphasize the role that researchers play in highlighting the complex relationships between governance and public service reform. From an African perspective, it is necessary to argue for a more comprehensive approach to this set of issues. Changing the structures of the regime is an important component of public service reform; the latter, in turn, is necessary to pave the way for a greater trust in public authority. The current crisis of legitimacy in African countries is both political and administrative in the sense that ordinary citizens have lost faith in their public services. Research and reform along the lines discussed in this chapter may be one way to proceed in the future.

Works Cited

Adamolekun, Ladipo. *Politics and Administration in Nigeria*. London: McMillan, 1986.

Adamolekun, L. "Parliament and Executive in Nigeria: The Federal Government Experience 1952–1965," in C. Baker and M. J. Balogun, eds. *Ife Essays in Administration*. Ile-Ife, Nigeria: University of Ife Press, 1975.

Adedeji, A. "Financing Local Government in Nigeria: An Overview," in A. Adedeji and L. Rowland , eds. *Local Government Finance in Nigeria*. Ile-Ife, Nigeria: University of Ife Press, 1973.

Adedeji, A., R. Green, and A. Janha. *Pay, Productivity and Public Service:*

Priorities for Recovery in Sub-Saharan Africa. New York: UNICEF, 1995.

Ake, Claude. "Sustaining Development on the Indigenous," in *Long-term Perspective Study of Sub- Saharan Africa*, Vol. 3. Washington D.C.: World Bank. 1990.

Ake, Claude. "Democracy, Governance and Development in Africa," Keynote Address Delivered at the Seminar of the African Development Bank Executive, Abuja, *A. M. News* (Lagos). June 12–15 1995.

Anyang Nyong'o, P. "Democratisation Processes in Africa," *CODESRIA Bulletin* 2 (1991):2–4.

Bahl, R.W, and J. F. Linn. *Urban Public Finance in Developing Countries.* New York: Oxford University Press, 1992.

Balogun, M. J. *Enhancing Accountability and Responsiveness of Local Government and Decentralized Units in Africa.* New York: United Nations Department of Economic and Social Development, 1993.

Balogun, M. J. "A Critical Review of the Changing Role of the Public Sector," in S. Rasheed and D. Luke, eds. *Development Management in Africa.* Boulder, Colo.: Westview Press, 1995.

Barkan, Joel, D. "Legislators, Elections and Political Linkage," in J. D. Barkan and J. J. Okumu, eds. *Politics and Public Policy in Kenya and Tanzania.* New York: Praeger Publishers, 1979.

Barkan J., and M. Chege. "Decentralising the State: District Focus and the Politics of Reallocation in Kenya," *Journal of Modern African Studies* 27, 3 (1989):431–453.

Beetham, David. "Key Principles and Indices for A Democratic Audit," in David Beetham, ed. *Defining and Measuring Democracy.* London: Sage Publications, 1994.

Beyene, A., and E. E. Otobo. "Public Administration in Africa: Past Trends and Emerging Challenges," *African Journal of Public Administration and Management* 3, 2 (1994):1–30.

Bird, Richard M. *Financing Local Services: Patterns, Problems and Possibilities.* Toronto: Center for Urban and Community Studies, Major Report No. 31, 1995.

Buijtenhuijse, Rob, and E. Rijnierse. *Democratisation in Sub-Saharan Africa: An Overview of the Literature.* Leiden: African Studies Centre, 1993.

Chantorrnvong, Sombat. "Tocqueville's Democracy in America and the Third World," in V. Ostrom, D. Feeny, and H. Picht, eds. *Rethinking Institutional Analysis and Development.* San Francisco: International Center for Economic Growth, 1988.

Cochrane, Glynn. *Policies for Strengthening Local Government in Developing Countries,* Staff Working Papers, Washington, D.C.: The World Bank, 1984.

Cohen, Ronald. "The State: A Lenticular Perspective," in D. Olowu et al.: *Governance and Democratisation in Nigeria.* Ibadan, Nigeria: Spectrum, 1995.

Commonwealth Secretariat. *Current Good Practices and New Developments in Public Service Management: A Profile of the Public Service of the United Kingdom.* London: Commonwealth Secretariat, 1995.

Dahl, Robert A. *Polyarchy: Participation and Opposition.* New Haven: Yale University Press, 1971.

Dia, Mamadou. *Africa's Management in the 1980s and Beyond.* Washington, D.C.: World Bank, 1995.

Emerson, Rupert. "The Prospects for Democracy in Africa: A Theoretical Statement," in M. F. Lofchie, ed. *The State of the Nations Constraints on Development in Independent Africa,* 1971.

Esman, M. J., and N. T Uphoff. *Local Organizations: Intermediaries for Rural Development.* Ithaca NY: Cornell University Press, 1984.

European Centre for Development Policy Management (ECDPM). *Democratisation in Sub-Saharan Africa: The Search for Institutional Renewal.* Maastricht: ECPDM, 1992.

Hadenius, Axel. *Democracy and Development.* Cambridge: Cambridge University Press, 1992.

Heller, P., and A. Tait. *Government Employment and Pay: Some International Comparisons.* Washington, D.C.: International Monetary Fund, 1982.

Huntington, S. P. *Political Order in Changing Societies.* New Haven: Yale University Press, 1968.

Huntington, S. P. *The Third Wave: Democratization in the Late Twentieth Century.* Norman, Okl.: University of Oklahoma Press, 1992.

Huntington, Samuel P. "Reforming Civil-Military Relations," *Journal of Democracy* 6, 4 (1995):9-17.

Hyden, G. *No Shortcuts to Progress: African Development Management in Perspective.* Berkeley: University of California Press, 1983.

Hyden, G., and M. Bratton, eds. *Governance and Politics in Africa.* Boulder, Colo.: Lynne Rienner Publishers, 1992.

Jacoby, Henry. *The Bureaucratization of the World.* Berkeley: University of California Press, 1973.

Manning, Nick. "Improving the Public Service: A Commonwealth Perspective," in CAPAM, ed.: *Government In Transition,* 1995.

Mccurdy, Howard E. Public Administration: A Synthesis. Menlo Park, California: Cummings, 1978.

Mihyo, Paschal. *Non-Market Controls and the Accountability of Public Enterprises in Tanzania.* London: Macmillan, 1994.

Mkandawire, T. "Further Comments on the 'Development and Democracy' Debate," *CODESRIA Bulletin* 2 (1991):11–12.

Mohiddin, Ahmed. "Parliamentarians and the Strengthening of Civil Society Institutions." Paper presented at Meeting of African Parliamentarians, Addis Ababa, April, 5–7, 1996.

Mujaju, Akiki. "The Conquest Syndrome and Constitutional Development in Uganda," in A. Beyene and G. Mutahaba, eds. *The Quest for Constitutionalism in Africa.* Berlin: Peter Lang, 1994.

Mwakyembe, H. G. "Democracy, Political Stability and the One Party System in East Africa," in A. Beyene and G. Mutahaba, eds.: *The Quest for Constitutionalism in Africa.* Berlin: Peter Lang, 1994.

Nwabueze, B. O. *Nigeria's Presidential Constitution: 1979–83.* London: Longman, 1985.

Oakerson, Ron. "Reciprocity: A Bottom-Up View of Development," in V. Ostrom, D. Feeny, and H. Picht, eds. *Rethinking Institutional Analysis and Development.* San Francisco: International Center for Economic Growth, 1988.

Olowu, Dele. *African Local Governments as Instruments of Economic and Social Development.* The Hague: International Union of Local Authorities, 1988.

Olowu, D. "Roots and Remedies of Governmental Corruption in Africa," *Corruption and Reform* 7, 3 (1992): 227–236.

Olowu, D., and P. Smoke. 1992. "Determinants of Success in African Local Governments: An Overview," *Public Administrative and Development* 12, 1 (1992):1–17.

Olowu, D., 1993. "Organizational and Institutional Mechanisms for Enhancing Accountability in Anglophone Africa: A Review," in S. Rasheed and D. Olowu, eds. *Ethics and Accountability in African Public Services.* Nairobi: ICIPE Press, 1993.

Olowu, D. (a) "Transition to Democratic Governance in Africa," in D. Olowu, K. Soremekun, and A. Williams, eds. *Governance and Democratisation in Nigeria.* Ibadan, Nigeria: Spectrum Books, 1995.

Olowu, D. (b) "The Challenge of Productivity Improvement," in S. Rasheed and D. Luke, eds. *Development Management in Africa.* Westview Press, 1995.

Olowu, D. *Bureaucracy and the People.* Ile-Ife, Nigeria: Obafemi Awolowo University Press, 1996.

Ostrom, Elinor. "Self-Governance, the Informal Public Economy and the Tragedy of the Commons," in P. L. Berger, ed. *Institutions of Democracy and Development.* San Francisco: Institute of Contemporary Studies, 1993.

Ostrom, Vincent. *The Intellectual Crisis in American Public Administration.* Alabama: Alabama University Press, 1974.

Ostrom, Vincent. "The Problem of Sovereignty in Human Affairs," in J. S. Wunsch and D. Olowu, eds. *The Failure of the Centralized State.* Boulder, Colo.: Westview Press, 1990.

Ostrom, Vincent. *Democracy.* Bloomington, Ind.: Workshop in Political Theory, Indiana University 1995.

Rasheed, S. "The Democratization Process and Popular Participation in Africa: Emerging Realities and the Challenges Ahead," *Development and Change* 26, 2 (1995):333–354.

Rasheed, S., and G. Demeke. "Democracy, Popular Participation and Good Governance: The Expanding Role of People's Organizations," in S. Rasheed and D. Luke, eds. *Development Management in Africa.* Boulder, Colo.: Westview Press, 1995.

Riggs, Fred. *The Ecology of Public Administration.* Delhi: Asia Publishing House, 1963.

Rowat, D. C. "Comparing Bureaucracies in Developed and Developing Countries: A Statistical Analysis," *International Review of Administrative Sciences* 56, 2 (1990):211–236.

Sartori, George. *The Theory of Democracy Revisited.* Chatham: Chatham House Publishers, 1987.

Saward, Michael. "Democratic Theory and Indices of Democratisation," in D. Beetham, ed. *Defining and Measuring Democracy.* London: Sage Publications, 1994.

Smith, B. C. *Decentralization: The Territorial Dimension of the State.* London: Allen and Unwin, 1985.

Stren, R., and R. White, eds. *African Cities in Crisis: Managing Rapid Urban Growth.* Boulder, Colo.: Westview Press.

Tordoff, W. "Residual Legislatures: the Case of Tanzania and Zambia," *Journal of Commonwealth and Comparative Politics* 15, (3 (1977):235–249.

United Nations. *Seminar on Decentralization in African Countries.* New York: Department of Economic and Social Development 1992.

Wescott, Clay. "Civil Service Reform in Africa," paper for AAPAM 17th Roundtable, Cairo, 1996.

World Bank. *Strengthening Local Government in Sub-Saharan Africa*, Senior Policy Seminar Report No. 21. Washington, D.C.: Economic Development Institute, 1989.

World Bank. *Sierra Leone: Policies for Sustained Economic Growth and Poverty Alleviation*. Washington, D.C.: West Africa Department, Report No. 11371-SL, 1993.

World Bank. *A Continent in Transition: Subsaharan Africa in the mid-1990s*. Washington, D.C., 1995.

Wunsch, J. S., and D. Olowu, eds. *The Failure of the Centralized State: Institutions and Self-Governance in Africa*. Boulder, Colo.: Westview Press, 1990.

Wunsch, J. S. "Foundations of Centralization: The Colonial Experience and the African Context," in J. S. Wunsch and D. Olowu, eds. *The Existence of the Centralized State*. San Francisco: ICS Press, 1995.

7

Problems and Prospects of Local Governance

Francis C. Enemuo

Introduction

In what has been theorized as "the collapse of the centralized state" (Wunsch & Olowu 1990) in Africa, it comes as no surprise that decentralization is currently a matter of much interest. Transferring power and resources to local-level government and non-governmental groups has been proposed as a means of restructuring the failed state system, a mechanism for consolidating the gains of the ongoing democratic reforms, and a strategy for conflict resolution. For their part, international donor agencies support decentralization on the expectation that it will promote an "enabling environment" for sustainable and equitable economic development.

Yoweri Museveni, the Ugandan President and author of a novel decentralization policy, articulates what may be taken as the expectations of African governments from the process:

> Our decentralization measures aim at undo-
> ing the harm that was done to local systems of
> governance by centralization. We want to unleash

181

local initiative and invigorate the local democratic process which, together, will sustain development and enhance local capabilities for self-governance and delivery of service. Given our historical backdrop, we believe that the devolution
of power, functions and resources will help us
achieve albeit cheaply, higher performance rates
in literacy, life expectancy, cash and food crop
production and other indicators of social development. (Museveni 1994: 4)

These are no doubt worthy objectives, but they are hardly
new. Much the same aims—the promotion of grassroots democracy and development—were announced as the *raison d'être* of
numerous local government reforms initiated in Africa since
independence. We may therefore ask the question: what are the
factors that have constrained popular participation, effective
service delivery and accountability in local governance in
Africa? In the main, this is the central question to be examined
in this chapter.

The thesis proposed herein is that the authoritarianism carried over from colonial rule, the privatization of leadership positions, their widespread use for primitive accumulation in post-
colonial Africa, and the resultant disillusionment among the popular classes, have denuded the legitimacy of the African state.
Since local government is but the representation of the state at the
local level, it has, likewise, been afflicted. In other words, the
problems of governance at the local level are a reflection and a
consequence of the crisis of governance at the center.

In addition to canvassing our major proposition, we shall
also examine the outlook for the future. We would, however,
wish to begin with a synoptic review of the concept of decentralization and a sketch of the background of local government in
Africa.

Conceptual Clarification and Historical Background

Interest in decentralization in the Third World is longstanding. International assistance agencies and even a number of African governments advocated it years ago as a strategy for eliciting popular involvement in development planning and in spreading the benefits of growth (Rondinelli 1981:133). What recent developments have done is to heighten this concern and to underline the political dimensions of decentralization. The constant reflection on the subject has yielded a rich corpus of literature. However, although opinions differ on the categorization of decentralization arrangements, there is a consensus on the view that decentralization involves the transfer of authority and resources from "the central government and its agencies to field organizations of those agencies, subordinate units of government, semi-autonomous public corporations, area-wide or regional development authorities; functional authorities, autonomous local governments or non-governmental organizations" (Rondinelli 1981:137).

Rondinelli (1981:137) has broken down decentralization into three categories—deconcentration, delegation and devolution—based on the extent of power that is delegated. In his view, deconcentration obtains when some amount of administrative responsibility is transmitted to lower levels within the central government. It is, he says, "the shifting of workload from central government ministry headquarters to staff located outside of the national capital." Deconcentration may also take the form of field administration which entails the transfer of decision-making discretion "to plan, make routine decisions and adjust the implementation of central directives" to field staff. Local administration, the other form of deconcentration, is the arrangement under which all subordinate levels of government within a country are agents of the central authority. As a form of decentralization, delegation, in Rondinelli's schema, implies the transfer of authority to plan and implement decisions over specific activities to organizations such as corporations which are placed under the indirect control of central agencies. Devolution, the third pattern of decentralization, involves the transfer of power to subnational units of government, which are autonomous, distinct from the central government and under only indirect supervisory control of the center. These units have responsibility for specific functions over defined areas and are under leaderships that are elected by the people. This is the form of decentralization with which we are concerned in this essay.

We shall adduce evidence from the Nigerian and Tanzanian cases to show that although African governments have repeatedly pledged to devolve powers and resources to autonomous local governments, their efforts have, at best, resulted in the establishment of local administrations.

The Colonial Antecedents of Local Government

Every one of the imperial powers instituted some form of local government in its African colonial holdings. It was a vital part of the administrative infrastructure exemplified by the British policy of Indirect Rule, which, as is widely known, informed local governance in British colonial territories. Under this policy, traditional political institutions were left in power but placed under the close supervision of British officials. The adoption of this system was dictated by the desire to reduce costs and maximize available personnel. The administrative hierarchy was headed by a Resident or Provincial Commissioner, assisted by a number of expatriate officials. Below him were the District Officers who were in more direct contact with the so-called "native authorities." The system was distinctly undemocratic, for there was no provision for direct popular participation. Under indirect rule, local government had no autonomy, but rather was subject to the control of the central government, for which it served as a local representative.

Important reforms were, however, introduced into the system in the years after World War II. This was as a result of sustained agitation by nationalist forces in the colonies. The new direction was ostensibly towards "an efficient and democratic form of local government," as indicated in the words of the epochal "Dispatch from the Secretary of State for the Colonies to the Governors of African Territories" dated February 25, 1947, which announced the new thinking. Accordingly, the elective principle was introduced in the composition of local government in many areas.

However, the changes envisaged by the Dispatch were hardly consolidated before the dawn of independence. And since those who inherited the reigns of leadership were determined to appropriate absolute power and its many perquisites, rather than transforming the state along the lines of the nationalist agenda, the move towards autonomous democratic local governance was halted and, in fact, reversed. This is a theme to which we shall return shortly.

Obstacles to Local Governance

A paradox shrouds local government in Africa. While almost every African government has, at one time or the other, declared its desire to establish an autonomous, democratic local government system as a mechanism for promoting popular participation and accelerating even development, none has permitted reasonable independence for local government. Most have turned local government into an agent of the national government, while others have banned it altogether. In certain countries local government has suffered both fates in turn.

Three reasons have often been given for the administrative marginalization of local government in Africa (Olowu 1988:109-110). The first is the argument that the multi-ethnic nature of African states and the ever-present threat of secession make a wide latitude of autonomy to local government untenable because it could be exploited by separatist movements. The second suggests that the limited human and material resources on the continent cannot support devolutionary decentralization. The third argument alleges the need to accelerate the development process and to economize scarce resources through centralized planning.

There may be some theoretical merit in these rationalizations. At the level of praxis, however, they have all been vitiated and shown to be self-serving. After thirty-five years of centralized rule, African states are more internally factionalized than in the period immediately after independence. Inter-ethnic tensions have led to bloody and chaotic collapse of the state in places such as Somalia, Liberia, and Rwanda. Communal antagonism has also resulted in the virtual socioeconomic paralysis of many other countries. The point being made is that centralized rule did not yield the dividend of national unity claimed for it, nor the development that it was supposed to promote.

The emergence of centralized rule could best be attributed to the fact that post-colonial African leadership, having charted a course different from the one it promised during the nationalist struggles, found itself isolated from the popular classes. Without solid mass support, its hold on power became tenuous, hence the tendency to centralize all power as a way of consolidating its rule. Further incentive to concentrate power was provided by the widespread practice of prebendalism, that is, the use of public offices for the personal benefit of office holders and their support groups (Joseph 1991:2).

Although the phenomenon of over-concentration of state power in the one-man or single-party system of government is now in retreat, there are still features of the African state that constrain accountability, popular participation, and the performance of local government. There are also policy and attitudinal impediments. Among the structural and policy problems are the following: (i) the "softness" of the state, (ii) institutional instability, (iii) dearth of financial resources and (iv) military dictatorship. We will comment briefly on each of these forces.

The "Soft," "Rentier" State as an Obstacle

As part of the formal, albeit subordinate, structures of governance, local government manifests and is affected by the notable weaknesses of the post-colonial state in Africa. Like its colonial progenitor, it has remained a state for domination and accumulation. Whereas to the power elite it is a vehicle for private accumulation and class consolidation, the mass of Africans have continued to experience the African state as a coercive, alien force to be avoided and cheated whenever possible. While nearly everyone can be most vociferous in making claims upon the state, exceedingly few citizens feel any duty to discharge civic obligations to the state.

According to Peter Ekeh (1978:317–319), this emphasis on citizen rights and neglect of civic duties by Africans derives from the colonial ideologies of legitimation which, in trying to justify colonial rule, encouraged the African to view his relationship with the government "not in terms of what he does for the government but in terms of what he receives from the government." The ideologies also served to disassociate rights and duties in the conception of citizenship by insisting that the Africans' "contribution did not support the government, that they amounted to very little, and yet that they benefited from the whole colonial deal." As a result of all this, there are now two publics in Africa, "an amoral civic public from which one expects benefits but which is not important in one's definition of one's duties," and a "moral primordial public, defined in terms of one's ethnic group, to which one's relationships were predominantly phrased in terms of duties."

Ekeh's insightful formulations provide a perspective from which to understand the absence of civic ardor among Africans. This, as Mabogunje (1995:2) has noted, is manifest in Nigeria, for example, where people who "strain themselves to pay levies and contribute or donate generously to the coffers of their community development associations" feel they owe local government no obligation, hence are unwilling to pay taxes or rates to it, and may even encourage or condone local councillors to mis-appropriate the funds meant for local services.

The widespread feeling of alienation towards the African state explains its "softness." Migdal (1988:4) posits that the strength of a state is measured by its capacity and capability to penetrate its society, regulate its social relationships, and extract required resources from it. Judged against this parameter, the inescapable verdict is that African states are weak because they are in varying degrees out of sync with society. They subsist, in the main, on incomes from external rents and aids. We are total-ly in accord with these formulations and observations. We would wish to add, though, that the imposition of the IMF/World Bank-inspired structural adjustment programs on African states, the coercion with which they have been implemented, and the severe privations which they have visited on the people have served to further delegitimate the state and alienate the citizenry.

What implications do the foregoing developments hold for governance at the local level in Africa? First, the widespread practice of rate and tax evasion and the existence of organizations in the "primordial public" to which the people owe more com-mitment constrain the capacity of local governments to raise resources from their environment. Secondly, the fact that the peo-ple do not fund the operations of local government disinclines them from participating in council affairs beyond the level of periodic voting. Thirdly, the perfunctory popular involvement in local affairs has served to weaken accountability. The point being made is that the problems of embezzlement and misappropriation that were rife in local councils in Nigeria and elsewhere would possibly have been minimized had the level of popular participa-tion in council activities been higher.

The Problem of Structural Instability

In a recent article on local government in Tanzania, Jwani Nwaikusa complained that the council has been reduced to the "status of the political guinea pig" of the central government. He adverts, of course, to the sharp twists in local government policies in Tanzania, which, according to him, have been dictated not by the desires of the masses, but "almost exclusively by the interests of centralized political power, keen to maintain a stable centralized state" (Nwaikusa 1994: 59). It is notable that local government has been established, abolished, and re-established again in Tanzania.

The turning point of the reform process in Tanzania was the announcement of what the government paradoxically termed a decentralization program in 1972. The policy led to the dissolution of extant local governments and their replacement with "highly qualified and, until then, highly-placed officers and experts from the central government." In effect, what happened was not devolution of power to the local level. Instead, central officials were decentralized by sending them to the regional and district offices of the central departments (Nwaikusa 1994:61). District councils were converted into district advisory committees dominated by party and government appointees, and district executive officers, previously in part responsible to their elected councils, were replaced by district development directors. Both bodies consequently became responsible to and dependent on the regional administration (Samoff 1989:3). The councils have since been restored.

President Nyerere, whose government initiated these reforms, was to describe the abolition of local government as a "mistake." As he explained it: "There are certain things I would not do if I were to start again. One of them is the abolition of local government and the other is the disbanding of the cooperatives. We were impatient and ignorant. . . . Those were our two major mistakes" (Nyerere 1984). Independent students hold a contrary view. It has been argued, for example, that the abolition was meant to facilitate the consolidation of a bureaucratic governing class at a moment when it was under great stress, and to pave the way for the implementation of a number of programs, particularly the villagization program, which would have been resisted by the council (Nwaikusa 1994:67).

In sum, the abolition and restoration of the local councils in Tanzania have occurred because:

> The interest of the central government have dominated local government policies and practices from the colonial times to the present. The demands and interests of the people have counted very little if at all, in the development of local government. As a result, the role and function of local government has been greatly distorted. People look at local authorities not as their institutions but as central government organs. The government, for its part treats local authorities like tools created for its use and disposal. Quite frequently, local government has been used to try out and experiment with new ideas and practices and sometimes rather adventurous policy decisions. (Nwaikusa 1994:67)

Very much like its Tanzanian counterpart, the Nigerian local government system has also been an object of repeated restructuring and reforms. From 301 in 1989, the number of local government units has increased to the current 589. This indiscriminate multiplication of councils has been justified on the ground that it is a strategy to bring government nearer to the grassroots and accelerate the pace and spread the benefits of development. It is true that the creation of these councils has narrowed the distance the citizen has to cover to reach the headquarters of his local government authority; it has not, however, translated into any significant improvement in service delivery to him nor has it enhanced his impact on the governance process. The more visible effect of the multiplication is the proliferation of avenues for members of the elite group for primitive accumulation through the prebendalization of their positions as local government chairmen and councillors.

It is to be noted that political considerations rather than economic calculations informed the establishment of a good number of the councils, particularly during the Babangida regime. Little, if any, thought seemed to have been given to the self-sustaining capacity of proposed councils. Indeed, apart from a handful of councils located in the urban centers, mostly in Lagos State, the overwhelming majority of Nigeria's local governments depends on statutory allocations by the federal and state governments for sustenance. Clearly, a reasonable number of the councils appeared to have been carved out to assuage powerful political interests and divert attention from the contradictions that emanated from the regime's subverted political transition program.

With respect to structural form, the single-tier, multi-purpose model is now in place across the country. This was introduced as part of the 1976 local government reform which abolished the various patterns in operation in different states of the federation. Prior to the reform, certain states in the country and the regions before them had experimented with the British conciliar model and the American council-manager format in the internal organization of the councils within their areas. All these were replaced with the portfolio-councillor pattern, under the 1976 reform. Another major reform of the management structure of local government was announced in 1991 following the extension of the principles of separation of powers to the local government system.

These constant reforms and re-reforms of the Nigerian local government system may have been well-intentioned. But their effects have not been totally salutary. Take, for example, the extension of the separation of powers principle to the system. The expectation that the councils would be able to exercise legislative oversight on the executive never fully materialized. They were simply unable to restrain the executives in many instances. In the places they were able to exercise control, they seem to have been motivated mainly by partisan political considerations rather than a genuine attempt to enforce accountability.

The drawing and redrawing of local government boundaries implicit in the constant creation of local governments have trivialized this tier of government into platforms used by individuals and primary groups to enhance their share of what, in popular consciousness, is described as "national cake," that is, oil rents. Local governments are hardly seen as vehicles for mobilizing local resources for the development of the individual council areas.

Furthermore, the point can be made that the frequent alterations in the composition of council territories, names, and locations of headquarters that usually follow each local government creation have aggravated the problem of nurturing the local roots and loyalties of councils. Wraith and Dent (1988:13) have noted that local government loyalty is like "a sapling" which "can only flourish if not continually transplanted, for its roots need time to grow."

The Problem of Weak Financial Base

Chronic underfunding and misappropriation of revenues have been cited frequently as the major causes of the uninspiring performance of local governments in Africa. The problems arise from lack of drive by councils to make maximum use of permissible funding sources, constricted tax base, and insufficient transfers from central governments.

The Nigerian case amply illustrates these observations. Local governments in Nigeria can raise funds from two major external sources (statutory transfers and loans) and from three major internal sources (property rating, user charges/fees, and local taxes). However, statutory transfers from the federal and state governments have grown to become the dominant source of local government revenue. While each state is required to allocate ten percent of its internally generated revenues to the local government within its territory, the federal government, in the wake of reforms under General Babangida, is obliged directly to transfer twenty percent of the Federation Account to the councils. This has greatly enhanced their fiscal capacity but the transfers have not come without problems.

In the first place, the ready availability of transfers is widely believed to have discouraged internal revenue drive by the councils, thereby making them excessively dependent on the federal handouts. Indeed, it has been suggested that no council, apart from a few in the Lagos metropolis, could afford to pay its staff without these transfers, since by the mid-1990s their independently-raised incomes hardly average ten percent of their annual receipts (Oye-lakin 1995:45). Second, in the wake of these transfers, the councils were assigned additional responsibilities often out of proportion with the grants. They were repeatedly directed to undertake unbud-geted tasks in support of programs of federal agencies such as the electoral commission and the mass mobilization agency. Third, transfers of funds were consistently late, causing the problem of budgetary bottlenecks for the councils.

It ought to be acknowledged that efforts made at generating revenue through local sources often ran into serious difficulties. In the case of property rating, for instance, although widely recognized as a possible source of considerable income to councils, its poten-tial is far from being realized. According to Gboyega (1990), the problems constraining the use of this income avenue include lack of political will to collect the tax for fear of generating popular oppo-sition, the widespread misconception of the tax as tax on the own-ership of property rather than on the use of services, the paucity of technical capacity to assess all properties and to collect the tax, the exclusion of too many categories of ratable properties, and the cor-ruption of collectors.

In general, the funds available to local governments in Nigeria have been inadequate to meet their assigned responsibilities and the expectations of their staff and constituencies. The grants from the federal and state governments proved insufficient, while the contri-bution of locally-derived revenue remained marginal. Besides, rev-enue from these sources was reduced by embezzlement and misap-propriation by council leaders and staff, and what remained was greatly denuded in value by the hyper-inflation engendered by the IMF Structural Adjustment Program.

The Problem of Military Rule

Of its thirty-six years of independent existence, Nigeria has been under military rule for a total of twenty-seven. It would there-fore be no exaggeration to say that every institution of governance and even civil society has been seriously impacted by sustained praetorian dictatorship. Local government has, however, often been mentioned as one of the institutions that profited from military rule. As one writer asserts, "successive military regimes have taken effective measure to fully revive, reform, revitalize and restructure the local government system in Nigeria as a tool for democracy and development" (Oyelakin 1995:30).

It cannot be doubted that the Babangida junta and also the Mohammed/Obasanjo regime introduced significant reforms in the processes and structures of local government as part of their different transition-to-civil-rule programs. For instance, the 1976 reform fostered by the Murtala/Obasanjo junta, which became incorporated into the 1979 Constitution and which provided for democratically-elected local councils across the country, specified the functions of local governments and guaranteed them federal and state allocations. General Babangida raised the portion of the Federation Account allocatable to local governments from ten to twenty percent, abolished the ministries of local government in the states to give the councils more autonomy, and reformed their internal management structures in line with the practices at the state and federal levels.

These military-sponsored reforms are certainly welcome. Having said so, it must also be emphasized that there are very important ways in which military rule has negatively transformed the Nigerian body politic and civil behavioral patterns, and thereby constrained the habituation of good governance in the country. In this regard, we agree with Ibrahim, who has observed that:

> Military regimes have succeeded in permeating civil society with their values—both the formal military values of centralization and authoritarianism and the informal lumpen values associated with "barrack culture" and brutality that were derived from the colonial army. The contemporary Nigerian elite has been acquiring a lot of "barrack culture" over the past few years, for example, many of them starch and press their clothing in a military style. . . . At a more significant level, there is a decline in civility and a rise in violence in social interaction. (Ibrahim 1995:7)

Both as a means of winning popularity and a strategy for undermining opposition, military regimes have found it valuable to restructure the Nigerian federation. Out of only four regions, the Gowon regime created twelve states in an attempt to undercut any renewal of the secessionist bid of the defunct Eastern Region. General Mohammed raised the number of states to nineteen, and Babangida to the present thirty states. What is to be stressed about these states is that they are all substantially dependent on federal allocations for their survival. They lack the fiscal and operational autonomy expected of a unit of a true federation. Indeed, under the military, a state government is little more than a willing agent of the federal government, or rather the vassal of the head of state and commander-in-chief of the armed forces. In this context, it is idle to expect local government to be autonomous and answerable to the people. What exists is local government in name only. Appointed by and operationally answerable to the state military government, which can dissolve and recompose them at will or on the order of the federal authorities, the councils have become local administrations *par excellence.*

Good governance requires adherence to operational rules and transparency on the part of state functionaries. In this regard, it is a matter for concern that what we have witnessed in Nigeria under the military is a sustained erosion of these values. Nigerian military leaders have shown a consistent disregard for the due process and the law of the land, including the laws promulgated by them. This phenomenon, often referred to as "executive lawlessness" (Oyebode 1996), is also manifested in defiance of court orders, promulgation of retroactive laws, ouster of the jurisdiction of the courts, and appointment and dismissal of public officials "with immediate effect." Perhaps the most dramatic display of this tendency is the annulment of the 1993 presidential election organized by the military and adjudged free and fair by local and international monitors. Even before this event, the junta had dissolved elected local councils before the end of their tenure.

It is true that the military did not invent corruption in Nigeria. The general view, however, is that they have taken the malaise to new depths. It has become so commonplace that it is now widely expected, demanded, and accepted by public officials. Its lucrative fruits are openly displayed in the mansions in the cities and village homes of serving and retired public officials, in their flashy cars and in their flamboyant dress. Corruption simply appears to have lost the moral disapproval of the Nigerian public, who euphemistically refer to it as "*egunje*," meaning "settlement" or "family support." The point to be made is this: good governance in the local public realm is impeded by the massive debasement of public morality in Nigeria under the military, the lawlessness displayed by military leaders at the federal and state levels, and the negative effects of all these on local government leaders.

The Resistance Council System in Uganda

On assuming power in 1986, after a six-year guerrilla war, President Yoweri Museveni and his National Resistance Movement introduced a novel pattern of local government based on Resistance Councils, or RCs. Barongo (1990) explains that every village (and in the case of towns and cities, every ward of not less than ten and not more than twenty resident families) was organized into a Resistance Council (RCI) in which all resident adults were members. From this base, a five-tier hierarchy of Resistance Councils was established at successively wider areas, at the levels of the Parish (RC II), Sub-County (RC III), County (RC IV), and District (RCV)[1].

Each RC had an elected nine-member executive committee which supervised local governance within its territory. An RC was expected to meet at least once a month to determine policies and at the level of RCI, the village, every adult resident was expected to be involved in the exercise. The executive committee was thereafter charged with the responsibility of implementing the plans through the central or local government bureaucracies. Until recent reforms, RCs at the county and divisional RCs in towns and cities elected 212 of the 278 members of the National Resistance Council (NRC), which served as the national parliament. It may be noted that the highest policy organ of the state, the National Executive Council was composed, in part, by people initially elected from the districts of NRC.

According to President Museveni, the RC decentralization policy was informed by the belief that "human beings can govern themselves in peace and dignity in pursuit of their collective well-being (public good) once they are entrusted with their own destiny." The policy was aimed at resuscitating the Ugandan local government system enfeebled by the 1967 Constitution and the Local Administration Act of the same year, both of which eroded its relative autonomy and capacity as enshrined in the 1962 independence constitution (Museveni 1994: 14).

The RC system has been lauded as being "successful in providing a form of political structure in which citizens are closely and actively involved at different levels, from the lowest village level to the top national lawmaking and policy organs of the state" (Barongo 1990:134). Despite the successes that have been attributed to it, the RC initiative is not without problems and failings. Among its constraints are the dearth of funds, insufficiently trained manpower, a holdover of dependency on the center, and the ambivalence and even hostility of certain central government officials to effective devolution of power. According to Nsibambi (1994), the uncooperative attitude of some officials to the RC initiative is partly due to the threat it poses to the income they derive from "administrative tourism," that is, making spurious visits to the provinces in order to submit questionable expenses for reimbursement. Notwithstanding these handicaps, the RC system remains widely recognized as a novel and relatively successful initiative.

Decentralization and Governance: What Future?

It has been suggested that four main factors affect the success or failure of decentralization policies in developing countries. These are:

i. the degree to which the central political leaders and bureaucracies support decentralization and the organization to which responsibilities are transferred;

ii. the degree to which the dominant behavior, attitudes, and culture are conducive to decentralized decision-making and administration;

iii. the degree to which policies and programs are appropriately designed and organized to promote decentralized decision-making and management; and

iv. the degree to which adequate financial, human and physical resources are made available to the organization to which responsibilities are transferred. (Rondinelli, Nellis, and Cheema 1984:47)

Our analysis indicates that these conditions were, in the main, absent in Nigeria and Tanzania. Insufficient funds and central government interference constituted major hindrances to meaningful decentralization. These impediments are, however, not insurmountable. As can be deduced from the experience of the Resistance Council system in Uganda, the most critical preconditions for successful decentralization efforts are the willingness of the center to devolve responsibility and resources and the readiness of local authorities to assume power and exercise authority responsibly and with openness.

If we wish to inquire into the future of decentralization in Africa, a key question to ask is: Are there forces on the continent that can enhance political commitment to effective devolution of power to local authorities? Our answer to this question is yes, and we can identify three such forces: (1) mass and ethnic minority agitation for rights and political inclusion, (2) liberal democratic reforms, and (3) donor pressures.

Agitation for Political Inclusion

A frica has, since 1990, witnessed numerous instances of mass agitation and crusades for ethnic minority rights and political inclusion. The latter have even taken the form of armed insurrection in some places. These movements may, no doubt, have been influenced by developments in the defunct Eastern bloc, but their immediate cause was resentment of prolonged political marginalization and worsening economic conditions. Africa's acute economic crisis has greatly depleted the capacity of the centralized state to provide the basic needs of the people. Structural Adjustment Programs implemented as antidotes to the crisis resulted in even steeper declines in living conditions, and eventually led to protests against the regimes implementing them and demands for more inclusive political arrangements. Our thesis is that the widespread disillusion with centralized rule and the calls for new forms of political order provide impetus for the movement towards effective devolution of power.

Liberal Democratic Reforms

C enter domination of local government in Africa was greatly facilitated by the emergence on the continents of dictatorships that concentrated power in the hands of one man, one party, or a military clique. However, with the onset of democratic rebirth in Africa, a number of these regimes have either been dislodged or compelled to introduce political pluralism. Although it is neither a sufficient precondition nor a reliable indicator of democracy, the existence of multiple parties and the conduct of periodic fair elections holds out the possibility that local councils may come under the influence or control of opposition parties. Under such a scenario, unrestrained center dominance of the councils would be greatly curtailed. We anticipate that councils under the control of opposition parties would challenge, within the constitution, acts of the central government that infringe on their legitimate powers. Furthermore, free and regular elections would require councils to justify their performance before their electors and thus enhance popular participation and accountability.

Pressures by the International Community

As is well known, progress towards democratization has been made a precondition for assistance by Western nations and financial institutions. Indeed, external pressures were critical in getting opposition parties to be allowed in places such as Kenya, Tanzania and Zambia. Western calls for democratization have also included support for decentralization of governance and the developmental process. For instance, a number of Western agencies now prefer to channel their aid through non-governmental organizations (NGOs). Resources have also been given for decentralization programs, for example the $31, 000 U. S. grant which the Danish government pledged towards the decentralization effort in Uganda (Nsibambi 1994:114). Western support for democracy and decentralization in Africa may not be totally altruistic, but it constitutes a critical boost to local grassroots pressures for reform in these directions.

Conclusion

In spite of its many travails since independence, local government remains a promising mechanism for promoting good governance and even development at the lowest level of the public domain in Africa. Although currently constrained by resource deprivation, structural uncertainty, and excessive central control, local government seems assured of a bright future considering the factors that favor its sustenance. In our view, progress towards the realization of its potential would be greatly facilitated by a number of reforms in its structure, funding, and functions.

With respect to structure, it should be noted that Africa is operating a system that is different from that of Western societies. Local governments are organic entities in the more stable societies of the West. Some even pre-date the central governments. African local governments, however, are creatures of the center. Often they have been carved out for cheap political reasons. Mutually suspicious communities have sometimes been lumped together, thereby eroding civic commitment to the councils. This is often justified as being necessary to attain a maximum size for viability, but, while a worthy objective, the wisdom of doing so has to be weighed against the need to inspire civic loyalty to councils. To this end, it is suggested that as much as possible organic communities be designated local councils, and where it is necessary to aggregate communities, only those that so desire and have a tradition of close association should be integrated. It is also necessary that local governments be allowed to function for an appreciable length of time, not less than a decade, before any major structural reforms are undertaken. This is necessary to engender civic loyalty and mass familiarity with their operations.

The widespread reluctance to pay local taxes and rates has often been justified with the argument that the councils have not made judicious use of what was paid hitherto, that the funds were misappropriated or embezzled. To encourage accountability and strengthen public confidence, it is suggested that local taxes and rates be collected for specified purposes. Our expectation is that if the public begins to see projects for which funds had been collected being executed, people will become more willing to discharge their financial obligations to councils.

Public interest in the activities of the council will also be greatly promoted through increased cooperation between the local authorities and grassroots non-governmental organizations, particularly the community-based organizations. What we propose is a form of agency arrangement whereby some of the most basic council functions are assigned to these organizations to undertake within their areas, with the councils providing the machinery and part of the funds. For instance, if the task of refuse disposal is assigned to community groups, the council could provide the trucks required by the different organizations. We anticipate that the high sense of morality that guides actions within these community organizations would result in more efficient use of these allocations and prompt performance of the assigned tasks.

Notes

1. The names of these councils were changed to Local Councils with the adoption of the 1995 constitution.

Works Cited

Aborisade, O., and Robert J. Mundt, eds. *Local Governments in Nigeria and the United States: Learning from Comparison.* Ile-Ife, Nigeria: Local Government Publication Series, 1995.

Barongo, Y. "Innovations in Systems of Governance in Africa: The Resistance Councils Experiment in Uganda," in The Carter Center: *African Governance in the 1990s.* Atlanta, Ga.: The Carter Centre of Emory University, 1990.

Ekeh, P. P. "Colonialism and the Development of Citizenship in Africa: A Study in Ideologies of Legitimation," in Onigu Otite, ed. *Themes in African Social and Political Thought.* Enugu: Fourth Dimension Publishers, 1978.

Enemuo, F. C. "Local Government and the Babangida Transition Programme: The Politics of the Reforms and the Performance of the Council as Parliament in Lagos State." Research report for the Governance Project of the University of Florida and the Obafemi Awolowo University, Ile-Ife, Nigeria, 1995.

Gboyega, A. "Property Rates," in I. Bello-Imam, ed. *Local Government Finance in Nigeria.* Ibadan, Nigeria: Nigerian Institute of Social and Economic Research, 1990.

Ibrahim, J. "Obstacles to Democratisation in Nigeria." Paper for Conference on "Dilemmas of Democracy in Nigeria." Madison, Wis., October 23–25, 1995.

Joseph, R. *Democracy and Prebendal Politics in Nigeria.* Ibadan, Nigeria: Spectrum Books, 1991.

Karuhanga E. "Local Self Government and the Right of the People to Development," in Donald Rothchild, ed. *Strengthening African Local Initiative: Local Self-Governance, Decentralization and Accountability*. Hamburg: Institute of African Affairs, 1994.

Mabogunje, A. "Institutional Radicalisation Local Governance and the Democratisation Process in Nigeria," in Dele Olowu, Kayode Soremekun and Adebayo Williams, eds. *Governance and Democratisation in Nigeria*. Ibadan, Nigeria: Spectrum Books, 1995.

Midgal, J. *Strong Societies and Weak States: State-Society Relations and State Capabilities in the Third World*. Princeton, N.J.: Princeton University Press, 1988.

Museveni, Y. K. "Challenges in Creating Institutions of Local Self-Governance in Uganda," in Rothchild, op. cit.

Nwaikusa, J. T. "Local Government Policies in Tanzania: The Political Guinea Pig," in Rothchild, op. cit.

Nyerere, J. Interview by *Third World Quarterly* 6, 6 (1989).

Olowu, D. "Strategies for Decentralization Within Developing Countries: A Nigerian Case-Study," in L. Adamolekun, D. Olowu and M. Laleye, eds. *Local Government in West Africa Since Independence*. Lagos: University of Lagos Press, 1988.

Oyebode, A. "Executive Lawlessness and the Subversion of Democracy and the Rule of Law," in M. Ayo Ajomo, A. O. Obilade, and A. Sambo, eds. *Democracy and the Rule of Law*. Ibadan, Nigeria: Spectrum, 1996.

Oyelakin, O. O. "Implementation of the Executive Presidential System at the Local Level: Its Logic, Merits and Constraints," in Aborisade & Mundt, op. cit.

Rondinelli, D. "Government Decentralization in Comparative Perspective: Theory and Practice in Developing Nations," *International Review of Administrative Science* XLVII, 2 (1981):318–336 .

Rondinelli, D., J. R. Nellis, and S. Cheema. *Decentralization in Developing Countries: A Review of Recent Experience*. Washington D.C.: The World Bank, 1984.

Rothchild, Donald. *Strengthening African Local Initiative: Local Self-Governance, Decentralization and Accountability*, Hamburg: Institute of African Affairs, 1994.

Samoff, J. "Popular Initiative and Local Government in Tanzania," *Journal of Developing Areas* 24, 1 (1984).

Wraith, R., and M. Dent. "The British Legacy of Local Self-Government in West Africa Revisited," in L. Adamolekun, D. Olowu & M. Laleye, op. cit.

Wunsch, J., and D. Olowu, eds. *The Failure of the Centralised State: Institutions and Self-Governance in Africa.* Boulder, Colo.: Westview Press, 1990.

8

Women, Development, and Governance

Funmi Soetan

Introduction

In recent years, increasing attention has been paid by internation-al donors, researchers, and the development community to the critical role of governance in economic development. Indeed, the crisis of development in Africa has been linked to the crisis of governance. Development models were previously dominated by quantitative measures of development which led to the neglect of crucial issues of governance and institutions. While the importance of women's role in development has been acknowledged subsequent to the publication of Ester Boserup's book; *Women's Role in Economic Development* in 1970, attention to the importance of women's role in governance only emerged in the late 1980s.

The central argument of this chapter is that the role of women as active participants in the governance process is critical for improved economic development in Africa. While Boserup's influential book and the writings of other researchers after her have drawn attention to women's unrecognized contributions to the development process, particularly in Africa, the same cannot be said of the relationship between women and governance. This chapter posits that women have vital contributions to make both to improved governance and to development by virtue of their long history of associating together as well as their increasing participation in new women's organizations which have begun to arise from: (1) the increased burdens borne by women under structural adjustment programs (SAPs); (2) the inequality experienced by women at every level of society; and (3) the exclusion of women from the public and economic sphere. This paper argues that, just as development experts have pinpointed the exclusion of women from development as a major reason for the limited success of economic development efforts in Africa (Whitehead 1991), the exclusion of women from the issues surrounding governance will have negative implications for Africa's political development as well.

In recent years, African states have been increasingly associated with corruption, lack of accountability, and repression of human rights. There is therefore a growing awareness that the state is important in molding the lives and choices of its citizens. The current economic crisis in Africa resulting from Africa's excruciating debt burden, which is exacerbated under SAPs, has been shown to disrupt major aspects of women's lives. Although women's lives are as affected by state policies as men's are, if not more so, women as a group are grossly underrepresented in political decision making, which continues to be largely an all-male preserve.

Attention to the interactions between economic development and governance came to the forefront in the late 1980s when Africa's economic deterioration worsened due to declining terms of trade and excruciating external debt. The IMF and World Bank remedy adopted by most African countries in the 1980s aimed at economic stabilization and structural adjustment. Policies to devaluate the currency, reduce real incomes, increase exports and reduce imports were put in place.

The negative impacts of SAPs on the poor, among whom women are in the majority, is well documented (Elson 1991; Commonwealth Expert Group 1989; Gladwin 1991; Vickers 1991). In the face of increasing poverty and declining standards of living under SAPs, calls rose from within and without Africa for a human- or people-centered participatory approach to development, a cause that was championed by (among others) the United Nations Economic Commission for Africa (ECA 1989) and the World Bank (World Bank 1989). Advocates of this fresh approach traced the root of Africa's development crisis to its problem of governance. The consensus in the development community and among donor agencies was that improvements in Africa's economic conditions were closely tied to improving governance, which involves—at a minimum—reduced corruption and better financial accountability, observance of human rights, an independent judiciary and media, participatory politics, and a liberalized market economy.

The ECA's human-centered approach is predicated on increased participation of the poor as a prerequisite for participatory development. A critical role is accorded civil society and grassroots groups in the ECA's governance strategy. While the human-centered approach acknowledged the important role of community associations, trade unions, women's groups, and other people's associations in bottom-up development, as well as their participation in decisions that affect their lives, it has been criticized for its lack of ideological clarity (Sandbrook 1993) and its failure to tackle the issue of female subordination (Elson 1993a).

In Africa, as in most regions of the world, development and governance are part of the public sphere, where men traditionally function. Women's contribution to development occurs at the subsistence, noncash level, and in the private sphere. However, women have been shown to have played an active role in the transformation of Latin America from authoritarian to civilian governments (Jacquette 1994; Karl 1995). This chapter examines gender dimensions of the current discourse on the relationship of development and governance in light of the existing (but small) body of literature that has addressed the issues of women's role in development and governance, specifically, lessons learned from comparative evidence of the participation of Latin American women. It identifies the gaps in research and proposes policies for enhancing women's sustained participation in development and governance in Africa.

Theoretical Perspectives

Three main theoretical perspectives—political science, feminist economics, and radical institutional economics—will be examined for their explanations of the relationship between women, development, and governance. Parpart and Staudt (1990) have demonstrated the exclusion of gender considerations from most theoretical analyses of development and crisis in Africa, a shortcoming this chapter seeks to help correct.

Political Science

In the 1970s, dependency theory and mode-of-production analyses seemed to point the way in understanding African development problems. These theoretical approaches have subsequently become unpopular, deemed inadequate for explaining the realities of the deepening African crisis. With the crisis in Africa, statist analyses focused on the political institutions that mediate economic outcomes achieved prominence. However, in spite of the dominant role of men in African states, neither gender conflict nor male domination of the state was central to the Africanist analysis of the state. As grand theories lost their prominence, less abstract middle-range theories came to the fore. Parpart and Staudt (1990) are part of the group of scholars who prefer theorizing on specific states, and who are, in addition, both historically sensitive and Africanist in orientation. In the course of elaborating a more gender-sensitive statist theory, they have highlighted the direction of the relationship between gender and the state, arguing that gender is central to an analysis of the African state because of the important role of gender struggle in molding states. They highlight how ensuing gender ideology influences resource allocation decisions and material realities. They stress that state mobilization of resources usually benefits men rather than women, sometimes thwarting female accumulation in the long run. In addition, compared to men, women's work is often outside the cash economy. Although the presence of contradiction among policies does provide women with loopholes to use to their advantage, and policies that grant women certain rights do coexist with those which guarantee male privileges and foster female dependency, overall the African policy process subsidizes male accumulation and assists capital accumulation by the state.

Feminist Economics

Feminist economists adopt a similar theoretical stance as their counterparts in political science. They seek to incorporate gender as an analytical category in macro-economics. For example, Elson (1993a) argues that neoclassical economics excludes women's issues at the macro level. Macroeconomic policies deal mainly with monetary aggregates, whose impacts are assumed to be gender-neutral. The main focus of macro-economics is on the equilibriating process of aggregate money supply and money demand. This "productive economy" is totally different from the "reproductive economy" which is assumed as a given and as able to function adequately whatever the disruptions or signals from the productive economy. Women contribute to the productive economy, albeit at a subsistence, often non-market level, undertaking, for example, food preparation, care of the sick and elderly, as well as the care and nurturing of children. Women are the main actors in the reproductive economy, with the main task of reproducing their nation's human resources. Gender is thus the basis for a fundamental division of labor in most societies.

Elson argues further that a major flaw in the SAP policies of de-emphasizing the role of the state and emphasizing the role of market forces is that the positive impact of SAP policies on the reproductive economy is taken for granted, with an implicit assumption of an infinitely elastic coping ability of the reproductive economy to accommodate itself to changes in macroeconomic policies. Evidence shows the assumption is unfounded. Since women are more active in the reproductive economy, the increased burdens of adverse changes in macroeconomic policies on women is totally neglected by neoclassical economics.

At the micro-level, Benaria (1995) similarly criticized neoclassical microeconomic policies for assuming that all economic activity was somehow linked with the market. This assumption has had the effect of rendering a large proportion of women's work invisible. Women's domestic unpaid activities in producing goods and services for family consumption did not qualify as economic work. The invisibility of women's work resulted in a neglect of the negative outcomes of the traditional sexual division of labor for women. While male labor was predominantly in the modern capitalist sectors of developing countries, women's work was concentrated in the subsistence sector. Women therefore constituted a source of cheap labor for the non-capitalist sectors of the economy. Hence, as a result of the traditional sexual division of labor based on gender inequalities, development policies had different impacts on men and women.

Radical Institutional Economics

Radical institutional economics is that branch of institutional economics mainly concerned with sexism and the economic status of women. It differs markedly from neoclassical economics. Peterson (1994b:x) criticized the dominant approaches to economic analysis for their inability to analyze the subordination of women and to prescribe policy responses. Radical institutional economists argue that the central concern of economics should be the process by which societies provision and reproduce themselves. In this way, their ideas overlap with those of feminist economists. Since the reproduction of the nation's human resources is predominantly carried out by women, radical institutional economics and feminist economic inquiry converge.

Peterson (1994b) examined the economic status of women in the context of public-private dualism. In her view, men inhabit the public sphere while women inhabit the private domain. The concept of public-private dualism, if extended to traditional economic theories of capitalism and socialism, is reflected adversely in definitions of the economy which exclude many of the private domestic and reproductive activities and tasks performed by women. Such activities are not considered economically relevant, which distorts both the contribution of women and the nature of the economy. Such distortion is seen in "gender-blind" policies which neglect the needs of women. Because men both have access to state power and are found in the public sphere directing resource-allocation decisions through policies which benefits them, the political power of men reinforces male status and male dominance while perpetuating female subservience.

Methods that incorporate women into existing categories of analysis are criticized for being merely "add-women-and-stir" approaches, which simply factor women in to the existing analysis of development, but which fail to propose concrete policies to address the fundamental issue of women's subordination (Peterson 1994b; Benaria 1995). In order for increased participation of women to bring an end to the subordination of women, radical institutional economists prescribe the transformation of existing institutions. However, no strategies are proffered for ensuring that such institutions are in fact transformed. This simplistic prescription assumes that institutions which have maintained the status quo for many years will be easily transformed.

A common thread running through the three theoretical perspectives is that the concept of gender is taken as an analytical category much like the concepts of race, class, and ethnicity have been used as analytical tools for understanding social relations. As succinctly put by Cagatay et al. (1995:1828) "gender is a stratifier of social life comparable to other stratifiers such as class, race, and ethnicity. As such, it is the basis for a fundamental division of labor in most societies."

However, the three theoretical approaches differ in the emphasis placed on the state and market forces as mediators of gender relations. While expectedly political science theorists tended to place more emphasis on the state as a mediator of gender relations, feminist economists concentrated on the role of market forces, although the operations of institutions such as markets, private sector firms, and public sector agencies are assumed to be "gendered via the social norms and networks which are functional to the smooth operation of those institutions" (Elson [undated]:11). Radical institutional economists accord greater recognition to the role of institutions rather than markets, but in addition emphasize the dualistic categorization of human activities. It is in this area that the ideas of feminist economists and radical institutional economists converge.

Conceptual Perspectives

In order to fully grasp the interrelationship between women, development, and governance, one needs to imagine the pendulum of development policy swinging sometimes in the direction of a greater reliance on market forces and sometimes toward a greater role for the state. Early approaches to development in the 1950s and 1960s focused on increasing gross national product (GNP). Quantitative measures of growth in the capital stock of a nation as well as growth in per capita gross domestic product (GDP) were then the main indicators of development. Individual well-being was expected to follow automatically from these through a naturally occurring "trickle down" process through which it was assumed that, over time, wealth would flow down to the poorest households, and within households to women.

The emergence of the Basic Needs Approach (BNA) in 1973 coincided with the focus on the informal sector by the International Labor Organisation (ILO). Basic needs were classified into two categories, comprising those that could be provided privately, such as food, shelter, and clothing, and those that had to be provided by public means, including health, sanitation, potable water, transportation, and education (Young 1993). Proponents of the BNA acknowledged women's central role (albeit sometimes through overwork) in providing their families basic needs for food, water, health, and education. Women's role as producers was however undercounted. Overall, the BNA differed from earlier quantitative approaches to development in one important way: it recognized women as independent economic actors and viewed the family not necessarily as a joint, autonomous economic enterprise. As changes in development strategies in the 1970s began to focus on reaching the poor majority, the male household head became the main target of development planning, with the benefits of development still assumed to trickle down automatically to other members of the household. However, increases in male incomes did not automatically result in improved incomes in their households. Thus, two main criticisms have been levied against the early approaches. First, they neglected issues of distribution and equity, both at the national and household levels. Secondly, they failed to explain why poverty in developing countries was growing to the point where more than sixty percent of the population was impoverished (Young 1993).

Issues of redistribution with growth and poverty-oriented approaches were subsequently emphasized (Chenery et al. 1974). These new perspectives took account of the heterogeneity of the poor, the constraints limiting their income and employment generation efforts, as well as the increasing feminization of poverty. Although a welcome corrective for gender blindness and altogether too optimistic assumptions about the distribution of wealth, the new perspectives were criticized for failing to propose concrete institutional strategies for wealth distribution. This is especially relevant for women, who continued to be a disadvantaged group in terms of access to resources.

While emphasizing the need for improvements in women's social and economic status, such improvements were to take place within the framework of women's traditional responsibilities of the prevailing sexual division of labor. This approach has been widely criticized as the "add-women-and-stir" approach to develop ment. The BNA has additionally been criticized for leaning too heavily on the state for meeting society's basic needs and for its neglect of the critical role of civil society.

African countries have experienced sluggish and sometimes negative rates of economic growth, with per capita income exhibiting negative growth since the 1980s. Major causes of the African crisis include declining rates of export demand, high debt burdens, and a fragile investment base. Beginning in the late 1970s, the IMF and the World Bank prescribed stabilization and structural adjustment policies to revive the ailing economies of African countries. The rationale for SAP was greater reliance on market forces. This was to be achieved through currency devaluation, public sector rationalizations, and trade deregulation. The impact of SAP on the poor and vulnerable groups is well documented. Similarly well documented is that women have borne the greatest brunt of adjustment efforts (Commonwealth Expert Group 1989; Elson 1991; Gladwin 1991; Aina and Soetan 1991; Elabor-Idemudia 1991).

The limited success of SAP and the human cost of adjustment led to calls for adjustment with a human face, championed, as noted earlier by the United Nations Economic Commission for Africa (ECA). The ECA subsequently proposed an African Alternative Framework to Structural Adjustment Programs. (AAF-SAP). The World Bank has joined in advocating a human-centered development since 1989. However, the ECA's model proposed a more radical approach which stressed the importance of reducing the continent's external dependence through self-reliant development within sub-regional markets. Unlike the IMF/ World Bank SAP, which placed a greater reliance on market forces, the ECA's model envisioned a larger role for the state. Popular participation was the proposed remedy for the major weaknesses of African states which included poor management, inefficiency, corruption and destructive political conflicts (Sandbrook 1993:137). Empowerment of people was the recommended strategy of the people-centered development for achieving goals. According to the ECA, empowerment of people at the grassroots level would enable people to participate actively in decision making which affects their daily lives. Collective decision making would be effected through indigenous organizations, which would be rallying points for hitherto disenfranchised groups. Such groups would not only mobilize people at the grassroots, but would enable them to amplify their collective interests and gain better access to resources. Civil society was thus accorded a major role in the ECA model.

While the objectives of the ECA model are attractive, the model made only a cursory reference or two to the issue of the subordination of women. They were supposed to be empowered through their membership in women's organizations through which they were expected to be able to question their subordination to men. Hence, the model neglected the dominance of male power and the need for transforming gender relations, if development in Africa is to be sustained (Elson 1993).

Sandbrook (1993) criticized the ECA's model on three grounds. First, the pace of progress toward collective self-reliance in Africa is constrained by limited trade among member countries. Second, the central government continues to dominate the political landscape, far overshadowing the weak local governments which are closest to civil society. In the ECA's view, strengthening local governments in a milieu of an empowered civil society should facilitate people-centered development. However, the growing incidence of repressive and often militarized leaders in Africa has reduced the prospects of power sharing between Africa's leaders and civil society. Finally, there is the lack of good governance by African governments. Good governance has been variously conceptualized. The ECA associated it with democratization, which was seen to be synonymous with greater accountability, local decentralization of hitherto centralized bureaucracies, and community self-management (Sandbrook 1993:137). Other writers conceptualized good governance as comprising accountability, openness, transparency, and the predictability of the rule of law (Brautigam 1991). Landell-Mills and Serageldin (1991:14) defined governance as the exercise of political power to manage a nation's affairs. The consensus since the late 1980s is that good governance is a critical determinant of the economic performance of developing countries. Indeed, the quality of governance is seen as the main predictor of a country's development performance, and donors are increasing concerned with promoting better governance. Five dimensions of good governance have been identified by Landell-Mills and Serageldin: freedom of association and participation, a sound judicial system, bureaucratic accountability, freedom of information and expression, and competent public agencies.

Discussions of good governance often neglect its gender dimensions, although it is highly relevant to the ongoing discourse in Africa. Governance is identified as a male affair from which women are excluded. As a result, development policies are formulated by men and the benefits of development are similarly distributed with a male bias (Elson 1991). Although access to the state and improvements in governance have profound effects on women's lives, women continue to be excluded from decision making at all levels of society. While it is true that women and men alike benefit from good governance, with a male-dominated political class men benefit disproportionately, while women's needs and priorities continue to be neglected and women's subordination perpetuated.

It is fair to ask if this has been the experience of women all across Africa. Are there variations between countries? What differences exist between the experience of African women and women in other regions? These questions are addressed next with empirical evidence from African and Latin American countries.

Comparative Evidence

In this section, the relationship between women, development, and governance is examined from the wider perspective of the experience of African women. A comparison is also made between the experience of African women and women from Latin American countries.

Three dominant themes can be identified in the empirical literature on the gender dimensions of development and governance. These comprise:

- male dominance of political power, its gender implications for resource allocation decisions, and the neglect of the gendered impact of state policies

- the extent of women's access to the state and the effect of regime type on the scope of political space available to women

* the consequences of the exclusion of women from political participation on alternative strategies employed by women to gain control on their lives

Male Dominance of Political Power

A common feature of the African state is that women are never central to state power. The outcome of women's marginalized political status is that women's interests are neglected in policy considerations. In other words, states play a major role in the mobilization and distribution of resources, and this role has a profound effect on people's opportunities, access to resources, and relationships to property (Parpart and Staudt 1990; Chazan 1990).

The contents of state policies, for example, have been empirically shown to neglect and sometimes discriminate against women's needs and interests. SAP is perhaps the best example of this. Empirical studies have amply demonstrated the gender-biased effects of adjustment. These emphasize that adjustment policies may be "gender blind," but their effects are not gender neutral. Studies have shown that women have borne the burden of adjustment efforts (Commonwealth Secretariat Expert Group 1989; Gladwin 1991; Meena 1991; Elabor-Idemudia 1991; Mbilinyi 1993). For example, Mbilinyi (1993) reported that the impact of retrenchments of public sector workers under SAP has hurt more women than men in Tanzania. This is because, in both private and public sectors, redundancies affected the low cadres of workers where women were concentrated.

Similarly, SAP policies encourage tradable cash crops produced by men to the detriment of subsistence, non-tradable crops which are mainly cultivated by women. This works through signals from currency devaluations which favor an increase in output of tradable compared to non-tradable commodities. This has had a negative impact on women in many ways. First, men have appropriated fertile lands for cultivating cash crops, leaving less fertile lands for women's subsistence crops. This has resulted in higher food prices in different parts of Africa, thereby exacerbating the food crisis in several African countries (Schoepf and Egundu 1991; Meena 1991; Gladwin 1991). Second, women have had to divide their time between assisting their husbands (who have increased cash-cropping) and working on their own farms. Egundu (1991) reported that in Zaire this jeopardized household food security as women spent less time on the family food gardens. As expected, the time spent by women in their husband's farms is not remunerated.

In addition, SAP policies have discouraged imports through currency devaluation, which has meant an increase in both import prices and in the prices of domestic substitutes. Higher inflation has been generated, which has further decreased women's income. The Commonwealth Expert Group reported a decline in consumer incomes in Zambia, Nigeria, and Tanzania. The result has been devastating for household expenditures, especially on food, rent, and transportation.

Devaluation of national currencies has similarly increased the price of food processing technology mainly employed by a large percentage of African women. It is estimated that African women provide about 90 percent of labor for food processing as well as for fetching water and for fuel wood gathering (O'Brien 1991). Although food processing employs traditional technology, imported mills are increasingly used for grain milling. Devaluation has increased the price of such technology and made replacement of equipment and procurement of spare parts very difficult, with dire consequences for the African food crises. For example, women engaged in food processing in a Nigerian study reported that prices of food processing mills increased four- or five-fold six years after SAP was introduced. This has resulted in accelerating prices and declining profits. Women in micro-enterprises have had a similar experience. Hairdressers and dressmakers expressed dismay at the astronomical increases in prices of technological inputs such as sewing machines and hair dryers. The major request expressed by the women was that government should control inflation as well as prices of equipment and spares (Soetan 1994).

Various studies have highlighted the coping strategies adopted by women for surviving the adverse effects of adjustments. "Studies have revealed an intensification of and an increase in women's reproductive work, an increase in women's labor force participation especially in the informal sector, an increasing bias against female education, deterioration of physical and mental health, and in extreme cases, disintegration of families and communities" (Cagatay et al. 1995: 1828). Mbilinyi (1993) reported that in Tanzania, household income has greatly eroded under SAP, which has forced women and girls to seek ways of compensating for the reduced income by increasing their activity in the informal sector, where they can obtain cash incomes which are not taxed or regulated by government. She also reported a high maternal mortality rate which increased from 190 to 215 maternal deaths per 100,000 births in 1990 and 1991, respectively. Worse still, a high rate of increase in HIV/AIDS infection was found among teenage girls between 15 and 19 years of age, probably as a result of increased prostitution to earn extra cash for survival.

As Ghanaian women have intensified their economic activities in the urban informal sector, Okine (1993) estimated that such economic activities take up to sixteen hours of their working day. This has negative implications for the health of the women. Available data show that more than one third of African women are economically active outside agriculture work in the informal sector. The percentage is as high as seventy-two percent in Zambia and sixty-two percent in the Gambia (The World's Women 1995:115).

A component of SAP programs is a reduction of government spending on education, health, and water supply. This has had a negative impact on the generality of African economies by increasing women's workload and reducing the quality of life of families. The family has had increasingly to finance the private costs of education and health care. This is borne disproportionately by women since, compared to men, women are re ported to spend a larger share of their income on food and children's education (Guyer 1980; Peters and Herrera 1989).

Women and female children also bear the burden of caring for the sick and aged. This has led to lost school days for girls and lost productivity for women. Kennedy and Cogill (1988) reported loss of a considerable number of working days in the sugar-growing region of Kenya due to sickness. Even members of relatively prosperous rural households spend a substantial part of their income on medicines, due to frequent recurrence of malaria, cholera, and other diseases. In Tanzania, an alarming increase in maternal deaths from a previous rate of sixty-five to seventy deaths per year to seventy-one deaths in thirteen weeks of 1988 was recorded at a medical center. Increasing malnourishment among pregnant women and declining quality of medical services were some of the reasons given for this poor state of maternal health (Meena 1991:178).

Elabor-Idemudia (1991) also elaborated on the adverse impact of SAP on Nigerian women and their coping strategies. As a result of SAP, women have had to work harder, sometimes working between fifteen and nineteen hours a day. Some women have also reduced the quantity of food per meal for their household, while others have eliminated protein food items. Higher incidences of malnutrition and disease have resulted and been exacerbated by the decline in health care services.

Women's Access to the State

Parpart and Staudt (1990) and other contributors to the volume addressed both the extent of women's access to African states as well as the extent of political space available to women under different regimes. The empirical studies in the volume established four findings that shall be treated one by one:

- Women are underrepresented and occupy minute numbers of decision-making positions in all African states.

- No conclusive evidence can be drawn about the effects of regime type on women's access to resources or on women's access to political power.

- The highly visible minority or core of women politicians engaged in a male-dominated political game are linked to the dominant political class and adopt the male political style, often as a survival strategy.

- The establishment of women's national machinery, such as women's wings of national parties, women's bureaux, and ministries of women's affairs do not represent a broader political agenda for women, but provide token considerations of women's issues. The primary role of women's wings of national parties is to provide support for male politicians and may sometimes be a male strategy to cause divisions among women.

Women in decision-making positions: Women are underrepresented in African governments. Table 1 (below) shows the limited representation of women in ministerial and sub-ministerial positions in 1994. In no African country did women occupy eleven percent of ministerial positions. In Ethiopia, Ghana, and Uganda women occupied about one-tenth of ministerial positions. Countries like Zimbabwe and Nigeria had about three per cent of ministerial positions occupied by women, while Kenya had none. Women were only slightly better off at sub-ministerial-level positions, where Ghana, Ethiopia, and Nigeria had around a tenth or a slightly higher fraction of subministerial positions held by women. In Zimbabwe, women occupied about one-quarter of sub-ministerial positions, but slightly more than three percent of ministerial-level positions.

Tripp (1994:156) reported that women made up a mere ten percent of Tanzania's eighty-two district commissioners and five percent of the eighty-two district executive directors. She also reported a slight improvement in 1992 at the CCM central committee level, which is a high level of political decision making in Tanzania, where one of the nineteen CCM Central Committee members was a woman and three of the twenty cabinet positions were held by women. However, affirmative action in Tanzania encountered hostility from men, as some men were openly hostile over the reserved seats for women at high levels of decision making. Compared with Latin American women, except for Chile and Guatemala (where women occupy 13.0 percent and 19.8 percent of ministerial-level positions respectively), very little differences exist in the percentage of women at both ministerial and sub-ministerial-level positions in Africa and in Latin American countries.

Table 1. Representation of Women at Ministerial and Sub-ministerial Positions, 1994.

Region/ Country	Ministerial-level positions, 1994		Sub-ministerial-level positions, 1994	
	Total No.	% filled by women	Total No.	% filled by women
Africa				
Cameroon	34	2.9	62	4.8
Ethiopia	30	10.0	20	10.0
Ghana	28	10.7	26	11.5
Kenya	28	0.0	81	3.7
Malawi	22	9.1	22	9.1
Nigeria	34	2.9	18	11.1
Uganda	30	10.0	41	7.3
Zambia	44	4.5	64	9.4
Zimbabwe	31	3.2	36	25.0
Latin America				
Argentina	10	0.0	67	3.0
Brazil	22	4.5	65	10.8
Chile	23	13.0	12	0.0
Guatemala	16	18.8	31	6.5
Mexico	20	5.0	60	5.0

Source: United Nations, *The World's Women.* New York 1995, pp. 171–175

Definitely a strong commitment by the higher political leadership to women's advancement in the measures taken by the National Resistance (NRM) government of President Museveni of Uganda for the political mobilization of women is a good example of government affirmative action in enhancing female participation in governance. Female representation at all levels of decision making was ensured through affirmative action, which included a reserved post for women as secretary for women at the village level. In addition, women could contest for other political posts. There had to be one woman representative on the National Resistance Movement (NRM) at the parliamentary level. Hence thirty-nine women representatives were in parliament with a good number of them subsequently appointed to either ministerial or deputy ministerial posts. In addition, a female vice-president was elected.

Women NGO leaders have also been prominent nationally and vocal against increasing incidents of child abuse as a result of fear of contracting AIDS from adults. Most female NGO leaders were active in supporting the bill against the rape and abuse of children. Legal assistance has been sought by such groups for victims.

Effects of regime types on women's access to resources and political power: In Nigeria's military regimes women appear to have been allowed greater participation than under civilian regimes. Mba (1990) traced the history of women's participation under both military and civilian regimes and pointed to the gender policies of "tokenism" whereby a few women would be appointed as advisers on education or social welfare. Even where women appear to have made major gains, as happened in Nigeria's Second Republic (1979-83), they were excluded from the commanding heights of politics which were still dominated by men. Many reasons have been advanced for woman's limited and unsustained participation in politics. These include the average women's lack of the financial resources needed to finance election campaigns, the lack of consent by husbands who anticipate the disruptive influence of politics on women's domestic activities, and the tendency for women to adopt an observer stance to politics since in the first place, they envisaged limited success (Chazan 1990).

Women's adoption of male political style as a survival strategy: Chazan (1990) stressed the vulnerability of the highly prominent but small group of women involved in the male-dominated political arena. Unfortunately, sometimes such women adopted the negative political tactics of the menfolk. Mama (1995) provided a good example of this from Nigeria's Better Life Programme (BLP) and the political maneuverings of its proponent, Mrs. Maryam Babangida, Nigeria's first lady from 1985 to1993. While the BLP had laudable objectives, the high profile, window-dressing style in which it was implemented was devoid of financial accountability and was criticized as an exercise in personal empire building or "femocracy" viewed as "a feminised autocracy running parallel to the patriarchal oligarchy upon which it relies for its authority, and which it supports" (Mama 1995:5, 41).

The rural women whom the BLP was meant to serve were clearly not involved in decision making and their priorities were assumed to be known by the First Lady and her advisers. Rather than assist in the creation and expansion of a political space for Nigerian women, the BLP only served the interests of the First Lady and the small caucus of wives of military governors around Mrs. Babangida. Frequent changes of government has also meant that Nigeria's first ladies have sought to remove all traces of the women's programs embarked upon by their predecessors, thereby creating discontinuity in women's programs to the detriment of the women beneficiaries.

The establishment of women's national machinery: As a result of international attention to women's issues during the UN Decade of Women (1975–1985), African countries were mandated to set up national women's machineries. By the end of the decade, fifty-one African counties had established women's machineries (Mama 1995). However, these are usually underfunded and sometimes their activities are duplicated by other institutions often leading to their ineffectiveness. In Nigeria, a Ministry for Women's Affairs was established in 1995 to oversee women's interests. However, there was no clear distinction between the roles of the new Women's Ministry and the existing National Women's Commission, which had previously been handling women's affairs (Sotade 1995).

In most African countries, national machineries were established by the government but in a few cases they were established either by or in conjunction with non-governmental organizations (NGOs). Malawi and Gabon are two countries where national machineries for women had both NGO and government input (Snyder and Tadesse 1995).

Although women participate actively in women's wings of political parties, when the time comes for them to run for political office they are often intimidated by male opponents. In addition, gender issues do not feature on the political agenda of some political parties. In certain instances, the party exercises overt and excessive control over women's leadership in the women's wing of the party. In other instances, divisive tactics by male party leaders intensifies rifts between educated and less educated women party leaders (Tripp 1994). In short, it has been difficult to establish independent national organizations of women. There has been a tendency for ruling parties and governments to treat such organized efforts under their paternalist wings.

Women's Exclusion From Political Participation

The exclusion of women from political participation has been associated with the adoption of collective strategies of involvement in their own informal associations by women (Tripp 1994). While generally not political in nature, women's organizations have been used for political purposes and are still a potent lobbying weapon at women's disposal (Mba 1990). Indeed, all over Africa, a proliferation of women's organizations has been documented (Tripp 1994). Trager and Osinulu (1991) reported increased participation by Nigerian women in women's associations as a strategy to ameliorate the adverse effects of SAP on women and their families. These associations provided resources and rendered assistance to their members.

In a study of the strategies employed for the empowerment of members of modern and traditional women's associations in Nigeria, women's associations were reported to be facilitating access to critical resources such as land, credit, agricultural inputs and training for their members. In the same stud, a control group of non-members of women's associations affirmed that access to such resources would be difficult for non-members (Soetan 1995). This is more critical where the states fail to provide access to critical resources, as occurs in most African states and is made worse by the SAPs. Modern women's associations such as women cooperatives and Better Life groups appeared to have fared better in ensuring access to resources for their members than traditional groups like market associations and informal credit societies. The higher educational status was the main reason.

Stamp (1989) argues that women's associations are central to decision-making role of women within African communities being the chief means by which women empower themselves politically. However, Soetan's study indicated that women's associations have had limited success at empowering their members politically. No difference was discernible between the political participation of members and non-members of such associations. A reason for this is the limited networking, and interactions between women's associations at the local, state, and national levels.

In contrast to the Nigerian case, women's groups in Kenya mobilized their members for increased political participation. Tripp (1994) reported the strategic meeting in February 1992 of 2,000 members and leaders of women's groups in Kenya to devise plans for greater political leverage in the December 1992 multi-party elections. Kenya's lack of women at ministerial and commissioner level might have fueled women's desire for greater political representation.

In the past decade, a greater success appears to have been recorded for women's networking at the international level. African women participated actively in the U.N. Decade (1975-1985) and the 1985 World Conference to review and appraise the achievements of the U.N. Decade that was held in Nairobi (Mama 1995; Snyder and Tadesse 1995). The ECA Fourth Regional Conference was held in Abuja, Nigeria to assess the progress of previous conferences held in Arusha and Tanzania. Another conference, the United Nations Women's Conference, was held in 1994 in Dakar, Senegal.

Perhaps the greatest gathering of the world's women took place at the internationally publicized Fourth World Conference on Women held in Beijing, China, in 1995. Women from 125 countries were represented. Country-wide strategies and platforms for action (PFL) were adopted on various issues including a greater role for women in politics, credit assistance for female entrepreneurs, the plight of the girl child and protection of women against rape, abuse, and war crimes. However, the achievement of these goals depends to a large extent on state assistance and international and NGO support. Similarly the impact of this on women at the grassroots level remains to be seen.

In contrast to the limited success of African women's grassroots efforts, the Latin American women's movements appear to have experienced greater success at grassroots mobilization and as a result to have achieved some measure of increased political leverage nationally. Latin American women's movements had recorded success and gained political space during the 1970s and 1980s when protest marches against military rule were popular. Of note was the case of human rights movements co-ordinated by Mothers and Grandmothers of the Plaza de Mayo of Argentina, who brought to international attention the poor human rights activities and corruption of the military regime of the day (Jacquette et al. 1994). A greater awareness of gender issues and the need to incorporate women's rights into democracy struggles have been incorporated into the agenda of the Latin American women's movement (Karl 1995).

In Uruguay, new women's consciousness developed in 1984 through the Plenario de Mujeres del Uruguay (Plenary of Uruguayan Women), which was a coordinating body to ensure women's struggles against dictatorship. Women participated in neighborhood groups, soup kitchens, cooperative movements, and support groups for the families of political prisoners which were initiated in most cases by housewives. Although this fostered gender consciousness in the political era of the mid-1980s by ensuring that political parties included programs for improving women's conditions, yet the underlying gender inequalities were not addressed. A manifestation of this was the absence of women in the list of political candidates and at any decision-making levels in the newly elected parliament and government (Karl 1995).

Similarly in Chile, although women's demands were incorporated in the agenda of political parties in the 1980s as a result of their struggle against a repressive military regime, yet the 1989 elections resulted in a male-dominated parliament and government.

Even in the African experience, women have struggled alongside men for political independence but have been excluded from the fruits of their struggle. Mba (1990) and Karl (1995:86) identified four reasons for this unfortunate outcome:

- Men view politics as an exclusive male club and discriminate overtly against any female intruders.
- Women are unfamiliar with political tactics and strategies.
- The financial demands of political campaigns is often beyond the means of most women.
- In-fighting and lack of internal cohesion among women's groups hinder the emergence of popular women's leaders movements.

Chilean women provide a good example of strategies for ensuring women's greater participation in politics. The importance of greater networking and training in political leadership for leaders and members of women's groups cannot be over emphasized. An interesting case is the formation in October 1992 of a women's political action group in Chile, Mas Mujeres al Parliamento (More Women in Parliament), with the sole aim of increasing women's representation in political and leadership positions. Both men and women committed to engendering political equity were members of the group. Another strategy adopted by the Chilean women's movement was the creation of Services National de la Mujer (SERNAM) or National Women's Services, which was a result of women's lobbying efforts. The director of SERNAM was subsequently made a minister in the new cabinet.

These examples of women's grassroots mobilization in Latin America prove that the gaining of greater political leverage is not beyond the reach of African women. Active networking of women's grassroots groups and persistent political lobbying appear to be the major channels for increasing women's participation in governance and development. Although Latin American women still need to put in more efforts at networking in order to bridge the gap between themselves and the men, yet their accomplishments are worthy of emulation by African women who have not made comparable strides in this direction.

Areas for Further Research

The discourse on the relationship between women, development, and governance in Africa is relatively new, having emerged only in the past few years. The previous sections suggest four main areas of empirical analysis. First, more information is needed on gender disaggregation of concepts of macro-economic models underlying SAP and future development models. For example, gender disaggregation of macro-economic variables such as savings, investment, and consumption would highlight the relevance of gender variables at the conceptualization stage of macro-economic models.

Second, the relevance of gender inequality and the sexual division of labor for micro-economic models should be pinpointed. Related to this is the need for account to be taken of women's domestic labor in GNP computations as is being done in some Western countries.

Third, comparative studies are needed to account for gender as an analytical category in the conceptualization and implementation of macro-economic policies. This is particularly pertinent for regional trade between African states. Gender-aware models of trade and investment should be developed both within Africa and in Africa's trade with other regions to ensure clear monitoring of the gendered impacts of macro-economic and development models.

Fourth, comparative studies of the strategies adopted by women's groups in gaining and expanding of their political space should be a priority for providing insights into both hindrances and strategies for women's political participation. Of particular relevance would be the identification of causes of lack of internal cohesion in women's groups and hence strategies to redress such problems would more easily be pinpointed.

Findings from empirical studies would diagnose and identify the prescriptions for engendering Africa's economic and political structures for sustainable development.

Policy Recommendations

The purpose of carrying out empirical studies in the stated areas is to come up with policies to vitalize Africa's development such that the hitherto neglected gender dimensions of development and governance will be incorporated for achieving development goals in Africa. To this end, policy makers need to ensure that statisticians, economists, and planners are trained in gender-sensitive macro economic data gathering and micro- and macro-economic modeling in order to account for gender perspectives of their economies. Policies should similarly be formulated and implemented to account for gender as an analytical category in development planning and to take into account policy impact on women, children, and other vulnerable groups.

Policies should be aimed at the gendered structures of different African countries to remove disabling structures and ensure gender equality in development and governance. In addition, policies are needed to ensure women's greater input in discussions of macro-economic policies and governance issues. Female political scientists, economists, and other women in related academic disciplines as well as NGO leaders have important roles to play in this regard.

Policies are needed for increasing public information flows through the media for empowering women with information. Policy makers, NGOs, and leaders of women's organizations should encourage greater alliance and networking among women's groups to strengthen women's political participation. Training of women leaders should be a major priority of such networking efforts.

Conclusions

In this chapter, the relationship between women, development, and governance has been explored from the theoretical perspectives of feminist political scientists, feminist economists, and radical institutional economists. Theorists argue that gender needs to be incorporated as an analytical category for understanding social relations as well as the impact of development and governance in Africa. In their view, gender is the main stratifier of social life in Africa. In addition, theorists agree that African women are excluded from political power, which continues to be dominated by men. The resulting gender bias in conceptualization, implementation, and impact of development policy has been highlighted.

Women's exclusion from formal politics has encouraged their active participation in the informal political arena of women's organizations. The comparative evidence from Africa and Latin American countries highlighted the importance of women's organizations for creating and expanding of women's political space. Women's experience in these organizations can contribute significantly to their participation in national politics. The experience of women's grassroots movements in Chile clearly demonstrates that in spite of initial setbacks and discrimination against women political leaders by male politicians, greater networking, and persistent lobbying eventually whittled down the obstacles to women's effective political participation. The forging of alliances at local, national, and international levels will work in women's favor as they seek to obtain and retain their political leverage.

Much empirical work still needs to be done to provide greater insights into these and other issues. The incorporation of gender at the conceptualization and implementation stages of development models and the monitoring of their gender impact would assist planners in the formulation and implementation of gender-sensitive policies. The removal of disabling economic and institutional structures which perpetuate gender inequality will increase women's contribution to sustainable development.

Works Cited

Afonja, Simi, and Bisi Aina, eds. *Nigeria Women in Social Change*. Programme in Women's Studies, Ile-Ife, Nigeria: Obafemi Awolowo University Press, 1995.

Aina, Bisi and Funmi Soetan. "Structural Adjustment Policy, Gender and Technology: The African Experience." Paper presented at the 1991 Annual Conference of the West African Technology Policy Studies Network, Lagos, December, 9–10, 1991.

Benaria, Lourdes. "Toward a Greater Integration of Gender in Economics." *World Development* 23, 11 (1995):1839–1850.

Brautigam, Deborah. *Governance and the Economy: A Review*. The World Bank Policy and Review Department, Washington, D.C., 1991.

Cagatay Nilufer, Diane Elsonn, and Caren Grown. "Introduction," *World Development* 23, 11 (1995):1827–1836.

Chazan, Naomi. "Gender Perspectives on African States," in Parpart, Jane, and Kathleen Staudt, eds. *Women and the State in Africa*. Boulder, Colo.: Lynne Rienner Publishers, 1990.

Chenery, H., et al. *Redistribution with Growth*. Oxford: Oxford University Press, 1974.

Commonwealth Secretariat Expert Group on Women and Structural Adjustment. *Engendering Adjustment for the 1990s*. London: Commonwealth Secretariat, 1989.

Elabor-Idemudia, P. "The Impact of Structural Adjustment Programmes on Women and their Households in Bendel and Ogun States Nigeria," in C. H. Gladwin, ed. *Structural Adjustment and African Women Farmers*. Gainesville, Fla: University Press of Florida, 1991.

Elson, Diane. "Micro, Meso, Macro: Gender and Economic Analysis in the Context of Policy Reform." Department of Economics, University of Manchester, England: undated.

Elson, Diane. *Male Bias in the Development Process*. Manchester, England: Manchester University Press, 1991.

Elson, Diane (a). "Gender-Aware Analysis and Development Economics," *Journal of International Development* 5, 2 (1993):237–247.

Elson, Diane (b). "Gender Relations and Economic Issues," in Barbara Evers, ed. *Women and Economic Policy*. Oxford: Oxford University Press, Focus on Gender 3, 1993.

Evers, Barbara, ed. *Women and Economic Policy*. Oxford: Oxford University Press, Focus on Gender 3, 1993.

Gladwin, Christina, H., ed. *Structural Adjustment and African Women Farmers*. Gainesville, Florida: University Press of Florida, 1991.

Guyer, Jane. "Household Budgets and Women's Income." *African Studies Working Paper No 28*, Boston: Boston University, 1980.

Healey, John, and Mark Robinson. *Democracy, Governance and Economic Policy: Sub-Saharan Africa in Comparative Perspective*. London: Overseas Development Institute, 1992.

Ingham, Barbara. "The Meaning of Development Interactions Between 'New' and 'Old' Ideas," *World Development* 21, 11 (1993): 1803–1821.

Jaquette, Jane, et al. " Women and the Transition to Democracy: The Impact of Political and Economic Reform in Latin America," *Latin American Program Working Paper*. Washington, D.C.: The Woodrow Wilson Center, 1994.

Jockes, Susan. "Gender and Macro-Economic Policy," *AWID Occasional Paper No 4*, AWID, Washington, D.C.: Association for Women in Development, 1989.

Karl, Marilee. *Women and Empowerment: Participation and Decision Making*. London: Zed Books Ltd., 1995.

Kennedy, E. T., and Cogill, B. "Income and Nutritional Effects of Commercialisation of Agriculture in South West Kenya," *Research Report No 63*. Washington, D.C: International Food Policy Research Institute, 1988.

Klemp, Ludgera. *Women Shaping Democratic Change*. Documentation of a Workshop at the Fredrich Ebert Foundation, Bonn, 21–22 October, 1992.

Landell-Mills, Pierre and Ismail Serageldin. "Governance and the Development Process," *Finance and Development*, September 14–17, 1991.

Mama, Amina. "Feminism or Democracy? State Feminism and Democratization in Nigeria," *Africa Development* 20, 1 (1995): 37–58.

Mba, Nina. "Kaba and Khaki: Women and the Militarized State in Nigeria," in Jane Parpart and Kathleen Staudt, eds. *Women and the State in Africa*. Boulder, Colo.: Lynne Rienner Publishers, 1990.

Mbilinyi, Marjorie. "Struggles over Patriarchal Structural Adjustment in Tanzania," in Barbara Evers, ed. *Women and Economic Policy*. Oxford: Focus on Gender 3, Oxford University Press, 1993.

Meena R. "The Impact of Structural Adjustment programs on Rural Women in Tanzania," in C. H. Gladwin, ed. *Structural Adjustment Farmers and African Women Farmers*. Gainesville, Florida: University Press of Florida, 1991.

O'Brien, Stephen. "Structural Adjustment and Structural Transformation in Sub-Saharan Africa," in C. H. Gladwin, ed. *Structural Adjustment Farmers and African Women Farmers*. Gainesville: University Press of Florida, 1991.

Okine, Vicky. "The Survival Strategies of Poor Families in Ghana and the Role of Women There," in J. Massiah, ed. *Women in Development Counties: Making Visible the Invisible*. Paris: UNESCO, 1993.

Parpart, Jane, and Staudt, Kathleen, eds. *Women and the State in Africa*. Boulder, Colo.: Lynne Rienner Publishers, 1990.

Peters, Pauline, and Herrara, M. G. *Cash Cropping, Food Security and Nutrition: The Effects of Agricultural Commercialization among Smallholders in Malawi*. Cambridge, Mass.: Harvard Institute for International Development, 1989.

Peterson, Janice (a). "Traditional Economic Theories and Issues of Gender: The Status of Women in the United States and the Farmer Soviet Union," in Janice Peterson and Doug Brown, eds. *The Economic Status of Women Under Capitalism: Institutional Economics and Feminist Theory*. London: Edward Elgar Publishing Ltd., 1994.

Peterson, Janice (b). "Introduction," in Janice Peterson and Doug Brown, eds. *The Economic Status of Women under Capitalism: Institutional Economics and Feminist Theory*. London: Edward Elgar Publishing Ltd., 1994.

Sandbrook, Richard. *The Politics of Africa's Economic Recovery*. New York: Cambridge University Press, 1993.

Schoepf, B., and W. Egundu. "Women and Structural Adjustment in Zaire," in C. H. Gladwin, ed. *Structural Adjustment and African Women Farmers*. Gainesville, Florida: University Press of Florida, 1991.

Snyder, Margaret, and Mary Tadesse. *African Women and Development A History*. London: Redwood Books, 1994.

Soetan, Funmi. "Technology and Women's Ventures in Nigeria's Urban Informal Sector," in Ogbu Osita, Banji Oyeyinka and Hasa Mlawa, eds. *Technology Policy and Practice in Africa*. Ottawa: International Development Research Center, 1994.

Soetan, Funmi (a). "Women, Small Scale Enterprises and Social Change: Implications of Changes in Industrialization Strategy," in S. Afonja and A. Bisi, eds. *Nigerian Women in Social Change*. Ife-Ife: Obafemi Awolowo University Press, 1995.

Soetan, Funmi (b). "Democratization and the Empowerment of Women The Role of Traditional and Modern Women's Associations in Nigeria," in D. Olowu, K. Soremekun, and A. Williams, eds. *Governance and Democratization in Nigeria.* Ibadan, Nigeria: Spectrum Books, 1995.

Sotade, Nike. "Setting an Agenda for the Women's Ministry," *The Guardian* (Lagos), November 23 (1995):13.

Stamp, P. *Technology, Gender and Power in Africa.* Ottawa: International Development Research Center, 1989.

Trager, L., and C. Osinulu. "New Women's Organizations in Nigeria: One Response to Structural Adjustment," in C. H. Gladwin, ed. *Structural Adjustment and African Women Farmers.* Gainesville, Florida: University Press of Florida, 1991.

Tripp, Aili Mari. "Rethinking Civil Society: Gender Implications in Contemporary Tanzania," in J. Harbeson, D. Rothchild, and N. Chazan, eds. *Civil Society and the State in Africa.* Boulder, Colo.: Lynne Rienner Publishers, 1994.

United Nations. *The World's Women.* New York: United Nations, 1995.

Vickers, Jeanne. *Women and the World Economic Crisis.* London: Zed. Books, 1991.

Whalen, Charles, and Linda Whalen. "Institutionalism: A Useful Foundation for Feminist Economics?" in J. Peterson and D. Brown, eds. *The Economic Status of Women Under Capitalism: Institutional Economics and Feminist Theory.* London: Edward Elgar Publishing Ltd., 1994.

Whitehead, Ann. "Food Crisis and Gender Conflict in the African Countryside," in Henry Bernstein et al., eds. *The Food Question.* London: Earthscan Publications, 1990.

World Bank. *Sub-Saharan Africa: From Crisis to Sustainable Growth.* Washington, D.C.: The World Bank, 1989.

Young, Kate. *Planning Development With Women Making a World of Difference.* London: Macmillan, 1993.

9

Structural Adjustment and Governance

Peter Wanyande

Introduction

Sub-Saharan African countries have implemented major economic and political reforms since the 1980s. This paper will argue that the economic reforms, generally known as Structural Adjustment Programs (SAPs), were largely forced on African countries by the international donor community led by the World Bank and the IMF, even in Nigeria (which describes its SAPs as "homegrown," implying that they were not dictated by the World Bank and the IMF). There were no significant, popular domestic forces which invited or welcomed the economic reforms. This is not true, however, of the *political* reforms currently underway in Africa. Though benefiting from the support of the international donor community, political reforms in Africa have in fact been to a large extent homegrown.

Both types of reform are intended to influence the nature and role of African states and economies in fundamental ways. The economic reforms aim to reduce the role of the state in the economy. SAPs eliminate the administrative controls through which the state once determined, for example, interest and exchange rates and

237

prices of various commodities. Structural adjustments leave these economic "signals" to be determined by the market forces of demand and supply. The role of the state is downgraded from the lofty management of the economy to merely providing non-state actors with an environment that is conducive to their participation in the economy, giving the private sector a greater role in the economy than was the case before. The political reforms aim to make the state more accommodating, open, transparent, accountable in its dealings with the citizens and tolerant of views from citizens that may not necessarily support the status quo. In short, they aim at introducing good governance. According to the World Bank, good governance is characterized by predictable, open, and enlightened policymaking; a bureaucracy imbued with a professional ethos; a strong civil society participating in public affairs; and all behaving under the rule of law (World Bank 1994:vii). The rule of law implies respect for human rights, such as the right to associate freely, the right to express political opinions, etc.

Background to the Two Reforms

Both sets of reform measures were necessitated by the socio-economic and political crises that engulfed Africa beginning in the late 1970s and early 1980s. The continent witnessed stagnating economies, with some countries experiencing economic decline or negative growth. The period also witnessed rising unemployment and deteriorating standards and conditions of living in which both absolute and relative poverty worsened. At the political level, by the 1980s governance in Africa was characterized by personalization of power, violation of human rights, widespread corruption, and the prevalence of undemocratic and unelected governments (World Bank 1989). African political systems, whether civilian or military, provided little room for economic development (Anyang Nyong'o 1991:30). They stifled the contribution of the private sector and also undermined the legitimate connection between state and society so central to sustained economic development (Rothchild 1994:206-

207). This was the crisis of governance which the international community and some domestic forces wanted to solve.

This chapter attempts to characterize the nature of the ongoing political and economic reforms in Kenya, Uganda, Tanzania, and Nigeria. It highlights the major issues, problems, and approaches that have dominated the reform process in the four countries, and assesses the extent to which governance during the ongoing economic and political reforms in these countries has changed from what it was in the pre-reform period, and whether such changes can be attributed to the economic reforms. Finally the chapter attempts to establish the linkage between governance and structural adjustment programs and to explain why governments in the four countries behave the way they do with regard to the implementation of SAPs.

Linkage Between SAPs and Governance

The attempt to relate the political and the economic is a long-standing one and predates the current discourse on the relationship between governance and structural adjustment programs. This discourse has historically been represented by two broad schools of thought. One school is associated with Marxist scholars, who argue that it is the economic relations that determine not just the political but all other human activities. Non-Marxist scholars who have contributed to this debate include Dankwart Rustow (1970), Gabriel Almond and Sidney Verba (1963), and Seymour Martin Lipset (1959). According to Rustow, democracy can only thrive when a country reaches a certain level of economic development. Almond and Verba, on the other hand, highlighted the cultural conditions necessary for democracy. They argued that only the "civic culture," characterized by a high propensity by citizens to participate in politics and high levels of trust and tolerance, was conducive to the emergence and growth of democracy.

Influenced by some of these essentially theoretical arguments, some scholars, for example, Samuel Huntington (1968) and Meddi Mugyenyi (1985), concluded that post-independence Africa was not yet ripe for democracy. According to Huntington, democracy would destabilize the fragile political systems in Africa, while, according to Mugyenyi, what Africa needed was development first and democracy second. According to this viewpoint, the current democratic changes and gains made in Africa so far are likely to evaporate. Only time will tell whether or not this will be the case. From the trends in some of the African countries that have introduced political reforms, we can judge that the near-term prospects for democratic consolidation are in fact rather slim. We are, however, not able to say with certainty whether this is due to the level of economic development or to cultural realities in Africa.

What we can say with certainty about the African experience so far is that the advocates of democracy are struggling against very strong anti-reform groups, including many current heads of state. Perhaps the most surprising example is Zambia, the first state in Africa to democratize following the dissolution of the Soviet Union. President Frederick Chiluba, who defeated Kenneth Kaunda by running on a pro-democracy platform, has recently begun to use undemocratic means to rule the country and to ensure that he remains in power; for example, by introducing a widely criticized law meant specifically to bar Kaunda from taking part in the presidential elections scheduled for November 18, 1996. Three of the four countries under study in this volume also exhibit this tendency. Nigeria, which began to introduce economic and political changes under President Babangida, has since begun to backslide, and is currently far and away the least democratic of the four countries. Since gaining power, Uganda's President Museveni has restricted political space by outlawing political contest based on political parties. Kenya began to introduce political and economic reforms in the 1980s and 1990s, but recently President Moi has demonstrated a tendency to drift back to the politics of the pre-reform period by restricting political space, making arbitrary decisions with far-reaching political consequences, and refusing to allow constitutional reforms to reflect the multiparty system of politics introduced in the country in 1992, thus continuing to defy calls for forms of change in line with democratic ideals. Only Tanzania shows no signs of straying from the path of democratization.

In the context of the current political and economic reforms, it has sometimes been suggested that there is a causal relationship between SAPs and democratization. The argument is that political reforms are the direct product of economic reforms. This relationship has, however, not been conclusively established. The mere fact that movements of political opposition have emerged in countries in which programs of structural adjustment are underway does not by itself say much about the nature of the links between the two phenomena. The actual demands raised in the course of the pro-democracy movements suggest quite a different interpretation: they may reflect to a significant extent a popular reaction against the socially painful effects of structural adjustment.

A slight variation in the debate about the relationship between SAPs and democratization is represented by the international donor community led by the World Bank and the IMF. This school posits that economic development can best be achieved in a liberal political environment. A senior official of the IMF has stated that the more open the political system, the greater the prospects that sound economic policies will be sustained (*Finance and Development,* March 1992). According to the World Bank, if sustainable development is to occur, a predictable and transparent framework of rules and institutions for the conduct of private and public business must exist. In other words, good governance is a *sine qua non* for economic development. The current thinking in the donor community is that economic development (read market-oriented reforms) and political reforms with emphasis on transparency, accountability, governmental responsiveness, and the rule of law should go hand in hand. It is the second part of this demand that presents problems for leaders like Moi of Kenya. Even though such leaders admire market principles, they do not feel comfortable with liberal political values such as transparency, accountability, and responsiveness to popular will. Quite clearly liberal political values threaten their use of office for personal gain.

The argument advanced in this chapter is that democratic struggles have been going on in many parts of Africa since the imposition of colonial rule. The independence struggles were waged on democratic principles. When, after independence, it became clear that post-colonial regimes were drifting toward authoritarianism, many pro-democracy forces emerged to oppose these tendencies. This was the case, for example, in Kenya where Oginga Odinga formed the first post-independence opposition party, the Kenya Peoples Union (KPU). In Tanzania, opposition to one-party rule was represented by Oscar Kambona, while in Uganda military rule led to a protracted war between Amin and democratic forces. Nigeria too was characterized by persistent demands for a return to democratic rule during the periods of military rule (Joseph:1987).

Unfortunately, most of these struggles failed to remove the despots from power. This changed in the 1980s and 1990s. During this period, Western powers, including donors who had previously supported regimes irrespective of whether or not they were despotic, used their foreign aid as leverage in support of the domestic pro-democracy groups to force African rulers to open up the political space to as wide a spectrum of viewpoints as possible. In Kenya, for example, it was not until donors withheld aid to the country in November 1991 that Moi felt compelled to introduce political pluralism. Thus, in contrast to the economic reforms which were forced on African leaders by the donors without any domestic support, in forcing political reform the international organizations have assisted domestic groups in opening up Africa's political systems. SAPs, therefore, have served at most to speed up a process of political opening that began independently. There is thus no necessary causal relationship between the two reforms currently underway in Africa.

It is also noteworthy that initially donor interest was limited to the poor economic performance of African countries. This may have been due to the fact that economic deterioration in Africa was affecting the donors directly, since they were the ones supplying the resources to sustain these economies. The donors initially wrongly assumed that the economic crises facing the continent were caused mainly or solely by economic factors, and avoided getting involved in the politics of the affected countries (see World Bank 1989). Indeed, the World Bank is forbidden by its charter from involvement in a country's internal political affairs. A recent publication by the Bank sums up its uncertain position:

> In analyzing governance, the World Bank draws a clear distinction between the concept's political and economic dimensions. The Bank's mandate is the promotion of sustainable economic and social development. The Bank's Articles of Agreement explicitly prohibit the institution from interfering in a country's internal political affairs and require it to take only economic considerations into account in its decisions. Thus, the Bank's call for good governance and its concern with accountability, transparency and the rule of law have to do exclusively with the contribution they make to social and economic development and to the Bank's fundamental objective of sustainable poverty reduction in the developing world. (World Bank 1994:vii)

In the early years the World Bank's position was that of the majority. So long as regimes appeared to be willing to implement economic reform, few of the donors showed any interest in political reforms when recommending adjustment packages for underdeveloped and vulnerable economies (Ihonvbere 1993:141). The donors only incorporated issues of political reform into their conditions for aid when it became clear that there was no necessary link between authoritarian regimes and the success of the economic reforms they propounded, as they had earlier assumed. As more and more donors began to incorporate issues of political reform, the Bank's apolitical stance become the minority position among the donors.

Few African regimes accepted the SAPs willingly. There was a general fear among their leaders of any liberalizing reforms that would weaken their control over the economic resources they required for ensuring their continued stay in power. They accepted structural adjustment programs, which had no domestic support, only because they had no choice. However, they resisted political reforms which did match clear popular aspirations as infringements on national sovereignty. Their resistance to political liberalization ended only when the donors made political reform a general condition for receiving aid. Thus, while both economic and political reforms have been imposed on African leaders, only the political reforms have matched the aspirations of the people.

It must be noted, however, that donors do not necessarily behave the same way when it comes to relating the two reforms. Some donors, such as Japan, have for a long time tried to treat political reforms and economic reforms as totally separate issues that should not be mixed as far as economic assistance is concerned. The Japanese government, for example, has been willing to provide economic assistance to Kenya even when other donors were tying economic aid to political reforms.

It is also important to note that some donors have been inconsistent in the way they treat different countries as far as economic and political reforms are concerned. Britain, for example, appears ready to let Uganda get away with superficial political reforms, while demanding that Kenya introduce far deeper political reforms. The point is that how a donor behaves toward any given country depends on what donor interests would be served by taking one position as opposed to another. This suggests that the origins of the two reforms are diverse, that the relationship between them is not very straightforward and is certainly not deterministic.

Economic Reforms and the SAP Debate

The current economic reforms continue to generate considerable controversy among academics and policy makers alike. First, there is controversy about the relevance of these reforms. Supporters of the reforms view SAPs as the panacea to Africa's economic and social crisis (World Bank 1981; Bates 1981, 1986; Sandbrook 1986). The Bank's position is based on the results of a study it commissioned and whose report was made public in 1981. The report and the World Bank literature that followed represent the first generation of the literature on SAPs (World Bank 1981, 1983, 1984, 1986). The thrust of this early literature is that Africa's social and economic crises were caused by faulty and inefficient economic policies pursued by African states since independence in the 1960s. According to this literature, SAPs are derived from considerations of economic efficiency; governments can more effectively achieve their development goals by reducing the commitments of the public sector and by encouraging the managerial capacities and potential of the private sector.

Among the opponents to the above position are those who write in the Marxist tradition, who attribute the economic crisis to Africa's weak and vulnerable position in the capitalist world economy (Onimode 1988; Goncharov 1990; Sawyer 1990; Stewart 1992). Bade Onimode, for example, rejects the Bank's and the IMF's prescribed solutions for not addressing the real issues that require restructuring in Africa

> the relevant fundamental structures that demand adjustment are those capitalist divisions of labor, of production, consumption, accumulation, technology and dependency in the poor countries and not the subsidiary or auxiliary ephemeral domestic structures of prices, trade, money and foreign exchange currently being addressed by SAPs. (Onimode 1988:291)

He goes further, observing that

> crude reliance on market forces under existing inequalities and noncompetitive conditions operate to intensify structural disparities, to weaken industrialization, to distort resource allocation, prevent national priorities and to increase existing bottlenecks and undermine the sovereignty of African countries. (1988:290)

Many political leaders in Africa share the position taken by these Marxist scholars. Their point of agreement is that the problems in Africa stem from causes beyond their control. A recent report criticized the assumptions behind adjustment as naive or simply ideological (Center for Development Research, March 1995:iii). The more correct position, in our view, is one of shared blame. The problems Africa is experiencing are caused by both faulty internal policies and external factors well beyond Africa's control.

The Impact of SAPs

Another area that has generated considerable controversy relates to the impact of SAPs. This is evident in scholarly literature as well as from reports of donor organizations and policymakers, both local and international. In one of the earliest studies commissioned by UNICEF on the impact of SAPs, a group of scholars reported that adjustment policies were causing untold suffering to vulnerable groups (Cornia et al. 1988). A similar conclusion was arrived at by the United Nations' Economic Commission for Africa (UNECA), which argued that SAPs not only brought suffering to the citizens in the adjusting countries, but also failed to meet the objectives for which they were introduced (UNECA 1991:16), namely, to reverse the deterioration of social and economic conditions in Africa and bring about economic growth. Many outside the UN agree that SAPs are not particularly helpful (Onimode 1992; Ihonvbere 1991; Center for Development Research 1995). In a recent survey of several adjusting countries in Africa, the Center for Development Research observed that

> Apart from increased aid dependency, most of the fundamental features of the current situation lack a strong correlation to adjustment, positive or negative. On the other hand, adjustment agendas have been heralded with grand claims to promote 'accelerated development,' or sustainable development. Nothing of the kind has occurred. Only a few countries have returned to even the low growth path of the 1960s and 1970s. Instead, there has been general contraction in per capita growth, accompanied by greater inequality. There is also little evidence of stabilization of the main pre-adjustment imbalances. (March 1995:iii)

The above position differs markedly from the conclusions of the World Bank. According to the Bank, SAPs are working and those countries committed to adjustment are realizing economic growth (World Bank 1994:1-7). The Bank's position finds support in the study by Hussain and Faruqee (1994), who observe that SAPs have improved the welfare of the poor in African countries under adjustment.

There is adequate evidence to show that many of assessments of SAPs, both positive and negative, are unjustified. Most of these studies either lack adequate data or simply ignore many other variables that may account for either the improvements in the economies of adjusting countries or the continued deterioration of conditions. Some studies neglect the impact of the nature of governance on the effectiveness of SAPs, while others generalize too much about SAPs, as if structural adjustment programs were a single, monolithic policy initiative. The 1994 World Bank study and the 1994 study by Hussain and Faruqee argue that the reforms work, but at the same time admit that they lack conclusive data to support their claim. The 1993 study by Ihonvbere on the other hand, while decrying the failure of the implementation of SAPs and their social costs in Nigeria, fails to relate the failures to the bad governance that characterizes Nigeria. Crispin Odhiambo-Mbai and Monica Neitzert (1995:36) argue that:

> it is misleading to equate the poor implementation and management of SAPs by bad governments, with failure of the programmes. It should be quite obvious that when SAPs are implemented by a bad government then they are bound to fail irrespective of whether the policies are good or not. Similarly it is misleading to claim that the adjustment programmes have improved the welfare of the poor in sub-Saharan Africa when there is no conclusive quantitative data for measuring that improvement.

We may add here that associating improvement or deterioration of economic conditions with SAPs may also be misleading if we fail, as do most reports, to consider possible intervening variables and events and pressures from the international environment. For example, adjusting nations have no control over such variables as falls in international prices or drought. In other words, unless we sift out

and separate the effects that arise directly from adjustment programs from those of other causes, we cannot conclude accurately
whether structural adjustment programs work or not.

Studies that have looked at the politics of adjustment in Africa
have examined the relationship between SAPs and regime type, the
role of interest groups, the effect of state capacity (Callaghy 1994),
and the impact of political elasticity (Wanyande 1993). Undemocratic regimes have been found to be better suited than democratic
ones to implement SAPs, although the variations in performance by
both democratic and non-democratic types of regimes suggest that
successful implementation of SAPs is dependent on the nature and
power of different interest groups in any sector under adjustment. In
a study of the politics of cost-sharing in education and health care
in Kenya, the present author observed that the behavior of implementing countries depends more on the degree or amount of political elasticity enjoyed by the country concerned. Regimes with
greater degrees of political elasticity available to them are likely to
avoid implementation of SAPs and vice versa (Wanyande 1993).
We will return to these issues in our discussion of the actual implementation of structural adjustment programs.

Our position is that it is wrong and misleading to blame
Africa's worsening economic and social conditions entirely on
SAPs. Many of the socio-economic problems that continue to
afflict the region were in existence long before the introduction
of SAPs. As we observed earlier, SAPs were introduced in Africa
as a way of solving the socio-economic crises in the continent,
some of which are now blamed on these policies. It is certainly
indisputable that SAPs did not give birth to problems of poverty,
disease, and unemployment in any of the three east African countries nor in Nigeria. The conditions that led to military coups in
Uganda in the 1970s, for example, were not the result of SAPs.

We also wish to argue that a distinction needs to be made
between the effects of SAPs on an individual's ability to gain
access to the services being affected by one SAP measure or
another, and the impact of SAPs on the quality of the service
itself. In this regard it is important to acknowledge that many of
the social services such as education and health care were in

pathetic condition long before SAPs were introduced. This was true of all the East African countries. Nigeria too had experienced deterioration in its social services long before SAPs (Ihonvbere 1993:141). There is also no evidence that these services would have improved if SAPs were not introduced. It is thus wrong to say that structural adjustment programs are the causes of the problems, just as it is not correct to say that structural adjustment programs were the catalyst for subsequent political reforms.

With regard to the consequences of SAPs on policy change, it is noteworthy that Tanzania has in the recent past been willing to change its socialist policy stance in favor of a market-oriented economy. As late as 1984 this was still unimaginable; Tanzania would not have undertaken this change if SAPs had not been presented as a condition for aid. Such a drastic change in policy orientation is, however, not evident in Kenya, Nigeria or, even Uganda, because these countries had been sympathetic to market economies even before SAPs. We discuss the impact of SAPs on politics in the four countries later in this paper.

Implementation of SAPs

We turn our attention now to the behavior of the governments of Kenya, Uganda, Tanzania, and Nigeria with regard to the implementation of structural adjustment programs. We wish to identify and explain similarities and differences in the ways these governments implemented SAPs.

The background to the current political and economic reforms in East Africa and Nigeria is common to Sub-Saharan Africa. The reforms represented a response to the deteriorating economic and social conditions in the four countries under study here, especially since the 1970s. After the initial economic boom in Africa in the 1960s and early 1970s, economic decline set in during the late 1970s. It was not, however, not until the 1980s that all these countries introduced SAPs. Political reforms came even later.

Kenya

Kenya first approached the World Bank and International Monetary Fund for adjustment lending in 1982. It, however, did not officially launch SAPs until 1985. One of the reasons for this was that the regime could still obtain financial assistance from its major donors, including the World Bank and the IMF. Kenya remained of strategic important to the West for a long time, and it did not occur to the Moi regime that this would change. When it did finally dawn on the regime that such assistance would not be forthcoming without certain economic reforms, the government began to implement the reforms. Since then the implementation of SAPs in Kenya has tended to be dictated by the amount of pressure exerted on the regime by its major donors. This is true to some extent with the political reforms as well, which came much later. For example, the Moi regime succumbed to the demands for multiparty rule only in December 1991 after donors threatened (in November 1991, at their Paris Club meeting) to withhold further aid unless the government introduced political pluralism. Only after this did the government begin to implement SAPs in earnest, albeit inconsistently and with a lack of commitment to these policies. As one study has shown, the implementation of these programs has been characterized by poor timing, inconsistency, lack of coordination and transparency, and corruption (Swamy 1994). The programs have also been implemented in a very haphazard manner, meaning that related reforms are not always taken together (Odhiambo-Mbai and Neitzert 1995:8-15).

It is instructive to note that the Kenyan government has learned how to manipulate the donors. Just before Kenya's finance minister is due to meet with donors over possible funding, the government typically undertakes major economic reforms or behaves in a manner to suggest it is changing its attitude towards the opposition parties. Clearly the maneuvering is an attempt to convince the donors that the country is committed to reform, in the hope that the donors will continue to grant money. It has sometimes worked. The meeting between President Moi and the opposition leaders in early 1996 is a case in point. The IMF released money to Kenya, pointing to the meeting as a sign that the regime was becoming more tolerant of the opposition. It is worth noting, however, that following the stage-managed meeting, the ruling party and the opposition remain poles apart.

Tanzania

The behavior of the Tanzanian leadership with regard to undertaking reforms is more or less similar to that of Kenya. The Nyerere government fiercely resisted attempts to enter into an adjustment agreement with the IMF and the World Bank, offering instead its own "homegrown" adjustment program. This position changed in 1985-86 when it became clear to the Tanzanian leadership that further assistance from other sources would be denied (Gibbon 1992:148). Nyerere stepped down rather than give in, and the new leadership under Ali Hassan Mwinyi accepted the IMF conditions. This represented a major policy shift in a country that was for two decades committed to socialism. Tanzania has subsequently continued to implement all reforms required by the donor community to continue to receive assistance.

Uganda

The Ugandan case was, however, different with regard to political reforms. While as strict with economic reforms as they are with other countries, the donors appear to be much more lenient toward the Museveni government as regards political reforms. The Ugandan government has refused to introduce multiparty politics, but, unlike in the case of Kenya and Tanzania, the donors did not make this a condition for aid and appear to have given up. In fact, President Moi has on several occasions wondered why the donor community required Kenya to implement political reforms while the same donor community did not ask or require Uganda to do the same. A possible answer to this is that donors are rather excited about the innovative system of governance being tried in Uganda. They may wish to see how it fares before condemning or dismissing it as undemocratic. Additionally, the situation in Uganda must be seen against the historical background of the Amin years. Since coming to power, Museveni has greatly improved the human rights situation in Uganda as compared with both itself and, for example, Kenya.

Nigeria

Nigeria represents a special case. Its government has been able to hold out against conditioned reform for one very simple reason. Its substantial oil revenue makes it significantly less dependent on donors than the other three countries. This point is especially relevant to the question of democratic reforms.

Governance in the Pre-Reform Period

The struggle for democratic governance and, in particular, against one-party rule in Africa has a long history (Anyang Nyong'o 1995:31). This is certainly true of Kenya and Tanzania and, to some extent Uganda. It is also true for Nigeria (Joseph 1987), although here the struggle has been more against military rule than against undemocratic civilian regimes. The current wave of democratization in Africa represents the most formidable effort yet witnessed in the quest for improved governance.

Opposition to one-party rule in Kenya began in 1966 when the first post-independence opposition political party, the Kenya Peoples Union (KPU), was registered, barely two years after the dissolution of the Kenya African Democratic Union (KADU), the party that lost to KANU during the 1963 independence elections, when Kenya became a *de facto* one-party state (Gertzel 1970,

Barkan 1992). KPU existed for only three years. In 1969 it was banned and its leaders detained without trial. As a result, Kenya became a *de jure* one-party state. In 1982 political pluralism was made illegal by an act of parliament passed for two reasons: the fear that some influential politicians were in the process of forming an opposition party (Barkan 1992:180), and the fact that by 1982 the Moi regime had lost much of its initial popular support and legitimacy and was suffering from a sense of insecurity. Making multiparty politics illegal and institutionalizing single-party rule was undertaken to preempt the formation of a particular party and as way of ensuring that the regime remained in office despite its waning popularity and legitimacy. After 1982 political dissent and opposition politics became criminal acts. The attempted military coup that same year can be seen as an expression of disapproval of the repression.

Post-independence political development in Tanzania has been more or less similar to that of Kenya. There were, however, some significant differences. Unlike Kenya, which attained independence under multiparty political arrangements, Tanzania achieved independence in 1961 under one party, the Tanganyika African National Union (TANU). Secondly, in Tanzania political pluralism and dissent were made illegal in 1965, four years before Kenya took similar steps. Tanzania therefore has had a longer history and experience of being a *de jure* one-party state than Kenya.

The main similarity between the countries is that political dissent has been dealt with very ruthlessly by both states. Many opposition figures have either been detained without trial (as happened in 1969 to Oginga Odinga and the entire opposition members of parliament from his party) or forced to go into exile (as happened to Oscar Kambona in Tanzania in the 1960s). This, however, did not completely silence the voices of dissent and opposition. It simply encouraged underground movements and opposition to the regime. In some cases courageous politicians went ahead and formed opposition parties. In 1988, for example, Odinga defied the ban on opposition politics and formed the National Democratic Party (NDP), which was, however, denied registration. This situation obtained until 1991 and 1995 in Kenya and Tanzania, respectively, when multiparty politic systems were re-introduced. In both cases the decision to allow multiparty politics was made possible by a combination of domestic and international forces and events (Rothchild 1994).

The situations in Uganda and Nigeria were different from what obtained in both Kenya and Tanzania in some important respects. In both Uganda and Nigeria, multiparty politics was not made illegal as such; its practice was simply undermined by the ruthless military rule that these countries have both experienced. The first coup in Nigeria occurred in 1966. The country saw unbroken military rule for thirteen years until 1979. After a brief period of civilian rule, the army took power again in 1983, and has ruled ever since. Uganda's first coup occurred in 1971. It ushered in the brutal rule of Idi Amin. After his overthrow following war with Tanzania in 1979, Uganda tried multiparty politics, but this was interrupted by a military coup that saw General Tito Okelo come to power. The accession of Museveni in 1985 after a protracted guerrilla war did not provide a conducive environment for multiparty politics. The new regime did not, however, outlaw multiparty politics until 1996, when a decision to make opposition parties illegal was arrived at through debate in the constituent assembly.

Current Trends

From the above discussion it is quite clear that democratic governance has been a rare practice in all four countries under study. In fact, in Nigeria, it makes no sense to talk of democratic political reforms at all, since the military regime has suspended all political party activity.

It is against the background of undemocratic malgovernance and the disappointing economic performance associated with it that the current attempts at good governance and economic reform were initiated. In the next several pages, we highlight the approaches to political reforms in the three countries where such reforms are going forward, discussing the major issues that have dominated the process.

Kenya

A major characteristic of the current democratization process in Kenya is that it has been perceived mainly as providing an opportunity for the capture of the presidency and state power. What appears to have been uppermost in the minds of the major political actors in the opposition has been to secure the seat of the incumbent leader. Organized opposition to Moi's one-party rule began to manifest itself in the 1980s through groups such as the Law Society of Kenya, the National Council of Christian Churches of Kenya (NCCK), and Odinga's NDP. Moi banned discussions on multiparty politics until the donors threatened to withdraw further aid (*The Guardian*, September 11, 1990). Multiparty politics was legalized in December 1991, by which time the prevalent view was that the ruling party (and Moi in particular) were too unpopular to win any election. For a time the protests remained largely fragmented and uncoordinated, as the state would not allow them to coordinate their activities. The state, for example, denied NDP registration. Nevertheless, a viable opposition movement began to form, ultimately coalescing in the Forum for the Restoration of Democracy (FORD), the first major organized opposition movement involving the masses. It became a political party in 1992 and posed the first real challenge to the Moi regime.

FORD faced several major problems. The first was ethnicity. For different ethnic groups, the race for the presidency had different objectives. For the Kikuyu this was an opportunity to regain the helm of leadership lost following the death of President Kenyatta in 1978 (Oyugi 1992). The Kikuyu were particularly bitter about Moi's systematic marginalization of their interests in the economic and public sector. Moi had, for example, done everything in his power to divert public resources away from Central Province, the home of the Kikuyu, to his own Rift Valley Province. For the Luo and the Luhya, the two other major ethnic groups who produced many of the key political actors in both the colonial and post-colonial eras, political pluralism was seen as their chance to have a turn at the presidency. The Luhya felt that, since the Kikuyu and Kalenjin had already had their chance, with the Luo having occupied the vice- presidency, it was now their turn to lead. Odinga, the leader of the Luo, argued that this time around the Luo would not be used to help others get the presidency, as had happened during the struggle for independence (Oyugi 1992). Odinga did this publicly during campaigns in Luo land and received overwhelming support.

The second problem faced by FORD was that it was made up of individuals with divergent shades of political opinion and ideological orientations. The membership was drawn from different political and professional backgrounds. They also had different objectives or reasons for joining the opposition, ranging from opposing one-party rule in general to opposing the Moi regime in particular. For the younger politicians from various professions such as law and the academic world, the introduction of multiparty politics provided an opportunity to restructure Kenyan politics and to introduce genuine democracy. The senior opposition politicians, however, had narrower agendas. Odinga, for example, who had been associated with opposition and radical politics for most of the independence period, was advancing in age and may have wanted nothing more than to have a last go at the presidency. Matiba, on the other hand, joined the opposition after a falling out with the Moi regime a few years earlier, before the pressure for multiparty politics became a global concern. He was, in other words, part and parcel of the one-party system until the 1980s. For him, the reason for joining the opposition may have had more to do with a desire to avenge his political detention than anything else. Owing to the personal ambitions of Odinga and Matiba and the great pressure they were under from elements in their ethnic constituencies who wanted a turn in the presidency, FORD split into two separate political parties (FORD Asili and FORD Kenya). After the split, FORD Asili's slogan was "Moi Must Go" while FORD Kenya adopted "Grand March to the State House" as its slogan.

The now-divided opposition faced a third problem. The incumbent President Moi saw them as a direct challenge to and attack on his ability and even personality. This was exacerbated by the opposition's threat that they would take Moi to court to account for misrule during his term of office. At a more general level, the ethnic groups that had benefitted from the regime in power saw the opposition movement as an attack on the structure of privilege that they had been used to, and rallied to Moi. Their support made the incumbent even more determined to retain power, and he used all the resources at his disposal—including state resources such as the provincial administration, the security forces, and the police—to frustrate the opposition. The provincial administration was used, for example, to deny licenses for political rallies to the opposition, while the police were used to disrupt opposition meetings that had been licensed.

The most damaging tactic Moi employed to frustrate the opposition was his manipulation of the electoral process. He kept the opposition in the dark regarding the date of the pending elections for as long as possible after the legalization of multiparty politics in December 1991, and did not announce the election dates until October 1992, two months before they were due to be held. The emergent pro-democracy forces thus had little time to debate and develop a coherent political program and arrive at a democratic consensus regarding the best approach and direction the political reforms should take. Their leaders did not get a chance to sort out their political and ideological differences before the elections were held. By the time the elections were announced, the parties had neither a coherent political and economic program, nor were they ready for the elections.

The resulting elections, held in December 1992, have since been described as neither free nor fair (NEMU 1993). Despite its apparent weakness, KANU retained power with only thirty-three percent of the votes; the remaining sixty-seven percent split among the opposition parties. The widespread feeling that the elections were not free and fair has meant that Moi's regime does not enjoy legitimacy. This has of course made him even more determined to contain any possible challenge and opposition to his rule. He has, for example, ruled out any dialogue with the opposition. In fact, it is very difficult for members of the opposition to share a platform with the ruling party. In parliament, the opposition and the government either talk past each other, or simply oppose each other for purely partisan reasons. This has made it hard for the leaders to debate the future direction of the country in matters of governance. The result is that there is no consensus about what rules of governance shall be established, which greatly profits the incumbent, who continues to govern as arbitrarily as before.

The three factors which divided and frustrated the opposition prior to the 1992 elections—ethnic hostility, the personal ambitions of the leaders, and Moi's ability to use state power to damage the opposition's chances—all combined to focus attention on capturing the presidency to the detriment of larger issues. It is no wonder that the two splinter groups of FORD, like other parties, chose to concentrate singlemindedly on the capture of the presidency to the exclusion of more abstract but fundamental issues such as constitutional reforms. Though fundamental to the introduction and functioning of democratic governance, these reforms may have appeared to the candidates as less likely to attract votes from the public.

We highlight this single-minded obsession with capturing the presidency for one important reason. The more vital issues fundamental to good governance have been subordinated to the pursuit of office. Principal among these issues are those determining the constitutional arrangements and the rules to be followed in the conduct of public affairs, including politics itself. In his addresses to mark the end of 1994 and to usher-in 1995, President Moi announced that the government would embark on a major constitutional revision during 1995 to make it conform to and reflect the multiparty political systems that had been introduced (*Daily Nation*, January 2, 1995). This promise was, however, broken later in the year when the president announced that such a move was unnecessary because, according to him, there was no constitutional crisis in the country—this despite the fact that the constitution as it stands best suits a one-party system of government.

The only major relevant constitutional changes that have been made since the introduction of multiparty politics in 1991 are those requiring (1) that a presidential candidate obtain twenty-five percent of the votes cast in five of the country's eight administrative provinces, and (2) that the president be limited to two five-year terms. The twenty-five percent rule has been particularly problematic. According to one lawyer, this provision should be abolished because provinces are not electoral areas (*Daily Nation*, April 26, 1996, p. 4). Since the provinces cannot be the basis of determining electoral results, the rule is undemocratic. A more democratic rule would be one requiring that the president win fifty-one percent of the votes cast in a presidential election.

The rule limiting the president to two five-year terms, as it stands, has also been criticized as one that could be manipulated to lead to a life presidency. According to some lawyers, "if the president dissolved parliament before the five-year period lapses, then he can extend his rule on the premise that he has not completed the stipulated five-year term" (*Daily Nation*, April 26, 1996, p. 4). The two relevant constitutional changes made thus far have both been controversial. Put differently, there is no agreement about the rules to govern Kenya's political practice, yet such agreement is crucial for the functioning of a democracy.

Apart from the two very controversial amendments, the one-party constitution remains basically intact. In particular, presidential powers remain unchanged. The danger here is the possibility that the incumbent president can use his vast constitutional powers to frustrate any attempts at democratic change if this is not in his best interests. An example is the appointment of the Electoral Commission. The current Commission was appointed single-handedly by the president with total disregard for the opposition parties. The Commission has had its term extended despite an outcry from the opposition and civil society that a new commission be named. This is but one example of the ruling party taking advantage of the constitution to do business as usual.

The apparent lack of progress in political reforms has been made possible by a number of factors. One is the fact that Moi retained power under the same party and constitution that has long served him well. He has been able to use the constitution to his advantage against his adversaries. This must be understood against the background that Moi saw the demands for democratic change as an attack on his personality and structures of privilege that he has built for his people since he came to power.

Another reason why the Moi regime has not been very enthusiastic about political reforms is simply that the international donor community has not been as strict and consistent in their conditions for political reforms as they have been with economic reforms. In fact, different donors seem to have different attitudes toward political reforms, not just in Kenya but in other parts of East Africa. For example, the British view has been that the absence of democracy is unacceptable in Somalia and Sudan but perfectly fine in Kenya (Gibbon 1992:143). On the other hand, the World Bank and the IMF have been less tolerant of one-party rule in Kenya but quite tolerant of Uganda's no-party rule. But even in Kenya, the IMF has been less insistent on political reforms compared to their demand for economic reforms. This has given the government enough elasticity and political space to decide the direction and pace of the reforms. It is true that the donor community has at times called on the government to improve its human rights record and to respect the opposition. The donors, however, have not been able to influence the government to stop harassing the opposition, nor have they insisted strongly that the government register all political parties that have applied, such as Safina.

The ideological and organizational weakness of the opposition parties has also contributed to the present ease with which Moi refuses to make further progress toward political reforms. The leaders of the opposition have preoccupied themselves with personal ambition and petty differences to the point that the ruling party is left free to ignore them and manage business as usual. The opposition parties have quite frankly failed to have the kind of impact needed to make the ruling party responsive to what the opposition represents both in and out of parliament.

Against this background, it is no surprise that the outcome of the 1997 elections of both president and parliament was a repeat of what happened in 1992. President Moi and his KANU party scraped through with a reduced majority in parliament and a smaller percentage of the national vote, largely thanks to the division within the opposition. This time there were no less than fifteen presidential candidates, although only four were serious national contenders. Yet, all four split the presidential vote along ethnic lines. In spite of its reduced power base, KANU emerged as the only party with a following in each province. For this reason, Moi was also able to secure the minimally required twenty-five percent of the vote in at least five provinces.

Tanzania

As in Kenya, the opening up of political space in Tanzania seems to have focused all attention on the race for the presidency to the detriment of any debate about the larger issues. This is reflected in the proliferation of political parties in the period leading to the elections. By the time elections were held in 1995, a total of thirteen parties had been registered and went on to take part in the elections (Maliyamkono 1995:25). It is doubtful that the manifestos and policies of these parties reflected any major differences. This is certainly true of Kenya, where parties such as Ford-Asili do not even have a manifesto. Another significant similarity between Kenya and Tanzania is that, in both countries, the ruling party retained power after the multiparty elections. A third is that in both cases the elections were believed not to have been free and fair.

An important difference between Kenya and Tanzania is that in Tanzania, although the ruling party retained power, it was under a new president. This seems significant as the new leader, Benjamin Mkapa, appears eager to demonstrate that he is a true democrat who is different from previous leaders, not just in Tanzania, but other African countries as well. He has, for example, declared his personal wealth, as one way of demonstrating his commitment to transparency and accountability. He has also announced that the government will fund all major political parties including the opposition. Both issues have been demanded in Kenya, but the Moi regime had not acceded.

Another important difference between the Tanzanian case and that of Kenya is that while in Kenya multipartyism was introduced so abruptly that it impeded progress toward genuine democratic reforms and governance, in Tanzania multipartyism was introduced gradually and was preceded by the establishment of a public commission (the Nyalali Commission) to look into the proposed system. Whether the debate was free is not the issue here. The important thing is that at least there were discussions, and the period between the decision to hold multiparty elections and the elections themselves was much longer than was the case in Kenya. Tanzanian opposition parties thus had a chance to think through the issues. The adoption of multiparty politics in Tanzania was given a further boost by the leading role played by Nyerere in the decision to introduce this system of government. Although the Nyalali commission reported that eighty percent of Tanzanians were not interested in multiparty politics, Nyerere went ahead and preempted the report by advocating the introduction of the system, a view that was eventually accepted (Maliyamkono 1995:23-24). Nyerere was such a respected and influential statesman that his involvement made multiparty politics look like it was not imposed from above. In the Kenyan case, on the other hand, multiparty politics was spearheaded by people who did not enjoy much respect outside their own ethnic groups.

Uganda

The situation in Uganda is different from both Kenya and Tanzania in many important respects. In Uganda, the ruling National Resistance Movement did not allow the participation of political parties in the May 1996 elections. In fact, multiparty politics is not allowed at all in Uganda. Instead, the elections were contested by individuals. This resulted in only three presidential candidates. It needs to be pointed out, however, that, as in Tanzania, the new system in Uganda was introduced after considerable public debate. The final decision in the Ugandan constitutional debate was taken by a specially elected constituent assembly. This debate gave the new system and the method of its introduction a feeling of being democratic.

Conclusion

It has been impossible to cover all four countries equally in terms of space devoted to their respective experience with structural adjustment programs, but some distinctive patterns are nevertheless possible to identify.

The first is that the approach to the need for economic reform has varied from country to country, with Uganda proving to be the most positive, Kenya and, especially Nigeria, being the most reluctant. Because structural adjustment policies have the tendency to reduce the basis for political patronage, it is no surprise that reluctance is particularly widespread in incumbent governments. Their representatives have institutionalized a patronage system on which much of their political legitimacy rests. Because the government of president Museveni came to power on a platform calling for reform in the corrupt system of government that was Uganda's during preceding regimes, it found it easier to embrace the economic reform agenda and rely on other grounds for establishing its legitimacy.

The second point is that contrary to expectations held when structural adjustment programs were first introduced in the 1980s, the style of governance in the four countries, with the exception of Uganda, has not really changed. As the section on governance above indicates, there has been a remarkable continuity ever since the days of independence. For example, the shift from one- to multi-party politics has not resulted in more democratic or effective forms of governance. In fact, there are indications that multi-party politics may have caused a deterioration, as reliance on consuming public assets for private political patronage has increased. The tendency for international agencies to strengthen their economic and political conditionalities is evidence that the response by African governments has been inadequate.

The African perspective on structural adjustment programs was initially outright negative and hostile. Intellectuals and politicians alike reacted against the "financial and economic policing" that was implied in these programs. Attempts by Africans, notably by the Economic Commission for Africa, to develop alternatives that work have not been successful. No such effort has proved viable. The result is that political leaders as well as academics have gradually accepted the programs as inevitable or as "necessary evils." Given the importance that these programs play in African economies, this mind-set is not very helpful. Scholars, in particular, should devote attention to how governance and structural adjustment of the economy are related and arrive at new insights that would promote anew both research and policy agenda.

Works Cited

Almond, Gabriel, and Sidney Verba. *The Civic Culture*. Boston: Little Brown and Company, 1963.

Anyang Nyong'o, Peter. "Democratization Processes in Africa," *CODESRIA Bulletin* (Dakar), 2, 3 (1991).

Anyang Nyong'o, Peter. "Discourses on Democracy in Africa," in E. Chole and H. Ibrahim, eds. *Democratization Processes in Africa: Problems and Prospects*. Dakar: CODESRIA Press, 1995.

Barkan, Joel. "The Rise and Fall of the Governance Realm in Kenya," in G. Hyden and M. Bratton, eds. *Governance and Politics in Africa*. Boulder, Colo.: Lynne Rienner Publishers, 1992.

Bates, Robert. *Markets and States in Tropical Africa*. Berkeley: University of California Press, 1981.

Callaghy, Thomas. "Lost Between State and Market: The Politics of Economic Adjustment in Ghana, Zambia, and Nigeria," in Joan Nelson, ed. *Economic Crisis and Policy Choice*. Princeton: Princeton University Press, 1990.

Center for Development Research. *Structural Adjustment in Africa: A Survey of the Experience*. Copenhagen, Center for Development Research Denmark, 1995.

Cornia, Andrea, Richard Jolly, and Frances Stewart, eds. *Adjustment with a Human Face*. Oxford: Clarendon Press, 1988.

Daily Nation (Nairobi), January 2, 1995 and April 26, 1996.

Dankwart, Rustow. "Transitions to Democracy: Towards a Dynamic

Model," *Comparative Politics* 2, 3 (1970).

Finance and Development (Washington, D.C.), March 1992.

Gertzel Cherry. *The Politics of Independent Kenya 1963-68.* Evanston: Northwestern University Press, 1970.

Gibbon, Peter. "Structural Adjustment and Pressures Toward Multipartyism in Sub-Saharan Africa," in P. Gibbon, ed. *Authoritarianism, Democracy and Adjustment: The Politics of Economic Reform in Africa.* Uppsala: The Scandinavian Institute of African Studies, 1992.

Gladwin, Christina, ed. *Structural Adjustment and African Women Farmers.* Gainesville: University Press of Florida, 1991.

Goncharov, Leonard. "The Critical State of the African Economy: Its Causes, Character, and Ways to Overcome It," in Olusegun, Obasanjo and Hans,d'Orville, eds. *Leadership Challenge of the African Economic Crisis.* New York: Crane Russak, 1990.

Hussain, I., and R. Faruqee, eds. *Adjustment in Africa: Lessons from Country Studies.* Washington, D.C.: The World Bank.

Huntington, Samuel P. *Political Order in Changing Societies.* New Haven, Conn.: Yale University Press, 1968.

Ihonvbere, Julius. O. "The Military and Political Engineering Under Structural Adjustment: The Nigerian Experience Since 1985," *Journal of Military Sociology* 20, 1 (Summer 1992):107–132.

Ihonvbere, Julius. "Economic Crisis, Structural Adjustment and Social Crisis in Nigeria," *World Development* 21, 1 (January 1993): 141–154.

Joseph, A. Richard. *Democracy and Prebendal Politics in Nigeria.* New York: Cambridge University Press, 1987.

Lipset, Martin, Seymour. "Some Social Requisites of Democracy: Economic Development and Political Legitimacy," *American Political Science Review* 53, 1 (March 1959):69–105.

Maliyamkono, T. L. *The Race for the Presidency: The First Multiparty Democracy in Tanzania.* Nairobi: Colour Print, 1995.

Mugyenyi, Meddi. "Development First Democracy Second," in Walter Oyugi et al., eds. *Democratic Theory and Practice in Africa.* Nairobi: Heinemann, 1988.

National Election Monitoring Unit (NEMU). *Report of the Multiparty General Elections in Kenya.* Homa Bay, Kenya: General Printers, 1993.

Odhiambo-Mbai, Crispin, and Monica C. Neitzert. "The Impact of Structural Adjustment Programmes on the Market in Kenya." University of Nairobi, unpublished paper, 1995.

Onimode, Bade. *A Political Economy of the African Crisis*. London: Zed Books, 1988.

Oyugi, Walter. "Ethnicity in Electoral Politics: The 1992 Multiparty Elections in Kenya." Unpublished paper presented at the Department of Government, Seminar on Elections and the Democratization Process in Kenya. August 19–2, 1992.

Rothchild, Donald. "Structuring State-Society Relations in Africa: Toward and Enabling Political Environment," in Jennifer A. Widner, ed. *Economic Change and Political Liberalization in Sub-Saharan Africa*. Baltimore: John Hopkins University Press, 1994.

Swamy, Gurushri. "Kenya: Patchy, Intermittent Commitment," in I. Hussain and R. Faruqee, eds. *Adjustment in Africa: Lessons from Country Case Studies*. Washington, D.C.: World Bank, 1994.

Sawyer, Akilagpa. *The Political Dimension of Structural Adjustment Programmes in Sub-Saharan Africa*. Accra: University of Ghana Press, 1990.

Stewart, Frances. "Short-Term Policies for Long-Term Development," in Giovanni Andrea Cornia, Rolph van der Hoeven, and Thandika Mkandawire, eds. *Africa's Recovery in the 1990s*. London: St. Martin's Press, 1992.

United Nations Economic Commission for Africa (UNECA). *African Alternative Framework to Structural Adjustment Programme for Socio-Economic Recovery and Transformation*. Addis Ababa: UNECA, 1991.

Wanyande, Peter. *The Politics of Structural Adjustment In Kenya: The Case of Cost Sharing in Education and Health Care*. Unpublished Ph.D. Dissertation, Department of Political Science, University of Florida, Gainesville, 1993.

World Bank. *Accelerated Development in Sub-Saharan Africa: An Agenda for Action*. Washington, D.C.: The World Bank, 1981.

World Bank. *Sub-Saharan Africa: Progress Report on Development Prospects and Programs*. Washington, D.C.: The World Bank, 1983.

World Bank. *Towards Sustained Development in Sub-Saharan Africa: a Joint Program of Action*. Washington, D.C.: The World Bank, 1984.

World Bank. *Financing Adjustment with Growth in Sub-Saharan Africa, 1986–90*. Washington, D.C.: The World Bank, 1986.

World Bank. *Sub-Saharan Africa: From Crisis to Sustainable Development*. Washington, D.C.: The World Bank, 1989.

World Bank. *Governance: The World Bank Experience*. Washington, D.C.: The World Bank, 1994.

10

The International Dimensions of Governance

Kayode Soremekun

Introduction

The post-Cold War era has ushered in novel values, attitudes, and aspirations in the international system. In a previous era that was dominated by the contending positions of Moscow on the one hand and Washington on the other, very minimal attention was paid to issues like governance and democratization. Rather, what mattered most in that Manichean[1] setting was the enlistment of allies on both sides of the ideological divide. Predictably, the entire process was attended by a measure of cynicism which ensured that the various entities in the international system were motivated more by convenience than conviction. However, the mutability of life is clearly demonstrated in the fact that new values and aspirations are now being actively promoted in the international system, one of which is governance (Barkan 1995).

The new prominence of governance is such that it continues to excite the interests of status-quo forces in the international system, as well as social forces in the various African countries. In fact, it has begun to wreak havoc on the once-close links between the metropoles on one hand and the ruling elites in the various African countries on the other. As the historic and mutually reinforcing bonds between the Western powers and African dictators have ruptured, new alliances between the metropoles and the various social movements in Africa are emerging to take their place. The immediate implication of this relatively nascent situation is that the study of international relations is being conceived of in new ways. The state, which was once the principal entity in our discourses, is gradually being displaced from center-stage. This is just as well.

The marginalized role afforded the state in theories of international relations is better reflective of the reality on the ground in Africa, where the state, far from approximating the classic attributes, is penetrated, hollow, and on the verge of collapse, as can be observed in seemingly diverse contexts like Nigeria, Zaire, Liberia, Somalia, and to a lesser extent in Kenya, Tanzania, and Uganda. The less than roseate status of the African state has prompted a lot of concern about how the African state can be reconstructed. One of the solutions currently on offer is that the quality of governance be more emphatically considered when shaping the public life of African countries. The seemingly pessimistic argument goes thus: Africa is in a rut because a critical variable like governance is missing in the leadership portfolio. It is no surprise, therefore, that the current crusade for improved governance in many African countries is championed by various social forces in the international system. As we shall see shortly, the specifics of this process (i.e., reification of governance), differ from one country to the other still, it is perfectly possible to dwell on both the universals on the one hand and the specifics on the other.

A major objective of this chapter is to explore the global dynamics which seek to enthrone governance in countries like Nigeria, Kenya, and, to a lesser degree, Tanzania and Uganda. It is a task that presents challenges and limitations to the analyst. The former derive partly from the fact that there is a great deal to be said for bringing these four countries together under the rubric of a single analysis, shot through as their various historical experiences are with the common heritage of the British colonial order—which, as we shall see, has done a lot to vitiate the question of governance, the current darling of the post-colonial powers. On the other hand, the limitations inherent in this task are obvious enough: we seek to compare one single country (Nigeria) with three different countries in East Africa. This limitation is offset partly by the fact that Nigeria's resource endowments are roughly equivalent to those of Kenya's, Uganda's, and Tanzania's combined, and partly by the fact that, as a country that enjoys regional hegemonic position, Nigeria has a tremendous influence far beyond its own borders.

The Issue of Governance

According to some writers (Hyden and Bratton 1992; Olowu et al. 1999), governance speaks in a direct way to the ruler-ruled relationship. In this sense it has three dimensions, the functional, the structural, and the normative. Functionally, governance deals with how rules are made, legitimized, and enforced. Structurally, it comprises three distinct institutions, the ruler or the state, the ruled or the society, and the rules or law. In essence then, governance embodies the quality of the relationship between the state and social institutions. Finally, the normative dimension of governance highlights the values associated with (good) governance. These include: transparency, organization, effectiveness, accountability, predictability, legitimacy, popular participation, and plurality of choices.

Marina Ottaway (1993) contends much less elaborately that both democratization and governance tend to be interpreted narrowly as the holding of (reasonably) free and fair elections. There is little to be said for this attempt to view democratization and governance in synonymous terms. Rather, it is more realistic to view them as gradated values on the continuum of state-society relationships. However, what is clearly beyond the pale of controversy is that governance and democratization have become buzzwords in contemporary policy and intellectual discourse.

Furthermore, the Western powers seem to acknowledge that good governance can be achieved without democratization; favored satellites of the international system who are yet to embrace democratization are usually excused on the grounds that, despite the fact that they lack democracy, they can seek improved governance. Uganda is a case in point. Its peculiar historical dynamics are such that its government cannot be said to be democratic, but it is tolerated by the Western world on the grounds that the there are indices of good governance present in the country (Wrong and Holman 1996). Against this backdrop it is possible to classify the notion of governance into two broad categories: (i) as an ideology and (ii) as an analytical concept. It is as the latter—as the functional means by which rules are made, legitimized, and enforced, the structural relationship between the state and social institutions, and especially the norms of transparency, organization, effectiveness, accountability, predictability, legitimacy, popular participation, and plurality of choices—that the term governance is employed here.

The grand irony in much of what we have said so far is that a lot of the global efforts that currently go into the attempts to foster improved governance in Nigeria and East Africa come from the very same forces which all along made strenuous attempts to thwart the consummation of governance in these countries. This is a contradictory position that is best appreciated in the context of the dynamics that attended the pre-colonial, colonial, and post-colonial phases in these countries. It is a circular phenomenon, which lends much credence to Oscar Wilde's concept of the past as being the present entered through another gate; or, in more prosaic terms: present, past, and future form one mighty whole. While it is possible to argue that the past resembles the present as far as this relates to the absence of governance in Africa, an exception can be made in that, despite the contentions of Malian writer Yambo Ouloguem (1972), the functional, structural, and especially normative dimensions of governance were all present in the ruler-ruled relationships in many parts of pre-colonial Africa.

Governance in Pre-Colonial Africa

Naomi Chazan (1991) shed much light on quality of governance in pre-colonial Africa when she asserted that despite the diversity of African politics, prior to the imposition of colonial rule several democratic strands were discernible in most traditional political formations on the continent. The first, according to her, was the principle of public involvement in decision making. In segmentary societies, such as the Kikuyu of East Africa as well as the Tiv and Igbo in present day Nigeria, adults participated in an almost Athenian fashion in the planning and implementation of communal affairs and in the adjudication of disputes. In more complex societies, she reveals, notions of representation were deeply embedded. Youths, traders, artisans, religious leaders, and heads of kin groups had their own delegates in ruling councils. Ashanti (West Africa) and Buganda (East Africa) furnish excellent case studies in this respect. Even in some highly centralized states, consultation was the norm, and the great empires of the Western Sudan (Mali and Songhai for example) practiced a form of indirect rule which allowed for a considerable amount of local autonomy. Values of participation, representation, and involvement (all indices of governance) were evident in a multiplicity of political settings. Closely allied to indigenous provisions for popular inclusions were notions of consensus. Decisions in many areas were arrived at through lengthy debates whose purpose was to blur opposites, to find the middle road, and thereby to ensure compliance. The rules of the political game among the Igbo and the Tswana, for instance, put a premium on compromise. At the same time, emphasis was placed on discussion (frequently termed palaver) and the public airing of different positions. Debate was an essential feature of the practice of politics in much of pre-colonial Africa.

Governance and Colonial Rule

At this juncture it is appropriate to pose the question: how and why did governance get marginalized in the various African social formations? This question is best answered by a dispassionate focus on colonialism—a phenomenon which effectively dislocated African societies such that, to date, the search for a recourse to governance remains elusive.

The argument here is that colonial rule did not promote the values associated with good governance in Africa. Despite the fact that the main colonial powers in Africa were themselves democratic countries, the institutions they created were first and foremost instruments of domination. Established to provide the means of control over vast areas containing disparate populations, they stressed functional utility, law, and order—but not participation and reciprocity. The colonial state also exemplified Western concepts of sovereignty and territoriality at the expense of notions like nationality and legitimacy. Within this highly authoritarian structure, connections between rulers and the ruled were strictly vertical: the definition of government lacked a popular component. Access to the colonial order was generally blocked and removed from the scrutiny of the people it purported to govern. A remote, bureaucratic, and patrimonial form of politics emerged under a state which violated as a matter of routine the values of the normative dimension of governance.

This pattern was reinforced through selective techniques of economic penetration. The encouragement of agricultural and mineral production for export, together with the creation of a cash economy and the opening of markets for European goods, brought the African continent into close and unequal contact with the global economy. To assist in the task of administration and to provide basic services, colonial regimes also encouraged the formation of new horizontal strata, dependent elites, usually the products of Western education and Christian religion, who enjoyed privileged access to the new centers and their resources. This tiny bureaucratic class was the outward expression of a new norm that placed particular value on the state as the primary source of social mobility. At the same time, however, some members of this Western-educated elite absorbed democratic ideals of participation, accountability, and popular mobilization and created urban-based groups through which they could be expressed. The colonialists in their respective ways unconsciously transmitted the theoretical connections between intellectual enlightenment, economic advancement, and democratic modes of thought. Ultimately, however, the reality of colonial rule was the antithesis of many of these ideas and conveyed quite different political messages.

It is against this background that we can appreciate not just the absence of good governance in the various social formations, but also the reality that such a void was actively fostered by global forces—a situation that carried over into the post-colonial order. In essence, then, there is much to be said for the culpability of international forces in terms of the fact that the colonial and post-colonial orders were not structured to promote the values of good governance (Ntalaja 1987).

In the absence of popular political control and other mechanisms of accountability, state officials were very arbitrary in their behavior; the only counter-weight to this arbitrariness was the constraint imposed by their hierarchical supervisors. Consequently, the colonial officers worked to please the latter, as well as to advance their own careers and material interests, rather than to carry out the duties associated with their offices. But there was still a major difference between the post-colonial state and the colonial state. Consistent with its order and revenue imperatives, the colonial state was relatively better organized than its successor to handle its specific administrative duties. Thus, in spite of its lack of legitimacy as an alien and oppressive structure, the colonial state achieved a high level of administrative performance and succeeded in establishing a stable—though unequal—order in which ordinary Africans enjoyed a limited—but regular—delivery of social services. On the other hand, the post-colonial state is best characterized by the coexistence of absolute power and administrative involution, or by the dialectic of power and fragility.

Governance and The Post-Colonial State

The post-colonial state is to all intents and purposes a *neo*-colonial state, a politically independent structure within a basically unchanged economic framework. In view of this reality, the neocolonial state, like its colonial predecessor, is primarily concerned with the maintenance of law and order and the accumulation of wealth in the interest of its ruling class. Since the state is a major avenue of wealth accumulation (as well as a source of wealth by virtue of its extensive control over economic resources), a major preoccupation of this class has been to expand and consolidate the state's role in the economy. Accordingly, the state is a major prize, the key object of intra-class fractional struggles. Power—and especially state power—is a zero-sum game; being in or out of power has serious consequences for one's well being, as well as for life itself. The emergence of patrimonial rulers as skilled arbitrators of the conflicting interests of various factions and groups is a necessary condition for establishing some form of effective rule under a neocolonial state. Relative stability requires that intra-elitist conflicts be reduced to factional politics under the control and manipulation of the top leader. Opposition parties and free elections are not allowed because they present real possibilities of political action by the masses, and it is precisely these possibilities that the neocolonial state strives to suppress. Thus, in view of their freedom from public accountability and popular political control, African rulers have used the state to serve their own interests, rather than those of the society at large.

In this light, the values of good governance were a rarity in many African countries, including the ones under study here. But its non-manifestation in Nigeria, Tanzania, Uganda, and Kenya was also largely conditioned by the specifics of the environment. As we shall see, the settler phenomenon in Kenya accorded this East African country its unique dynamics in which the normative dimension of governance was most notably absent.

Kenya

In its own way, the historical dynamic of Kenya embodies a measure of irony. Despite the violence leading up to Kenyan independence, governance in independent Kenya was expected to be characterized by transparency, openness, and organic bonds between the government and the governed. Such expectations have largely turned out to be euphoric, however, because the nationalist movement was hijacked by a coalition of repressive forces made up of status-quo forces in the international system (the United States, Britain, and Israel) and the members of the ruling class in Kenya.

The socioeconomic structure in the country could be summed up in this terse and poignant statement by a Kenyan nationalist: "Kenya is a country of ten millionaires and ten million beggars." The post-colonial state that emerged under Jomo Kenyatta was essentially a replication of the colonial structure underpinned by political repression. According to Victoria Brittan (1988), Kenyatta started the authoritarian trend which his successor Daniel arap Moi later took much further—muzzling the parliament; turning the country's ruling party, the Kenya African National Union (KANU), into a cipher; and detaining those who attempted to air the issues of foreign domination in the culture, the judiciary, the press, and the economy, as well as the government's corruption and mismanagement. It is pertinent to ask here: What was the response of the international community to the negation of the values of governance in Kenya? Unfortunately, it was one of cold complicity and active collaboration with the ruling class.

This symbiosis was strengthened by the Manichean logic of the Cold War, by which authoritarianism was seen as a shortcut for new nations such as Kenya to achieve rapid development. The specifics of the Kenyan situation were such that, over time, an organic relationship developed between Kenya and the Western world, with Washington in the vanguard of the latter. In view of the atmosphere of fear which characterized the ruler-ruled relationship under these circumstance, the Kenyan ruling class came to rely increasingly on foreign powers for their own security. Ngugi Wa Thiongo (1988) rendered the situation accurately:

> Both the Kenyatta and Moi regimes were afraid of their own army and police force. They relied instead on secret military and defence pacts with foreign powers. Kenyatta started it with a military pact with Britain, which allowed a British military presence in Kenya. Moi completed it on a grand scale by giving military bases to the United States.

Perhaps the most interesting aspect of the Nairobi-Washington linkage, particularly from the perspective of governance, is that the evolution and consequent growth of the relationship was characterized by secrecy. The Kenyan president accounted to no one but himself for the character and scope of the American presence in Kenya. Thus when Kenyan and American forces engaged in joint maneuvers off the Northeast coast of Kenya, they were treated as a national security secret. Similarly, when the American Navy gained access to Kenyan bases and other facilities, the President refused to debate the issue in Parliament. From the foregoing it is evident that the status-quo forces of the international system, especially the United States, were not only indifferent to the values of governance in Kenya; they were also active collaborators in the negation of same, since the linkages forged with Kenya were not open to scrutiny by either the Kenyan media or populace or its accredited representatives.

But Western governments were not alone in this posture of complicity. Much of the blame lies with the scholarship that focused on the country. The overall image of Kenya filtered to the outside world was until recently that of a peaceful, prosperous country whose values were grounded in democracy and economic liberalism. Again Victoria Brittan (1988) described this aspect of Kenyan life when she pointed out that "the myth was born of a Kenya, which was multi-racial, liberal, tolerant—a stable haven for Western investment and tourism. Central Nairobi, with its high-rise office buildings, international chains of hotels, traffic jams, shops full of imported European goods . . . cinemas and theatres offering Western low-brow entertainment exuded prosperity and stability."

This fictitious profile was also accorded a measure of credence by the Western media, which systematically suppressed information about the reality of life in Kenya for many years. Apart from South Africa, by the mid-1990s there was nowhere on the continent home to so many Western journalists.[2] With a few exceptions, they lived in the white colonial-style ghetto and made a practice of not writing about Kenyan politics. When they did, it was usually in the misleadingly crude terms of power struggles between personalities and tribes, (usually Luo versus Kikuyu) and the economic problems supposedly caused by a high birth rate or by the arid and semi-arid nature of much of Kenya's land.

However, in a curious turn of events following the dissolution of the Soviet Union and the end of the Cold War, circumstances changed. The same global forces which actively collaborated with the Kenyan ruling class in negating the values of governance began nudging the Kenyan government along the very path of governance. Most prominent in this drive, particularly at the global level, was U. S. Ambassador Smith Hempstone. In the run-up to the December 1992 elections, for instance, Ambassador Hempstone was in the vanguard of the drive to ensure what he called a "level playing field" for Moi and the opposition candidates. This posture was complemented by the drive to enhance the human rights climate in Kenya. The visibility and consistency of Hempstone in these and other offensives were such that, increasingly, he came to be viewed as the leader of the opposition movement (*Abuja Times,* November 12, 1992). Not to be out-done, the European Community and the Commonwealth lent their weight to the fostering of improved governance and democratization, sending observers to the elections and providing logistical support. Moi, with remarkable flexibility, was able to adapt to the new situation, and won the elections. It was, however, a kind of pyrrhic triumph, aptly described as victory without cymbals (Olukotun 1993). What made for the turn-around on the part of the erstwhile handmaidens of "malgovernance" in Kenya? Before attempting to answer this question, we will turn to a discussion of Nigeria, where, until recently, global forces nurtured dictatorship and mal-governance when, as in Kenya, they began belatedly to scrutinize the governance situation in Nigeria.

Nigeria

Upon the attainment of independence, Nigeria passed peace-fully and uneventfully from colonialism to nationhood. The enterprise of black traders and businessmen based on cocoa and palm oil exports was well established by then. There was a small, educated middle-class, a lively press that had been functioning for more than a century, an active parliament, a sound economy, and an agricultural sector that produced enough food to feed the nation. But the high hopes surrounding West Africa's largest nation soon degenerated into despair as Nigeria declined into conflict and turmoil. In the first sixteen years of independence there were three *coups d'etat,* the assassination of two heads of state, and one civil war which claimed nearly a million lives. The country's oil revenues were squandered in a binge that has seri-ously questioned the thesis which links national development to the size of the natural resource base. The military proved to be more corrupt and less efficient than the civilians they had over-thrown for their corruption and inefficiency.

Nevertheless, in the 1970s the country began to emerge (at least in narrow terms) as a regional super-power. By the 1980s Nigeria enjoyed towering stature and influence on the continent and was viewed as the only country in Africa that had enough clout to influence policy in major world capitals (Lamb 1987). The Nigerian state became remarkably dependent on oil exports. Petro-leum exports accounted for only 10 percent of export earnings in 1962. These rose to 82.7 percent of total export earnings in 1973, and peaked at 93 percent while production reached a peak of 2.05 million barrels a day. There was a dramatic rise in public expendi-ture. Government spending rose from U. S. $ 1.1 billion in 1970 to 6.5 billion in 1975, thus raising state expenditure as a percentage of GDP from 15.5 percent to 30.5 percent. With high levels of expenditures and dependence on oil revenue, when the price of oil fell (by 1986 from around U. S. $40 to about U. S. $10 per barrel), the country became mired in debt (Ibrahim 1995).

Prior to the 1990s, Nigeria was seen by some as a model of good governance in Africa, for several reasons. Because the political elite, coming as they did from different backgrounds and regions, were culturally and politically different, a unified hegemonic bloc was impossible. Indeed, Nigeria's heterogeneity hindered the emergence of a tyrannical system of the sultanic or oligarchic type that became the norm in so many other African societies. There was a relatively robust civil society which effectively counter-posed itself to the Nigerian state. But gradually the state began to make attempts to overwhelm civil society, such that the twin values of governance and democracy were negated (Ibrahim 1995). Nigeria's lofty stature was short-lived. The fall was dramatic. The lone super-power of the continent in the mid 1980s came to replace South Africa in the mid 1990s as the pariah of the international system.

Good governance, as defined in this context, has become elusive in Nigeria, ironic when one considers the high hopes Nigeria engendered, held up as it was until recent times as the one country in Africa that had what it takes to sustain and nurture the culture of good governance. Nigeria's fall is grimly reminiscent of the Kenyan situation. In Nigeria, too, global forces were partially responsible. With an economy similar to that of the Arab states, which revolves around petroleum revenues, and with the complicity of global actors, Nigeria transformed itself into a rentier state, which in turn spawned a sociopolitical formation whose hallmarks negated the ideals of governance.

A rentier state bears many of the same traits as a patrimonial state with one important difference: the rentier state is amply funded by external rents. Most rentier states are oil exporters. In a rentier state, those in control of state power and bureaucratic offices use their positions for private appropriation. In the process, rentier states create structural constraints that erode the impersonality and the rule of law that are necessary for democratic practice. Political reform, governance, and other civic values are viewed as personal privileges that are granted or refused by the ruling clique. The rentier character of the Nigerian state ensures a disjuncture between the ruler and the ruled because, enjoying high annual rents as it does, the state does not have to wrest taxes from the citizens. This has implications for political reform, or the lack thereof. Whenever the state relies on taxation, the question of democracy becomes an unavoidable issue. With taxes comes a strong current in favor of democracy. A slogan from the American Revolution—"no taxation without representation"—shows the link between the imposition of taxes and the demand for democracy.

The point being stressed is that the absence of taxation engenders an apathetic populace on the one hand and an irresponsible government on the other. Moreover, the neopatrimonial state promotes what has been called booty capitalism. The neopatrimonial bourgeoisie in the rentier state is both parasitic and predatory, with no particular interest in indices of governance like transparency and accountability. The consequence is the virtual collapse of governance. In the process, the state is rendered more fragile. A neopatrimonial regime fully expresses itself in military rule. In the case of Nigeria, military rule has been actively fostered and promoted by global forces.

The military has been in the saddle of power for three-quarters of the whole period since Nigeria's independence. The military has had a tremendous impact on the country's culture and institutions. Jibrin Ibrahim (1995) has argued, for instance, that military rule ultimately traumatizes society by generalizing its authoritarian values, which are in essence anti-social and destructive of politics. He argues further that politics in this sense is understood as the art of negotiating conflicts related to the exercise of power. Military regimes have succeeded in permeating civil society with their values and brutality. At a more fundamental level, there is a decline in civility and rise in violence in social intercourse. In terms of governance, the most devastating impact of the military is the illusion that it has a useful political role, particularly in terms of its capacity to deploy force in the face of anarchy. It is this illusion which effectively underpins a situation in which the Nigerian military constitutes the most important segment of the power elite. They are the most wealthy people in the country and they occupy the summit of the most powerful organizations in the country's polity and economy. Predictably, in view of its large role in the nation, the military bears a major share of the blame for anti-governance values. It is instructive to mention here that, in this significant respect, the Nigerian military has been aided and inspired by certain forces in the international system. Such support can be observed in different ways.

One does not have to look far beyond the colonial origins of the Nigerian army to uncover the dynamics of malgovernance. The Nigerian army, like other African colonial armies, was not structured to combat external threats. Rather, the basis for its existence was internal pacification—a task which it has diligently carried out from the colonial era till date.[3] Secondly, owing largely to the climate of the Cold War era, the Western powers were not particularly fussy about the character and tenor of military regimes. Rather, the soldiers who displaced elected civilians in Nigeria, Uganda, and other African countries (including countries which moved into the Soviet camp, such as Congo and Somalia) could count on the support and recognition of their regimes by the great powers. Such a routine endorsement of military rule was also complemented by scholarship in the West, where the military was viewed as the vanguard of development in the various African polities. Invariably such a perspective did much to transform apolitical soldiers into political gendarmes.

Another way in which Western countries contributed to the ascendancy of the military in politics in Africa can be observed in the type of training-cum-socialization processes to which the soldiers were exposed. David Jemibewon (1978) in his memoirs reveals that, in the course of his military training in Western institutions, he and his colleagues from other African countries were consistently introduced in formal and social circles as future leaders of their respective polities. This Macbethian seed ultimately took root, germinated, and flowered such to that many of the products of Western military training institutions went on to seize power in their home countries. Thus, in deliberating on the role of the military in negating good governance in Africa, it is appropriate to remember and appreciate the culpability of the great powers.

But when we look beyond Nigeria to East Africa, what emerges is a contrasting situation as far as the role of the military is concerned. In Kenya, there is very little to be said for the role of the military in political life. Save for the aborted coup of 1982, the soldiers have refrained from intervening. This is not to say that attempts have not been made to draw them into it; only that they have largely remained aloof from a situation that is arguably very contagious in Africa. On the other hand, however, in Uganda, armed or military rule was for many years the defining hallmark in that country. As in the Nigerian situation, the role of global forces cannot be underestimated. As we shall see shortly, Idi Amin—both in the early and the later stages of his misrule—derived a measure of support and nourishment from the international system.

Uganda

Uganda is another African country that has had to contend with values that are antithetical to governance and democracy. Starting with the Obote years, through the dreadful Amin era, to the return of Obote and the subsequent ascension to power of Yoweri Museveni, it is possible to contend that Uganda epitomizes some of the worst aspects of the African crisis (Rupesinghe, 1989).

The apparent reprieve that the country is going through is largely owed to the efforts of Yoweri Museveni, the former guerrilla leader who shot his way to power in January 1986 after a five-year guerrilla war. Since then, he has managed to distance Uganda from its horrendous past such that the erstwhile pearl of Africa is on its way to regaining its status, since the country is currently regarded as something of a model by the the international financial institutions (*This Day*, May 3, 1996).

Nevertheless, it is still possible to observe a fly in the Ugandan ointment. This relates to both the substance and dynamics of the constitution, which undergirds the country's democratic renewal. The assembly which was supposed to debate the new constitution was viewed as a mere clone, specifically structured to endorse Museveni's vision for Uganda. Among other things, this vision entails a unitarian system that is designed to be broad-based, non-partisan, and (ostensibly) to give all citizens access to all positions of leadership on the basis of individual merit. On the face of it, this non-party system has much to recommend it, since it is clearly designed to break with the familiar trappings of Uganda's past.

Museveni's critics think otherwise. They see the entire plan as a mere ploy designed to perpetuate Museveni's hold on power. At the global level, similar reactions can be discerned. The donor community has been very vocal in contending that Museveni's no-party system of government will not be accepted in the long run. In the short-run, however, it is clear that Uganda is regarded as something of a favorite in the international system. How long this status will last no one can foretell. It is safe to say it cannot last forever. Given Museveni's recent election as President for a five-year term, come the year 2001 he will have ruled the country for a total of 15 years and should he decide to go for a second term, it means that he would have been in power for 20 years!

In Uganda, as in all the countries here under scrutiny, and indeed throughout Africa, a fundamental shift can be observed in the external environment. Tin-pot generals, illiterate sergeants, and other shades of dictatorship are no longer routinely and automatically endorsed. Rather, they are being scrutinized and held up against values whose defining and definitive features are governance and democracy. A number of reasons have been advanced for this visible and palpable shift in the international system (Soremekun 1999). Perhaps the most obvious is the demise of the Soviet Union and the subsequent demise of super-power rivalry. Other factors include the changed role of the Catholic church, the contagious effect of the democratic momentum, as well as the changed focus of the international financial institutions. Individually and collectively, these factors have ensured a prime place for measuring governance in the relationships between the status-quo forces in the international system and African countries like Nigeria, Kenya, and Uganda. This relatively new situation has fostered a climate in which the democratic and governance credentials of African states are being scrutinized by Washington and its Western allies. This relatively novel situation continues to produce new alignments and re-alignments in the international system. In the process, the epistemological basis of international relations is also being questioned. In a previous era, international politics was largely perceived as an activity between one government and the other. But in a new global climate which seeks to promote governance, intergovernmental or state-state relations are being actively complemented (or even counterposed) by linkages between the state and the various social forces in Africa. In practical terms, the implication is that a typical Western ambassador, such as U. S. Ambassador to Nigeria Walter Carrington, does not only try to forge linkages with his host government; he also attempts to transcend this traditional preoccupation by forging links with the various organizations of civil society in his host country.

Predictably, such flexibility on the part of Western countries has brought them into sharp collision with a number of African dictators. For instance, the rather cozy relationship between the Kenyan government and previous American ambassadors in Nairobi has since been replaced by a relationship which alternates between iciness and hostility. Indeed, at one point in time, the tenor of the relationship between the American envoy and the Kenyan president was such that the former was described as the leader of the opposition in this East African country. Meanwhile, very much the same thing can be said for the relationship between the American ambassador in Nigeria and Sani Abacha, the head of the military junta. Indeed, it is arguable that Western nations currently come across as opposition members in the minds of contemporary Nigerian rulers. In any event, in their bid to articulate their relatively novel vision in Africa, global forces have taken more than a casual interest in the attempts to enshrine governance in various African countries. These days the electoral process is incomplete without the presence and participation of international observers.

From what we have explored thus far about Kenya and Nigeria, it is evident that status-quo forces in the international system were partly responsible for sustaining their different cultures of malgovernance. Very much the same thing can be said about Uganda, particularly in the post-colonial era. The British routinely endorsed every change of government in consonance with the ethos of diplomatic craft. The worst excesses of Idi Amin were condoned by London; even when Amnesty International in conjunction with the Ugandan Human Rights Committee detailed the atrocities of the regime and urged that Amin be accorded a leprous treatment, Britain continued to support this infamous regime. The most notorious form that this took was the famous "whisky run," with regular flights to Entebbe from Stansted Airfield in England. With (significantly) U. S. pilots, these twice-weekly flights were loaded with luxury goods and morale boosters from British suppliers. Very much the same pattern could be discerned during Obote's second coming. Till the end, and in spite of the atrocities committed under this regime, Britain stuck to its policy of giving succor and support (Rupesinghe 1989).

As we have already indicated, however, there are attempts by the status-quo forces in the international system to ensure that governance occupies a prime place in both the practical and thinking processes of the Ugandan and other African rulers. One way of achieving this is through the transformative process of democratization, a phenomenon that is in turn linked to the multiparty electoral processes. A standard and relevant item, particularly in the context of this topic, is the presence and participation of international observers. Indeed, but for the decisive role and influence of these external actors, it would have been unlikely for the Kenyan government to permit the formation of multiple parties and for the consequent elections that were held. Similarly, much the same thing can be said about the unfolding situation in Nigeria. A close look at the successive regimes of Ibrahim Babangida and Sani Abacha cannot help but reveal the significant influence of the global forces. In various ways, international players have played a large role in nudging these dictators along the routes of governance and democratization. However, as in the Kenyan situation, the rainbow is not yet in sight, if only because Kenyan and Nigerian leaders have succeeded thus far in thwarting the aspirations of both the international and domestic forces which seek to wean them away from the malevolent values of dictatorship and tyranny.[4]

Prospects for Governance in Kenya, Nigeria and Uganda

Despite positive gains, it is possible to contend with a measure of confidence that as decisive as the global system appears to be in its efforts to nurture governance in Nigeria, Kenya, and Uganda, the outlook is still very bleak. Nigeria's hegemonic influence in the sub-region, for example, has made it both a rallying point and a Mecca for dictatorship in West Africa.

A key point for skeptics is the governance credentials of the Western world itself. Although the ruling classes in the United States and Europe are certainly not in the same league with Moi, Babangida, and Abacha, still it must be appreciated that European and North American societies display evidence of increased xenophobia, racism, and rightist surges. Second, it must be noted that the conversion of the West to the project to instill the values of governance has largely been fueled by the dissolution of the Soviet Union. Should a new enemy appear on the horizon for the Western world, will they revert to the former policy of blind support for African dictators? Third, the Western world continues to employ double standards. Various shades of dictatorship continue to thrive in the Arab world, and in a relative sense they are not under any pressure to democratize or improve the quality of their governance. It is also necessary to appreciate that old friendships die hard. For instance, despite the several irregularities that were noted during the casting and counting of votes in Kenya, the various elements in the external environment of that country endorsed the flawed result and consequent reelection of Moi. Very much the same thing can be said about Uganda, where Museveni's governance credentials are not being held up to close scrutiny (Sachs 1996). A similar situation can be observed in Nigeria, where the response of sections of the international system is to vacillate between perfidy and ambiguity. Predictably, African dictators have caught on to the game. Many of them seem to realize and appreciate that, as long as they comply with formalistic rituals of multiparty elections, the Western countries will let them be. Andrew Purvis (1996), writing from a significant and telling locale like Nairobi, captures this phenomenon of motion without movement: "The end of the cold war and mounting pressures from Western donors for political reform as a condition for on-going aid led to a flurry of multiparty elections. But now reactions have set in, and entrenched leaders are using a variety of tactics from judicial maneuvering to fudged voter lists and voter intimidation to retain their position."

The implications of this unflattering scenario are significant, and external actors should take due note. The route to improved governance and democratization does not lie in elections alone; rather, sustained efforts should also be directed at empowering aspects of civil society with a view to ensuring the emergence and consolidation of commonly accepted prerequisites of effective governance. Such prerequisites include a thriving middle-class, high literacy levels, and an expanding economy. Indeed, if the Nigerian experience is anything to go by, governance is partly hampered by the fact that getting on the bandwagon of the state is virtually the only route to a decent existence. There are instances in which such subversive blandishments from the state have been effectively spurned by social forces and individuals who derive their succor and sustenance from external forces.

Closely related is the fledgling and impoverished condition of what passes for the opposition in many African countries. Their governance credentials are as suspect as the credentials of those holding office. Many who have managed to displace incumbents have not lived up to the minimum ideals of what they profess.[5] Their fragile status is further weakened by the fact that they are counterposing themselves against status-quo forces which continue to rely on the instrumentalities of the state. Thus, in the absence of sustained support from the external environment, the current drive for governance in Nigeria, Kenya, Uganda, and the African continent at large will continue to contend with daunting obstacles.

On balance, however, if explicit comparisons are to be made among the three countries under study, it is arguable that Kenya and Uganda have brighter chances of nurturing and consolidating governance in their respective polities. This perspective that can easily be qualified by the fact that, although the donors have done a lot to push Kenya along the path of democratic governance, there is a tendency for the country to regress into the patrimonial trap, since, according to Goran Hyden, "No society escapes its past." In Uganda there is the possibility that Museveni's rather long tenure may degenerate into the forms of dictatorship well-known in Uganda's past. It is partly this fusion of the past with the present that renders the Nigerian situation more problematic. Specifically, two factors largely absent in Kenya are at work here—oil and the military. In a sense, they are inter-related; oil revenues constitute one major reason why Nigeria remains under the jack-boot of the military. Any successful coup-maker comes into vast oil revenues, such that the highest rank in the Nigerian army is not (as many would suppose), General or Field Marshal; rather, it is the Presidency itself. The situation has been worsened by the fact that the military draws much of its political sustenance from what Ken Saro-Wiwa called the colluding elite, which until recent times could be located in not just its domestic arena but in the global environment.[6]

The bestiality of the Nigerian military regime is such that, in view of Abuja's hegemony in West Africa, its inclination to subvert the twin values of democracy and good governance clearly go beyond Nigeria's borders.[7] Oil has constrained the policy choices that are open to the Western world in terms of its efforts forts to bear down on the Nigerian Military government. Sanctions continue to dominate the tenor of the threats that are being directed at Nigeria, such that what distinctly comes across is a measure of buck-passing. Owens Wiwa, in a plaintive piece titled "The Agony of the Ogonis" gave voice to this situation when he noted how both the United States and the European Union continue to claim that they are waiting to take a cue from each other as to who will lead the sanctions drive, but neither moves. But for the execution of Ken Saro-Wiwa, the status-quo forces in the global system might still be wringing their hands and issuing diplomatic bromides and platitudes.

There is certainly very little cheer in this chapter. Still, there is a basis for hope. This qualified optimism derives from what can be called the unintended consequences of intended action. Although the military and the patrimonial essence continue to thwart governance in Nigeria and Kenya, respectively, there have emerged in recent times a number of human rights bodies and non-governmental organizations which, in their respective ways, are challenging the bestial and sadistic inclinations of the Kenyan and Nigerian state systems. They are auspiciously placed to do much more, if the global system can complement their efforts in imaginative and creative ways. Such creativity is evidenced in countries like Botswana and India. They share with both Kenya and Nigeria a British colonial heritage, yet the two countries are democratic polities and quality governance is clearly enshrined in them. The success of these two countries impels us to expand our search for explanations as regards the absence of good governance and democracy in Kenya, Nigeria, Uganda, and other parts of Africa. While we cannot totally disregard the neocolonial factor, Botswana and India clearly indicate that psychological and cultural variables go a long way to explain differing outcomes in places like Nigeria, Kenya, and Uganda on the one hand and Botswana and India on the other (Sisson 1994; Soremekun 1994).

In an oblique way, the evolving situation throws light both on the changing concept of sovereignty and the rather "flexible"' character of the relationship between Africa and the Western powers. In the previous era, and admittedly in probably more rhetorical terms at least, sovereignty was an absolute attribute of states. But such is the transcendental and seemingly unfettered reach of the Western powers that the sovereignty of the African states (in the Cold War era) is largely seen in qualified terms. These days, the tenor of the post-Cold War era is such that, it is in place for the ambassador of a Western country to voice concerns which relate to the fact that his host government is making a departure from the norms of good governance and democracy.[8] This is not to suggest that the donor countries have the upper-hand in their quest to enshrine these norms in African states. Rather, current events appear to reflect a more intriguing and rather interesting relationship between African countries and the donor community. In some cases (notably Kenya and Uganda) where aid is a major variable, the respective leaderships in these East African countries have (despite their being recipients of aid) succeeded in dictating both the pace and outcomes of the democratization processes. The specifics of the Ugandan situation are worth recalling. In spite of certain pointers which suggest that Uganda is traveling on an old road, the country has become virtually a showcase of the international financial institutions. It remains to be seen whether the country will not turn out to be a newer, less jaded model of dictatorship. However, what is evident in much of the foregoing is that, despite the deep convictions of the Western powers regarding the need for Africa to improve governance and join the global stream of democratization, the onus and responsibility for such an outcome lies largely on the various social forces of each country in Africa. It remains to be seen whether these countries can rise to meet the challenge.

Conclusions

Much of the literature on Africa's relations with the rest of the world has been cast in terms of an emphasis on the structural constraints inherent in the global economic system. This was, of course, particularly pronounced in the 1970s when the influence of dependency theory reached its peak, but it continued throughout much of the 1980s as analysts dealt with the implications of World Bank-imposed conditionalities. Because there was little recognition of African autonomy to act, there was a corresponding lack of interest in governance. How African countries governed themselves was not a high priority of scholarly analysts.

This has changed in the 1990s. With growing demands for political reform of the autocratic and corrupt mode of governance that developed in the first three decades of independence, there is also an enhanced recognition that Africans can make a difference to their own predicament. Even if the language is not assuming revolutionary changes, it is full of references to reform and improved governance, all implying human agency. From an African perspective, it is hard to see the irony in this situation: scholarly critics embraced structuralist explanations at a time—the Cold War—when the prospect for autonomous action existed because of the opportunity of playing one power bloc against the other; they are turning to agency-inspired models of explaining politics in Africa at a time when dependency on economic structures in the global economy has reached an all-time record depth. It is no surprise, therefore, that the position of African scholars on the role of externally driven democratization is ambivalent: some embrace it uncritically; others oppose it as another indication of the West's interest in recolonizing the continent. None of these more extreme positions, however, is likely to be very helpful—to scholarship and political practice alike. There is a need to identify a position that recognizes the inevitability of international forces in shaping Africa's destiny while at the same time assumes that within existing institutional and structural limits, African actors can make a difference to the political future of the continent.

Notes

1. The Mancihees were adherents of a third-century doctrine holding Satan to be co-eternal with God.
2. There are more than eighty foreign journalists normally resident in Nairobi, whence they travel to the rest of Africa.
3. Margaret Vogt made this point at the conference on "The Dilemma of Military Rule in Nigeria," Lagos, November 1995.
4. There is a lot to be said for the incumbency factor here. Moreoever, Western powers are ambiguous in their reactions to the current wave of democratization in Africa.

5. In Zambia, for instance, President Frederick Chiluba regressed into anti-democratic tactics against his predecessor, Dr. Kenneth Kaunda.
6. As noted above, in the Cold War era, both the Western powers and the Soviet Union actively supported dictators for cynical and self-interested reasons.
7. Nigeria has a near-imperial status which means that it is able to dictate the tenor and pace of events in the sub-region
8. At the independence celebrations of the United States on July 4, 1996, Walter Carrington, the then U. S. Ambassador to Nigeria, gave voice to these concerns.

Works Cited

Abuja Times. November 12, 1992.

Barkan, Joel D. "Can Established Democracies Nurture Democracy Abroad? Lessons from Africa." *Working Paper No. 10, MSU Working Papers on Political Reform in Africa.* Department of Political Science, Michigan State University, East Lansing, Michigan, 1995.

Brittan, Victoria. Contribution in Ngugi Wa Thiongo, ed. *Barrel of a Pen: Resistance to Repression in New Colonial Kenya.* London: New Beacon Books, 1988.

Chazan, Naomi. "Between Liberalism and Statism: African Political Cultures and Democracy," in Larry Diamond, ed. *Political Culture and Democracy in Developing Countries.* Boulder, Colo.: Lynne Rienner Publishers, 1994.

Hyden, Goran, and Michael Bratton. *Governance and Politics in Africa.* Boulder, Colo.: Lynne Rienner Publishers, 1992.

Ibrahim, Jibrin. "Obstacles To Democratization in Nigeria." Paper presented at the "Conference on Dilemmas of Democracy in Nigeria." African Studies Program, University of Wisconsin-Madison, Nov. 10–12, 1995.

Jemibewon, David. *A Combatant in Government.* Ibadan, Nigeria: Evans Publishers, 1978.

Lamb, David. *The Africans.* New York: Vintage Books, 1987.

Ngugi Wa Thiongo. *Barrel of a Pen: Resistance to Repression in Neo-Colonial Kenya,* London: New Beacon Books, 1988.

Ntalaja, Nzongola. "The Crisis in Zaire," in N. Ntalaja et al., eds. *Africa's Crisis.* London: Institute for African Alternatives, 1987.

Olowu, Dele, K. Soremekun, and A. Williams, eds. *Governance and Democratisation in West Africa.* Dakar. CODESRIA Press, 1999.

Olukotun, Ayo. Column in *Sunday Times* (Lagos), October 1, 1993.

Ouloguem, Yambo. *Bound To Violence.* African Writers Series. London: Heinemann Publications, 1973.

Purvis, Andrew. Contributing article in *Time Magazine,* April 1, 1996.

Rupesinghe, Kumar, ed. *Conflict Resolution in Uganda.* London: James Currey and Athens, Oh.: Ohio University Press, 1989.

Sachs, Jeffery. Contributing article in *The Economist.* June 29, 1996.

Sisson, Richard. "Culture and Democracy in India," in Larry Diamond, ed. *Political Culture and Democracy in Developing Countries.* Boulder, Colo.: Lynne Rienner Publishers, 1994.

Soremekun, Kayode. "The Media and Public Opinion as Complements of a Successful Ombudsman System," *International Ombudsman Journal* 2, 2 (1994).

Soremekun, Kayode. "International Dimensions of the Democratic Ferment in Nigeria," in Olowu et al. *Governance and Democratization in West Africa.* Dakar, CODESRIA Press, 1999.

This Day (Lagos). May 3, 1996.

Wiwa, Owens. "The Agony of The Ogonis," *Africa Notes.* Ithaca, N.Y.: Cornell University, 1996.

Wrong, Michaela, and Michael Holman. Contributing article in *This Day,* May 3, 1996.

11

Intellectuals and Governance

Adebayo Williams

Some Conceptual Clarifications

As a conceptual tool, democratization involves the study of the mechanism whereby the people are gradually empowered to have a direct say in how they are governed. Democratization, then, is the process by which political rights are extended to the populace by their rulers. The dynamics are often extremely complex and contradictory. The process by which subjects become full citizens in any society do not obey straight, geometrical progression; on the contrary, it is informed by complications, detours, and occasional setbacks. In some cases, democratization occurs as a result of peaceful negotiations between the rulers and the ruled. In other cases, it is the result of bloody conflicts and violent upheavals in the society. Invariably, these conflicts are a precondition for negotiation. The momentous convulsions which heralded democratization in modern Europe are a classic example.

In light of this, many scholars prefer to explain democratization as a process that takes place in waves (Huntington 1991). Others see it in terms of critical conjunctures, that is, through the instrumentality of historical actors seizing the initiative in propitious political circumstances (Diamond et al. 1988; Collier and David 1991). However, these views always tend to overlook the state and nature of the concrete structures on the ground, which may either serve as accelerating levers or structural clogs in the wheel of democratization. These include the level of literacy, the average income, the degree of urbanization, and the level of communications development, and, perhaps most important, the level of ideological homogenization of the middle class. As Hyden (1995) perceptively observes, "the possibility that political elites may have undemocratic ambitions gets overshadowed by the overarching concern to bring democracy to fruition."

Governance, on the other hand, implies the ability and competence of the government to use the structures of the state for the betterment and upliftment of the populace. The concept has three major components: systemic, political and administrative. In an influential definition, Hyden (1992) suggests that governance is "the conscious management of regime structures with a view to enhancing the legitimacy of the public realm."

Hyden has been criticized for enlisting the parameters of liberal democracy in defining governance (Bratton and Rothchild 1992). Indeed, some scholars have gone as far as dismissing the whole idea of governance as a strong arm of the economic imperialism of the Bretton Woods institutions. The idea, they contend, arose as part of the political conditionalities of the World Bank and the gradual negation of the independence of the Third World. According to Leftwich (1993): "the general but simplistic appeal for better governance as a condition for development is virtuous but naive . . . it has been politics and the state rather than governance or democracy that explain the differences between successful and unsuccessful developmental records."

The activities of the Bretton Woods institutions in Africa, especially their controversial structural adjustment programs, have elicited some severe but not entirely unjustified criticism. Yet whatever one's sympathies for this Third World intellectual nationalism and its reflex hostility to the imperatives of the World Bank, it is clear that this criticism obscures one fundamental fact.

There is an organic linkage between democratization and governance. However authoritarian and repressive it may be, a government which succeeds in putting down the shoots of good governance in terms of raising the level of literacy, expanding the middle classes, providing adequate medical care, and enhancing communication also creates an enabling environment for democratization irrespective of its own internal dynamics. The collapse of communism is a direct consequence of the social upheaval engendered by the profound contradiction between authoritarian rule and societal development. So is the stirring in South East Asia and the current face-off in Indonesia between the forces of repression and those of political liberalization.

The dialectic of democratization is often not without its great ironies. In Uganda, Museveni's disdain for liberal democracy is underwritten by a record of tolerable governance which has seen war-torn Uganda transformed within a relatively short period into an oasis of stability, relative prosperity, and accountability in a region marked by strife, poverty, and official corruption. In Ghana, where Jerry Rawlings achieved a similar feat, a grateful nation endorsed the extension of his tenure and provided his regime with legitimacy even though the election could not stand the rigors and full scrutiny of liberal democracy. This was also the case in South Korea, Singapore, and, at least for some time, Suharto's Indonesia. Yet the fundamental lesson to be learned from the Asian tigers' experience is that, as the socio-economic structures put in place by the rulers assume an independent existence of their own, the rulers'—or their parties'—plans for millennial rule are ultimately circumscribed by resurgent forces of democratization.

The role of intellectual forces in these struggles is quite critical. In many Western and non-Western societies the intellectual class or the intelligentsia constitutes a crucial if not the most crucial segment of civil society. It must be stressed that the role of the intelligentsia is not limited to literate societies. In his study of the Ujaama phenomenon in Tanzania, Hyden (1980) drew attention to an as yet "uncaptured" African peasantry that is also intellectually sophisticated. Despite the objection of Bayart (1993: 254) to what he called "a suggestive but nonetheless unfortunate expression," Hyden's assertion is not without its solid merits.

As a continent, Africa is teeming with traditional philosophers, sages, and savants with great powers of articulation and conceptualization. The importance of indigenous philosophical systems to traditional African societies cannot be lightly dismissed. They often undergird political conduct and the struggle for supremacy. For example, among the Yoruba of Nigeria the concept of Omoluwabi provides a gentlemanly code of conduct for political struggle and social transactions. It is not entirely coincidental that many members of the first generation of African political leaders preferred to be known by appellations which validated their roles as teachers and repositories of wisdom. Chief among these were Mzee Jomo Kenyatta of Kenya, Mwalimu Julius Nyerere of Tanzania, Mallam Aminu Kano, and Mazi Mbonu Ojike.

Yet despite their importance within the structure of civil society, intellectuals also serve as functionaries and crucial allies of the state in its hegemonic projects. This introduces a dual or even contradictory perspective to the role of the intellectual. The dominant classes in society do not maintain their position solely or primarily through the use of force or other modes of coercion, but often through persuasion and more insidious forms of intellectual propaganda. In this war of ideas and conflicting worldviews, the state deploys its intellectuals to establish its ideological outlook as all-embracing and universal; and to shape its interests and the needs of subordinate groups in the polity. This is what Gramsci has described as the battle for hegemony.

For every Socrates who was forced to drink the hemlock for being a "corrupter of youths," there was a Plato who was an instructor of princes. For every Thomas More "the turbulent priest" who was murdered for his principled opposition to the king, there was a Machiavelli who would go to any length to extend his intellectual retainership at the court. Despite this fine balance, it is the ease with which intellectuals succumb to the blandishments of powerful states, the haste by which they capitulate to ascendant factions of the ruling class which are often the subject of controversy and bitter polemics. This is what Said

(1983), echoing Julien Benda, has called "the treason of the intellectual."

A way out of the emotive dispute is to adopt Gramsci's seminal distinction between traditional intellectuals, who support the status quo out of political and ideological necessity, and organic intellectuals, who are both the products of a new historical tendency and the producers of its ideological needs. The aim of this paper is first to elaborate the intellectual milieu in which the struggle for democratization and good governance takes place in Nigeria while informing the study with the cases of Kenya and Tanzania; second, to demonstrate that while many members of the African intelligentsia have acted as intellectual enforcers of an authoritarian status quo, others have acted as catalysts for democratization and good governance; and third, to analyze the effects of subsequent events on the institutions and systems which engaged the intellectuals in the first instance.

Nationalism and its Intellectual Dimensions

The first movements against colonial rule in Africa were peasant-based and predominantly rural in orientation. They were led by traditional chieftains who resented the encroachment of the colonial lords on their fiefdoms and the erosion of their influence and authority. These traditional rulers were mainly interested in the restoration of their authority and the revalidation of precolonial ethnic boundaries. They did not and could not come to terms with the colonial nation-state, a strange and perplexing idea which welded together linguistically disharmonious and culturally incompatible nationalities under the rubric of one nation. Their resistance to colonial rule was therefore ethnic in orientation. In a sense, their bewilderment was justified. The colonial partitioning of the continent was an *ad hoc* and arbitrary affair. The old Kongo kingdom, for example, suddenly found itself dismembered into three different countries—Zaire, Congo and Angola. As if this was not enough, each country now came under a different colonial power—Belgium, France, and Portugal, respectively. Very few ethnic groups escaped this process of dispersal. It was therefore perfectly understandable that the scions of the pre-colonial empires hankered after the restoration of what they must have considered the old (but far more benign and sensible) order.

The second wave of movements of resistance and revolt against colonialism was an urban-based and, unlike the first, predominantly elitist wave of movements. These movements were led by educated town dwellers who were in most cases products of colonial and missionary education. Unlike the first movements, the second wave was forced to come to terms with the colonial nation-state. Whether the leaders of the anti-colonial movements liked it or not, the new nation was a compelling reality, and there was nothing they could do about it. These leaders were therefore forced by the political and historical circumstances to transcend their ethnic roots in order to forge a pan-ethnic identity. Unlike the cultural Africanism already glimpsed in the works of Casely-Hayford and Sekyi Kobina of the (then) Gold Coast, and the eighteenth-century Olaudah Equaino (which was principally devoted to the cultural emancipation of the black man), this was the first stirring of political nationalism in Africa.

These new anti-colonial movements gave the first indication of the arrival of a new elite class in Africa. Their formation owed little or nothing to the dynamics of the pre-colonial traditional African societies. They were a direct consequence of colonial incursion. In all but one or two cases, such as Sekou Toure of Guinea and Ahmadu Bello of Nigeria, the leaders of these independence movements had no blood relationship with the old kingdoms. They sought alliance with the traditional rulers only to the extent that they needed them to maintain a cultural linkage with the past in order to be able to confront the harsh realities of colonial rule. In any case, by that point in time many of the traditional authorities had sought compromise and accommodation with the colonial rulers and had effectively become liabilities to the struggle.

The struggle against colonialism required the articulation of alternative visions, the formulations of rival motifs, tropes and myths, the conceptualization of a more rational and humane world-view, which could only come from thorough intellectual analysis. This was the kernel of nationalism in Africa. Only an intellectualized elite could have pulled it off. In light of this, it should not be surprising that the heroes of African independence and the final struggle against colonialism were mostly intellectual figures and cultural producers in their own right. A cursory glance will suffice: Senghor, Toure, Nkrumah, Cabral, Neto, Mugabe, Kenyatta, Nyerere, Azikwe, and Awolowo were all educated and erudite men. Some of these leaders, notably Kenyatta, Cabral, Mugabe, and Neto, combined their intellectual sophistication with outstanding military abilities.

Such was the staking-out of territorial ambitions and the crucial need to delimit the spheres of influence and authority that anti-colonial African leaders felt compelled to devise alternative blueprints for the political and economic transformation of their respective countries and peoples. In tracts, pamphlets, polemics, essays, autobiographies, political pastorals, and the odd fictional output, African leaders spelled out their plans of action and their vision for the continent.

This rich drama of ideas has been succinctly captured by Mazrui (1995) and he bears quoting at some length:

> Tapping on modernized versions of the sage tradition a number of founding fathers of independent Africa tried to become philosopher-kings. They attempted to philosophize about man and society and about Africa's place in the global scheme of things. Some leaders attempted to establish whole new ideologies. Julius K. Nyerere of Tanzania inaugurated Ujaama, intended to be indigenously authentic African socialism. Kenneth D. Kaunda initiated what was called humanism. Gamal Abdel Nasser had previously written The Philosophy of Revolution and subsequently attempted the implementation of "Arab socialism". The modernized version of the Western tradition also popularized the use of honorary doctorates as regular titles of Heads of State.

This was the intellectual context in which the struggle for independence took place in Africa. It was also to affect the complexion of the post-colonial state. Nationalism became the organizing principle of the newly independent nations. Since such nationalism was forged in the crucible of the continental struggle against colonialism, it quickly became, within the context of the new nation, a nebulous ideal or a vague anti-imperialism. There are two sides to this development. On the one hand, it allowed African nations to avoid the uglier and nastier side-effects of nationalism that had proved very costly to Europe and parts of Asia in the nineteenth and twentieth centuries. On the other hand, it allowed emergent African leaders to lay sole proprietary claims to the new nations. It is quite revealing that only one or two post-independence leaders of Africa were possessed of a supra-national pan-African outlook: Nkrumah of Ghana and Nasser of Egypt were alone among leaders who dreamed of a Pan-African state. African leaders developed a cautious and healthy respect for the national borders they have inherited from colonial rule. It is not surprising that the first principle governing the OAU charter is the recognition and respect for individual countries' frontiers and right to self-determination.

There are interesting developments from this. While there are occasional border disputes and the odd armed skirmish, inter-state wars are virtually non-existent in Africa. Yet the post-colonial state in Africa is marked by a series of bloody intra-state conflicts, such as those in the Sudan, Zaire, Nigeria, Ethiopia, Angola, Mozambique, Liberia, Sierra-Leone, and Somalia. The reason for most of these wars is not difficult to discern. As the new rulers seized their countries and cornered their resources, they made it clear that they would brook no opposition to their rule. Since interference from other African states was already a taboo, the new rulers were able to pull curtains of silence around their countries, within which rulers were accountable to no one but themselves, and corruption and mal-governance quickly blossomed. The dispossessed opposition whose leading members also contributed to the struggle for independence, found it had no alternative than to throw down an armed challenge to the state.

The Intellectual Context of Post-Independence Governance

The strategies for domination and the containment or liquidation of oppositional forces by the new African ruling elites assumed different forms and took different dimensions in many countries. Emergent intellectual formations played a crucial role in the formulation and execution of these strategies. In post-independence Nigeria, for example, while the country remained a nominal democracy, the energies of the Balewa-led Federal government were devoted to schemes aimed at staying in power at all costs. These ranged from deliberate subversion of the Federal constitution, and outlandish rigging of elections to the instigated take-over of the government of Western Nigeria, which was ultimately to prove fatal to it.

In Ghana, despite Nkrumah's intellectual pretensions and pan-African outlook, opposition to his regime was brutally suppressed. By the time he was overthrown, Ghana had become a virtual one-party state with notable members of the opposition languishing in dungeons. Ali Mazrui (1995) thus had reason describe the former Ghanaian leader as a "Leninist Czar." In Francophone West Africa, while most of the countries became multi-party democracies on paper, they were in reality one-party states. Attempts were made by many of the rulers to co-opt members of the intelligentsia to become part of the shared destiny of the ruling class. Arguably the most successful of these was Houphuet-Boigny of Ivory Coast. Bayart's (1993:118) comments on his manoeuvres are quite illuminating: "One of Houphouet-Boigny's main worries seems to have been how to maintain his guardianship of the intellectuals in order to avoid the development of a 'learned bourgeoisie' and to prevent them from questioning the pre-eminence of his faction, which had been gained since the Second World War."

The situation in East Africa was remarkably different and varied from country to country. Despite the fact that up until independence Makerere University had been the intellectual hub of the sub-continent and was to provide much of its bureaucratic and intellectual manpower, each leader appeared to have forged a distinct political identity for his country and then looked for intellectual resources to justify this. Thus in Kenya Kenyatta, and then Moi, virtually outlawed the opposition and turned the country into a one-party state. In Uganda, Milton Obote did the same thing and turned the country into a unitary state after the federalist experimentation with the Buganda kingdom broke down. The intellectual justification for this personalized autocracy was often that multiparty democracy was a Western luxury, an indulgence which in Africa promotes ethnic divisions and centrifugal forces which might prove fatal to a fragile multi-ethnic nation. It must be admitted that the philosophy behind the one-party state is not without its eloquent defenders in Africa.

The situation in Tanzania was, however, remarkably different. Julius Nyerere adopted as a political ideology an African variant of socialism known as Ujaama, which was based on African primordialism and rigid, centralized economic planning. As it has been noted by several acute observers (Randrianja, 1996:25), this was merely another version of a one-party state. Dictatorship—whether of the proletariat or the peasantry—is still dictatorship. However, notable African intellectuals came to Nyerere's defense. Even conservative intellectuals who could not warm up to the idea of socialism professed admiration for the patriotism and unique integrity which Nyerere brought to bear on the project.

Despite the fact that Nyerere's continental defenders were many, his most sturdy intellectual support came from within Tanzania itself. Many Tanzanian intellectuals fell under the spell of Nyerere's charisma and selfless dedication. The University at Dar es Salaam, particularly the Faculty of Arts and Social Sciences, became the laboratory for Ujaama socialism. The intellectual ferment grew notable scholars such as Babu and Nabudere. The debate between proponents of African Socialism or Socialism in Africa echoed throughout the continent.

If the intellectual opposition to Nyerere was negligible, this was not the same thing in other East African countries and Nigeria.

In Nigeria shortly after independence a steadfast and sizable intellectual opposition emerged. It was crystalline around the figure of Chief Obafemi Awolowo, the opposition leader. As premier of the Western Region, Chief Awolowo had been able to attract to himself a formidable group of intellectuals who had helped to formulate the policies of the Action Group government. After independence, this group came together again with new recruits to fashion a coherent Social Democratic blueprint for the Action Group. According to one notable insider (Ige 1995:201-202), this was to serve as a political and philosophical challenge to what was then considered the conservative and uninspiring leadership of the National People's Congress-led Federal government.

After Chief Awolowo was imprisoned, the core of this intellectual coterie remained. Some of its notable members had to resign their university appointment as a result of what was perceived as political persecution. Members of its radical wing forged an alliance with workers, farmers, artisans, and sundry groups which were to make the Western region totally ungovernable until the military take-over in January 1966 (Ige 1995; Soyinka 1994). In several other countries, notably Cameroon, Senegal, Mali, Burkina Faso, and Uganda, there was also intellectual revolt against the dominant parties.

In Kenya the intellectual opposition to the dominant party blossomed at the university in Nairobi. In several respects this opposition was to take on a socialist or, in fact, Marxist hue. The opposition charged the ruling party with betrayal and accused its leading members of being unworthy heirs of the Mau-Mau tradition. The situation was hardly helped by the mysterious murders of some leading politicians, notably Tom Mboya, a flamboyant former trade unionist, and Joseph Karuiki an outspoken parliamentarian. The role of African writers as the vanguard of this intellectual resistance to authoritarian rule cannot be discounted. I have dealt with this at length elsewhere (Williams 1995, 1996). Suffice it to say that, in Kenya, Ngugi, Micere Mugo, and others became thorns in the flesh of the authorities. In Uganda Okot P'Bitek became a literary one-man assault squad. In Nigeria, Soyinka, Achebe, and Okigbo lambasted and lampooned the authorities for their inefficiency and corruption.

The inefficiency, corruption, barely disguised graft, and auto-cratic temperament of the majority of post-independence African governments made them sitting ducks for the critical arrows of the intellectual opposition. Their dire failings quickly stripped them of whatever legitimacy or authority they had at the time of inde-pendence. The illiberal political atmosphere made them vulnera-ble to armed challenge or bloody military intervention or both. But since military rule merely revalidated the evils of corruption and authoritarianism, the fundamental crisis remained—and, in some cases, deepened. The few countries that managed to avoid military intervention or armed challenge simply stalled, caught as they were in an economic and political morass.

This was the situation when the second wave of liberation hit Africa at the end of the eighties. African countries found themselves at a political and economic dead-end. If the struggle for independ-ence was all about liberating Africa from external colonialism, the post-independence struggle was about liberating most African countries from the internal colonialism that had replaced it. With whispers about failed states in the air, it became increasingly clear to African rulers that there was now no alternative to good gover-nance and the resumption of the process of genuine democratization which had been put on hold shortly after independence.

The Intellectual Context of the Current Struggle for Democratization

The renewed clamor for democratization witnessed by most African countries at the beginning of the nineties benefited immensely from two conjunctures, both internal and external. By the mid-eighties most African countries faced an economic implo-sion as a result of years of waste, mis-management, corruption, and the crushing debt burden consequent upon these. A few countries, like Cote d'Ivoire, witnessed declining revenues as a result of declining demand for cacao produce. In Tanzania, decades of rigid, centralized planning ended in heroic failure and national misery.

In their helpless and prostrate condition, African countries had no alternative other than to turn to the Bretton Woods institutions. The IMF and the World Bank naturally saw this as a golden opportunity to impose their version of economic and political discipline on errant African countries. As a precondition for help, African countries were forced to accept certain political and economic conditionalities. These included structural adjustment, massive devaluation, the trimming of bloated bureaucracies, accountability and transparency in governance, and political liberalization. As the harsh side-effects of these measures began to bite harder, fuelling discontent and urban misery, pro-democracy groups sprouted all over Africa calling for the heads of the corrupt and tyrannical regimes which were responsible for the crisis in the first instance. The stage was set for a violent confrontation between the corrupt and decadent authoritarian regimes and resurgent forces of democracy in Africa.

The pro-democracy forces in Africa were aided by a propitious external conjuncture: the collapse of the Soviet Union and communist regimes the world over. The global cry was for freedom and democracy, and not even the most hardened of autocrats was willing to be caught on the wrong side of history. With his twin policy of glasnost and perestroika, Gorbachev set in motion an irreversible process. As the Soviet glacier cracked, strange monsters emerged from the icy waters to devour the communist giant. With the collapse of the Soviet Union, corrupt and autocratic African leaders found that they no longer had any communist card to play against the West. The threat "to go red" was often enough to stop Western powers from moving against them. By the same token, America saw no need to support "strong men" to act as a bulwark against communism. From then on the Mobutus, Bandas, and Mois were on their own. America emerged as the undisputed superpower and global law-giver and felt no compulsion about imposing its political and economic doctrine of multi-party politics and economic liberalization on the world. As Hobsbawm (1994:9) has noted, it was only in this sense that Fukuyama's (1992) thesis about the "end of the world" and other such triumphalism could be said to have a case.

In Francophone Africa, with the quiet (but far from altruistic) nudging of France, most of the leaders, particularly the long-serving ones, acceded to popular demands for Sovereign National Conferences. It was a device to get them out of power with minimum chaos and bloodshed. Many such conferences met with varying degrees of success, but that is beyond the scope of this paper. Suffice it to say that the intellectual resources that went into these democratic revolts against the entrenched status quo in the former French territories were considerable. Virtually all of them were led by notable intellectual figures with an axe to grind. Some had suffered imprisonment and torture under the ancien regime. A few had been forced to spend considerable time in exile. One or two had survived assassination attempts. However, a number of them were also former allies who had rebelled against their former masters.

In Uganda, after the harsh and repressive regimes of Obote and Amin, power became completely privatized. Armed challenges to the government proliferated and the state lost its fundamental raison d'etre: the capacity to organize superior violence. After his conquest of the nation in 1986, Yoweri Museveni refused to have anything to do with liberal democracy claiming that it was an open invitation to tribalism religion or regionalism.. A man of considerable intellectual gifts himself, Museveni has gathered a hard core of intellectual loyalists who have provided rationalization for his unique political experiment. Among his innovations are elections on a non-party basis, which have earned him cautious praise from sympathetic observers, but which have been dismissed by one of his critics as nothing but "autocratic rule enforced by the military" (Omara-Otunnu 1992:463).

Kenya, on the other hand, is a classic illustration of old habits dying hard. After finally succumbing to a combination of internal agitation and persistent Western pressure for political liberalization, President Daniel arap Moi reintroduced multi-party democracy in 1992. He was, however, able skillfully to exploit the old ethnic divisions in the country and the frailties of a badly divided opposition to hang on to power after a bitterly contested and controversial election. The political tensions have hardly disappeared from the surface. The opposition groups, FORD and its splinter association, are led by Kenyan intellectuals who have survived years of harsh intimidation. In the case of the Safina Party, it is led by the scion of an illustrious white settler family. President Moi's public response to Safina has been to dismiss Richard Leakey, one of its leaders, as a "foreigner," a categorization which could hardly help race relations in an already racially and ethnically polarized society. The fact that President Moi has been forced into this kind of self-delegitimizing offensive remains one of the quiet gains of the current struggle for democratization in Kenya.

Despite the collapse of the socialist experiment, neighboring Tanzania has been able to make a cautious and guarded transition to multi-party democracy without a major incident. There are many factors responsible for this. Socialism might have brought economic decline, but a strong sense of national identity was forged in the crucible of shared privation and equality of want. A strong cultural bonding was fostered by an outstanding visionary and selfless leadership. The personal authority and moral prestige of Julius Nyerere helped to smooth over the rough edges of the transition. By voluntarily relinquishing power, Nyerere led by example. Tanzania was also lucky that, unlike the situation in Kenya, there are no dominant ethnic groups to upset the delicate ethnic and racial equation. The majority of Tanzanian intellectuals who had rallied round Nyerere did not find it difficult to make the transition from socialism to multi-party democracy. There are, however, a few who persist in the belief that the introduction of multi-party democracy is a shameful capitulation to donor blackmail (Martin 1993).

Of all the countries under study, it is perhaps Nigeria which presents the most interesting spectacle of democratic recession or remilitarization by subterfuge. This unique phenomenon, in which a nascent military state promises democratization only to promptly subvert it as part of its internal logic or organizing principle, has also been described as "permanent transition" (Diamond et al. 1997). It is a development worthy of serious study in all its ramifications, if only for the light it throws on the democratic project in Sub-Saharan Africa.

Nigeria became independent on the first of October 1960. It succumbed to its first military putsch on the 15th of January 1966. In Nigeria's almost forty years of existence, the military has ruled for three-quarters of the whole period. In the light of this, many cynical commentators have concluded that in Nigeria it is civilian rule that is an aberration rather than military dictatorship. Thus, rather than military interlude the actual reality is that of civilian interregnum.

Yet no military ruler has come to power in Nigeria without at some point unfolding a program for a return to democratic rule—Gowon in 1971, Mohammed in 1976, Babangida in 1986, and Abacha in 1994. The only exception was General Buhari, whose regime initially enjoyed widespread popular legitimacy as a result of the corruption and crass inefficiency of the civilian regime it ousted. Almost without exception, these programs for democratization were either deliberately aborted, deliberately stalled, or their products swiftly terminated by another military uprising. In short, since 1966, Nigeria has been in a democratic "transit camp." The most remarkable of these unique power games—the one that raised most hope, only for it to be cruelly dashed at the last post—was the transition program of General Ibrahim Babangida. Its failure also provided rich insights into the behavioral patterns of the intelligentsia in a neo-patrimonial postcolonial state.

General Babangida seized power in a palace coup at the end of July 1985. Before then, there were reports of sharp and bitter disagreements among leading members of the military government led by General Buhari. After some apparently stage-managed public debates, the new government rejected an IMF loan but accepted its conditionalities. A structural adjustment program was thus imposed on the country in July 1986. Before then, General Babangida also unfolded a Transition Program initially designed to last until 1990. If the economic measures were a response to the perilous state of the Nigerian economy, the promise of political liberalization made without popular pressure was an elaborate bluff dictated by Babangida's celebrated political savvy and survivalist instincts. When the global wave of political liberalization hit Africa almost three years later, regime advisers would openly crow that it had already been anticipated by Nigeria's military authorities. With canny prescience the General had been able to pre-empt unfavorable international attention to his self-perpetuating maneuvers.

Nigerian intellectuals played a major role in formulating and executing the policies that underpinned Babangida's grand political deception. Never in the history of the country had members of the intelligentsia been deployed on such a massive scale. It was a total power project. Right from the inception of his administration, President Babangida left no one in doubt that intellectuals would be quite crucial to his regime. His cabinet was stuffed with the best and the brightest of Nigeria's intellectual class. It was arguably the most intellectually intimidating team ever put together by a Nigerian leader. As if this were not enough, the team was augmented by a kitchen cabinet known as the Presidential Advisory Committee, which was headed by a noted intellectual: the committee was chaired by Professor Ojetunji Aboyade, an internationally renowned economist and former Vice-Chancellor.

In 1986 President Babangida inaugurated a Political Bureau with the sole aim of initiating what he himself described as the "collective search for a new political order." The membership read like a Who's Who of Nigeria's leading political scientists. Many of them were university teachers who had made a name for themselves as ardent defenders of civil societies. One or two had made famous interventions against the iniquities of military dictatorship. By this time also a hazy pattern began to emerge: a steady hemorrhage of the university system as a result of General Babangida's relentless head-hunting.

By the middle of 1990, particularly after an abortive military uprising, discerning Nigerians, especially members of the intelligentsia who remained uncoopted, began to alert the nation to the possibility of a self-perpetuating design. A new phrase crept into Nigeria's political lexicon: "hidden agenda." In an interview, Yesufu Bala Usman, the noted Marxist political scientist, alleged that General Ibrahim Babangida had plans to be succeeded by Alhaji Ibrahim Babangida. As a response to the whispering campaign, General Babangida publicly stated that although he did not know who would succeed him, he already knew who would not. It was clear at that point that even if the general did not wish to succeed himself he definitely intended to play gate-keeper with the transition.

Seeds of doubt germinated fast. An engineered minority report which extended the tenure of the government till 1992 was given pride of place over the majority recommendation of 1990. According to a member of the Political Bureau its report was "manipulated, twisted out of context for the subversion of the process of the transfer of power to elected civilians" (Oyediran 1995:10). At this point, a process of ideological differentiation or "carpet-crossing" began among the members. The normally conservative sided with the government. After being physically prevented from submitting a minority report, a radical member, Dr. Edwin Madunagu, promptly returned to the barricades. A few who had been known for a robust identification with civil society started singing a different tune. They had in effect ceased being free-floating members of the intelligentsia and had become functionaries and ideologues of a military state.

The reasons for this shift are numerous. By the time General Babangida was imposing a two-party system on the country, he had also created several organs of the state which were filled with his intellectual loyalists. Among the various institutions so created were: The Constitution Review Committee, The Constituent Assembly, The National Electoral Commission, The Centre for Democratic Studies, The National Council for Inter-Governmental Relations, The Centre for Peace, The Movement for Mass Mobilization for Self-Reliance and Economic Recovery (MAMSER), etc. It was a moveable political feast. It must be remembered that by the time General Babangida took over power, the material circumstances of most university lecturers had become quite strained. Such was the level of pauperization that during the regime of General Buhari, university teachers became permanent fixtures in queues for essential commodities. General Babangida improved the material circumstances of virtually all of his intellectual advisers. Intellectuals had become not just functionaries, but stakeholders in the state.

The enormous financial resources needed to maintain this bloated and unwieldy bureaucratic Leviathan, the massive bribery of the military, and influential members of the political class who were encouraged either to turn a blind eye to the political chicanery or to become willing pawns on the gigantic chess board, led to the swift erosion of the gains of the country's structural adjustment program. The resulting hardship and harsh economic climate turned many members of the emasculated middle-class against the government. The ensuing intellectual revolt against the Babangida government was led from the university.

The university teachers' organization (ASUU) became the only national body successfully to resist General Babangida's attempts to destabilize it both from within and from without. For its pains, it was proscribed and then de-proscribed on two occasions. Some of its leaders were compulsorily retired from the university. At the onset of the siege, the then Minister of Education accused some university teachers of "teaching what they were not paid to teach." This ominous indictment was widely seen as a prelude to a massive ideological purge of the universities, which failed to materialize due to the steadfastness of the lecturers' association. ASUU's political independence, the refusal of its leadership to consider monetary inducements, its sharp and well-informed commentaries on the true state of the nation, and its constant dismissal of the Babangida Transition Program as an epic swindle cost the government a substantial part of its legitimacy.

Disaffected intellectuals were also at the vanguard of the revolt against the Babangida government in the larger civil society. Some of them had found their way into the press as pioneers of a new phenomenon—intellectual journalism. This was both a direct and indirect response to the gradual destruction of the facilities of scholarship in the Nigerian universities. It was a development which led General Babangida on one occasion to wonder aloud with unintended irony as to why university teachers should abandon their lecture theaters for the arena of public discourse. Many of the intellectuals also found their way into the nascent human rights organizations that had sprouted in the country in response to widespread violation of human rights by the government.

When all these forces of opposition finally were able to link up in the aftermath of the annulment of the June 12, 1993 presidential election, this was to prove fatal to General Babangida's ambition to remain in power. Yet, till the bitter end, his intellectual loyalists continued to defend his Transition Program even when it was obvious to the most casual observer that the whole thing had collapsed. Against all the weight of concrete evidence, the most ardent of them declared: "For once in the history of Nigeria, power has been authentically democratized and the experience now entrenched can hardly ever be reversed" (Olagunju et al, 1993). In the same year that this was published, General Abacha struck in a military coup that swept off all the remaining vestiges of the "authentic democratization." It was a compelling intellectual disaster.

Quite unexpectedly, Abacha's rule came to an end in 1998 as a result of his sudden death. His successor, General Abubakar, realizing the costs to himself and other professional soldiers of trying to continue ruling the country, initiated a transition process, which resulted in a series of elections that brought civilian rule back in early 1999. It is too early to say what the Third Republic may have in stock for Nigerians, but it is an encouragement that a former military head of state, Olusegun Obasanjo—who had paved the way for the Second Republic in 1978-79—has returned as a civilian ruler. The challenges that he and his government face are enormous, given the damage to the country's economy and system of governance that has been caused by successive governments, both military and civilian in the past. It becomes especially important for Nigeria's intellectuals to take an active interest in how the new system of governance can be sustained and improved upon.

Conclusion: Towards a Paradigmatic Shift

Several broad conclusions can be drawn from this paper. First, intellectuals in Africa do not have a fixed and uniform behavior as far as governance and democratization are concerned. Contrary to what could be expected from members of a profession whose fundamental tenets should make it a natural ally of democratic rule, many intellectuals often harbor undemocratic views and are easily enlisted for autocratic projects. While many oppose autocratic rule, especially military dictatorship, many intellectuals also end up as enthusiastic supporters of authoritarian rule, depending on the circumstances. These circumstances are determined by a constellation of forces—ideological, material, religious, ethnic, and psychological. Given this, it is impossible to talk of an intellectual group in Africa with a unified worldview.

Second, the kind of cohesion and sense of duty and mission that allow intellectuals in advanced countries to bury ideological, personal, and political differences and come together to take concerted action, especially when their broader interests are threatened, has not appeared in Africa. The severe snub which Oxford University handed to Margaret Thatcher by denying her an honorary degree over what was considered to be the destructive and philistine nature of her educational policies is inconceivable in Africa. Indeed, the contrary is often the case. While the destruction of the university system continued apace, Nigerian universities were falling over themselves to honor General Babangida, his wife, and top members of his administration. In such circumstances, it is impossible to talk about an intellectual class or even a caste of learned people. It can be argued that whoever pays the piper dictates the tune, but if that were an historical truth, there would never have been a proletariat or workers' class.

Third, there are certain intellectual-led organizations that are peculiarly suited to combat military dictatorship and authoritarian rule. As the example from Nigeria has shown, while not being models of democratic arrangement themselves, and being susceptible to the cancerworms of ethnicity, corruption, and intolerance, the association of university teachers and the various human rights organizations fought the military dictatorship to a standstill. Yet when these organizations, particularly the human rights organizations, attempted to transform themselves from pressure groups to mainstream political organs, they quickly unravelled. Thus, while not actually expanding democratic space, these organizations, by contracting the space available to authoritarian projects played a valuable role in democratization.

There are, however, certain inferences to be drawn from these broad conclusions, and they should serve as a lesson to intellectuals who serve authoritarian regimes. In Nigeria, the Babangida and Abacha years engendered an almost total destruction of the university system. In the end, there was unprecedented infrastructural deterioration and severe collapse of morale and self-respect which led to a massive internal and external braindrain. What began as a trickle at the end of the eighties suddenly became a bitter flood in the nineties. Nigerian intellectuals fled to the sanctuaries of learning in the west.

But this is not the end of the story. It also tells us that the programmed self-destruction of both the state and its intellectual functionaries is a function of weak states and even weaker civil societies. As many commentators have noted, the epidemic political crisis of Africa stems from the weakness of both the state and civil society, irrespective of ideological coloration. In advanced nations, civil societies exist both as a check and as an ideological bulwark for the state. Indeed, in these countries, the state carries out its insidious penetration of the societies through certain mediating institutions of civil society, or what Althusser (1972) has described as the ideological apparatuses of the state—e.g. the church, the family, the educational system, and other institutions of socialization. The collaboration is neither mutually destructive nor predatory; it is quite the contrary, mutually reinforcing.

Authoritarian malgovernance destroys the university system and the basis of intellectual self-respect. In the process, civil society suffers a serious setback. This was not restricted to Nigeria; it was also the case in Ghana, Liberia, Uganda, and (to a lesser extent) Kenya. It was only when there was tolerable governance and a degree of political liberalization in both Ghana and Uganda that the university system in the two countries began to flourish in the ruins. Good governance and democratization provide needed soil, sunlight, and rain for a healthy and thriving university system.

The concluding point of this volume, therefore, is that a first step towards reversing the downward trend in many African countries must be to provide a political environment in which personal freedoms are respected and the accountability of leaders can be upheld. The actual forms of political democracy may be secondary in African at this juncture. Elections have not proved to be the "founding events" of democracy that African intellectuals and others so widely expected in the early nineties. Africa must find a way forward of its own. In this regard, intellectuals have not been very helpful so far. Not only have they sided with corrupt political leaders for opportunistic reasons, but they have also allowed their own home institutions—the universities around the continent—to deteriorate to a point where the social reproduction of a professional class of intellectuals—at least for the foreseeable future—is at risk.

Works Cited

Althusser, Louis. *Lenin and Philosophy and Other Essays.* New York: Monthly Review Press, 1972

Bayart, Jean-Francois. *The State in Africa: Politics of the Belly.* London: Longman, 1993.

Bratton M., and D. Rothchild. "The Institutional Bases of Governance in Africa," in G. Hyden and M. Bratton, eds. *Governance and Politics in Africa.* Boulder, Colo.: Lynne Rienner Publishers, 1992.

Collier, Ruth B., and David. *Shaping the Political Arena.* Princeton, N.J.: Princeton University Press, 1991.

Diamond, L., J. Linz, and S. M. Lipset, eds. *Democracy in Developing Countries: Africa.* Boulder, Colo.: Lynne Rienner Publishers, 1988.

Diamond, L., A. Kirk-Greene, and O. Oyediran, eds. *Transition Without End: Nigerian Politics and Civil Society under Babangida.* Boulder, Colo.: Lynne Rienner Publishers, 1997.

Fukuyama, Francis. *The End of History and the Last Man.* New York: The Free Press, 1992.

Huntington, Samuel P. *The Third Wave: Democratization in the Late Twentieth Century.* Norman, Okl.: Oklahoma University Press, 1991.

Hobsbawm, Eric. *Age of Extremes: The Short History of the Twentieth Century 1914–1991.* London: Michael Joseph, 1994.

Hyden, Goran. "Governance and the Study of Politics," in *Governance and Politics in Africa.* Boulder, Colo.: Lynne Rienner Publishers,

1992.

Hyden, Goran. "Conjunctures and Democratisation," in D. Olowu, K. Soremekun, and A. Williams, eds. *Governance and Democratisation in Nigeria.* Ibadan, Nigeria: Spectrum Books, 1995.

Ige, Bola. *People, Politics and Politicians of Nigeria, 1940–1979.* Ibadan: Heinemann, 1995.

Leftwich, A. "Governance. Democracy and Development in the Third World," *Third World Quarterly* 14, 3 (1993):605-624.

Martin, G. "Democratic Transition in Africa," *Issue* 21, 1–2 (1993):6–7.

Mazrui, Ali. "Political Leadership in Africa: Seven Types and Four Transitions," in Hans D'Orville, ed. *Leadership for Africa: Essays in Honour of Olusegan Obasanjo on the Occasion of his 60th Birthday.* New York: African Leadership Foundation, 1995.

Olagunju, Tunji, et al. *Transition to Democracy in Nigeria, 1985–1993.* Ibadan, Nigeria: Safari Books, 1993.

Omara-Otunnu, A. "The Struggle for Democracy in Uganda," *The Journal of Modern African Studies* 30, 3 (September 1992):443–465.

Oyediran, Oyeleye. "Transitions Without End: From Hope to Despair." Unpublished paper presented at University of Wisconsin-Madison, November 10–12, 1993.

Randrianja Solofo. "Nationalism Ethnicity and Democracy," in Stephen Ellis, ed. *Africa Now.* London: James Currey, 1996.

Said, Edward. *The World, the Text, and the Critic.* Cambridge: Harvard University Press, 1983.

Soyinka, Wole. *Ibadan: The Penkelemus Years.* Ibadan, Nigeria: Spectrum Books, 1994.

Williams Adebayo. "The Fictionalisation of Democratic Struggle in Nigeria," in D. Olowu, K. Soremekun and A. Williams, eds. *Governance and Democratisation in Nigeria,* Ibadan, Nigeria: Spectrum Books, 1995.

Williams, Adebayo. "African Writers and the Crisis of Governance," *Third World Quarterly* 3 (June 1996):349–362.

Index

319